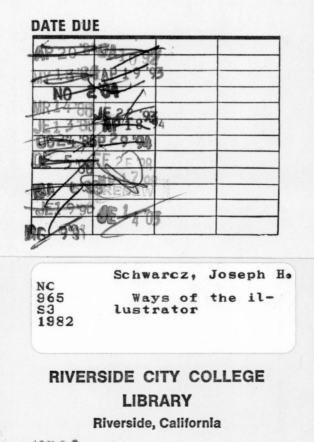

WAYS OF THE ILLUSTRATOR

Ways of the Illustrator

Visual Communication in Children's Literature

by JOSEPH H. SCHWARCZ

AMERICAN LIBRARY ASSOCIATION

CHICAGO · 1982

Text designed by Ray Machura

Cover designed by Ellen Pettengell

Composed by Modern Typographers, Inc.
in Linotron 202 Palatino

Printed on 60-pound Antique Glatfelter,
a pH-neutral stock, and bound in
B-grade Holliston cloth by
Malloy Lithographing, Inc.

Title page illustration is taken from *Das Grosse Liederbuch*, illustrated by Tomi
Ungerer, edited by Anna Dieckmann. All rights reserved by Diogenes Verlag,
Zurich. © 1975 by Diogenes Verlag, Zurich.

Library of Congress Cataloging in Publication Data

Schwarcz, Joseph H.
  Ways of the illustrator.

  Bibliography: p.
  Includes indexes.
    1. Illustration of books—Technique.   2. Illustrated
books, Children's.   I. Title.
  NC965.S3   741.64'2   82-6722
  ISBN 0-8389-0356-8   AACR2

Contents

Illustrations

Acknowledgments

My gratitude goes to those whose encouragement and assistance furthered this project:

Professor Sara Innis Fenwick who, when I studied with her at the University of Chicago, taught me in that inimitably courageous and yet tactful way she had to see the importance of children's literature.

Betsy Gould Hearne, of the American Library Association, whose wholehearted fascination with children's books has been, over the years, a constant inspiration.

Batya Guggenheim, who continually discovered provocative books, substantiated my ideas, and produced creative ones of her own.

Herbert Bloom, senior editor, American Library Asociation, whose perspicacious comments improved the manuscript.

Mary Huchting, production editor, American Library Association, who edited the manuscript admirably.

Helen Cline, managing editor, American Library Association, who furthered the book with utmost care.

The International Youth Library in Munich, a unique institution, with thousands of children's books from dozens of countries and treasures of resource materials. During several stays there I was aided by grants and by continuous help in my research. Special thanks go to IYL's director Walter Scherf, assistant director Jess Moransee, and all members of the staff, especially Erika von Engelbrechten whose assistance was invaluable.

Professor Klaus Doderer, head of the Institute for the Research of Juvenile Literature of the University of Frankfort on the Main, who encouraged my efforts and put at my disposal the wealth of materials found in the Institute, and to the staff.

Publishers all over the world who permitted use of their copyrighted illustrations and texts. The large majority did so without charging a fee.

Werner Küffner, Sara Melzer, Abraham Ophir, Poldina Stigler, Nedda Strashas, and Abraham Yinonn for their translations of poems from the

Serbo-Croat, Polish, Czech, Italian, Lithuanian, and Afrikaans, respectively.

Tamara Beris, who prepared the typescript with uncommon dedication.

I dedicate this book to Hava, my wife, as a token of gratitude for the many stimulating concepts she contributed and for her belief in the validity of my search for meaning in the illustration.

1

Introduction

From a very early stage in their lives the children of our time are surrounded by sounds and voices, by forms, figures, and colors coming to them from radios, television sets, and record players, and from books, magazines, pictures, and the like. The media are a constant part of the environment. As children grow up they slowly become aware that the media are capable of transmitting and representing another reality in contrast to the more tangible one of people, objects, and actions. The two domains, the real and the symbolic, supported by that dependable intermediary, the toy, mix in puzzling ways. Their mutuality enriches the children's world and heightens the sense of magic that life holds, a sense that for a few lucky ones will never completely disappear.

In this abundance, books with their wealth of stories and pictures have become an outstandingly important factor in initiating children, on a broad basis, to literature and visual art. Much thoughtfulness has been invested in the development of the illustrated books, as it ramifies in ever new directions of content, form, and style. There are countless ways in which books aid children in sharpening their grasp of themselves and gaining experience to solve the riddles of existence and discover new ones. Books lead them from their confined spheres toward a wider and more profound perception of life by confronting them with their present and their future and offering them joy and beauty. As a guide to leisurely activities, today's illustrated children's book moves far ahead of other means and media, especially the schematism of television, in ingenuity and versatility.

One prominent aspect of the spectacular growth of children's literature is the increasing importance of the illustration. Many factors have contributed to the process in the course of which pictures have practically become an integral part of books published for children. Evolving styles in art, changing concepts in education, new artists' materials, and diversified and improved printing techniques, on an unprecedented scale, in other fields of mixed verbal-visual media all have had a share in this development. By now,

The generic pronoun has been used freely in *Ways of the Illustrator* for succinctness but is intended to refer to both males and females.

the illustration has proliferated in quantity and attained impressive heights. It has become an indispensable means of symbolic communication and a rich vein of artistic expression created for the child. It can justifiably be asserted that the pictorial material in children's books reaches a degree of intricacy and reflects an abundance of individual styles far beyond what can be found in accompanying texts. Therefore, it offers more to and demands more of the child's mind. The growth and spread of the illustration in children's literature is one of the conspicuous changes in the child's world and one of the achievements of art in our era.

The flourishing of the illustration has not been received completely uncritically. One concern is what has often been termed "inundating the child with pictures." Some observers have even expressed the opinion that the flood of illustrated books is certain to damage or stifle the child's power of imagination beyond repair. Now, it is no doubt correct that the quantity of books that are being published and reach children is excessive; even if one is convinced of the importance of the genre and full of admiration for its accomplishments and its liveliness, he has to agree that less would be more. But the problem is, as we all know, not an isolated one. The flooding of the market with visual and visual-verbal messages is a comprehensive phenomenon; the children's book is just one element of it, vying for attention with many others. One has to adjust to this rapid development of the media, for good or ill. Restricting the flow of illustrated books would not achieve any objective, because other visual-verbal media would immediately fill the void, capturing more of the children's time and interest.

It is true that too many pictures may limit the viewer and detach him from his internal and external reality, and especially hurt his imagination. But is it less true that the imagination needs to be stimulated and that pictures can liberate the viewer from his own narrowness and improve his perception of the world? To a great extent it all depends on the cast of those who create and distribute the pictures and on the quality of the latter.

Another critical point raised frequently is the claim that the proliferation of individual styles in children's book illustration has reached such a high level that the child has to be ready to adjust to a different stylistic expression with practically every new book, and that this is too much of a good thing. There is justification for this. When, as in the course of preparing this book, one reads and looks at hundreds of books, he is apt to feel that the demands on the child to adapt to techniques and styles are not easy. One possible result of these demands might be superficial viewing. One also gets the impression that while many illustrators arrive at their personal styles quite naturally, sometimes the effort comes out a bit forced.

Yet in this context, too, we have to remind ourselves that the concept that creativity means, among other things, developing a unique, recognizable style of one's own pervades all fields of communication and art in our civilization. We would not want illustration for children to be a stagnant field while other means of communication generate new styles and techniques. Present conditions enable that new type of artist, the illustrator of children's books, to grow in importance and social status and to attract singularly gifted artists. Although there are many illustrators who do not develop a style of their own, and there is widespread application of repetitive stereotypes and imitation of the stereotypes of television and comics, especially in the cheaper books which are quantitatively dominant, the flexibility of individual expression displayed by the superior artists can be taken in stride, and accepted as one of the more felicitous introductions of children to the diversities of our culture.

While children's literature as a special field of writing attracted the attention of critics and scholars who began to analyze and evaluate its literary contents and structures relatively early in the century, the illustration suffered from neglect for a long time. Even after it became a ubiquitous component of children's books it continued to be treated, in reviews and critical appraisals, as an appendage, as part of what used to be called "the physical appearance of the book." At most, it was remarked upon briefly in simple dichotomic terms such as beautiful-undistinguished, tasteful-drab, aesthetic-lacking in appeal; or it was said to "harmonize" with the text, which is an epithet for stating that the illustration is a subordinate, not an integral, part of the book.

Yet the illustration grew in stature, scope, and complexity. At the same time other verbal-visual media developed beyond anticipations. Parallel with these processes, new branches of scientific research, iconology, semiology and schools of art appreciation based on Gestalt psychology and information theory devised the tools and the framework for the investigation of these media. These developments, together with the growing awareness of the powerful influence of the media on children, stimulated interest in the illustration and induced writers on children's literature to give more attention to it.

After 1945 one can detect a growing concern for the illustrator's work. Beginning with the first edition, Arbuthnot's *Children and Books*, later guided and developed by Zena Sutherland, has treated the illustration as an important element. Then came the outstanding books which examined the history and present state of the American and German picture book, by Bader and Doderer and Müller, respectively, and Hürlimann's work on the modern picture book. During the same period there began to appear books whose specific subject was the illustration, Baumgärtner's anthology, Künnemann's profiles of artists of many countries, Cianciolo's introduction and Holešovský's book on illustration in Czechoslovakian children's books. *The Horn Book* of Boston continued its concentrated efforts to spread the message of the illustration's distinction and significance.[1] Also, books treating the

---

1. Recent examples include:
   Lee Kingman, ed., *The Illustrator's Notebook* (Boston: Horn Book, 1978).
   ———, Grace Allen Hogarth, and Harriet Quimly, eds., *Illustrators of Children's Books, 1967–1976* (Boston: Horn Book, 1978).

general theme of children's literature increasingly began to include extensive chapters on the pictorial aspects.[2]

The fact that the illustration is now being recognized as a serious matter and the artist as an equal partner in the production of the book[3] highlights the necessity for looking at the artist's work with a carefulness analogue to that accorded other visual messages and aesthetic objects.

The present book is intended to contribute to the trend of leading away from condescending appraisal or rejection, toward the examination of the illustrator's work as a means of symbolic communication. Two main issues will be considered:

> In what ways does the illustration, an aesthetic configuration created for children, express its contents and meanings? How do its elements combine and its structures operate so as to carry the messages to which we are asked to relate?
>
> How does the illustration relate to the verbal text? In what ways does it influence, clarify, enhance, weaken, or comment on the impact, mood, and intention of the written word?

This endeavor requires a double approach. On the one hand, the illustration is a work of visual art and has to be looked at as such. On the other hand it is one of the two elements in the book. Each of these elements represents persons, objects, environment, events, actions and developments, by description and depiction, respectively. These representations reflect, explicitly and implicitly, aesthetic, psychological, and educational attitudes. This cooperation of word and picture implies that the two issues we have referred to—the illustration as a picture and as an element related to the text—cannot be dealt with separately. The combination of the two forms of communication into a common fabric where they complement each other creates conditions of dependence and interdependence. In other words, the full meaning of the illustration can only be revealed in context.

We shall offer no theory of the illustration. No such thing seems possible, or useful, with a rapidly expanding and changing form of artistic creation. Rather, we shall develop a framework for the treatment of various aspects pertaining to the artist's ways of expression and communication. Our discussion of these aspects will move through specific stages:

Chapter 2 will introduce a number of concepts relevant to the perception of basic relationships between word and picture, and of functions the illustration fulfills in the context.

The common motif of chapters 3 to 8, brought together under the heading

---

2. See, for instance:
   William D. Anderson and Patrick Groff, *A New Look at Children's Literature* (Belmont, Calif.: Wadsworth, 1972).
   Constantine Georgiou, *Children and Their Literature* (Englewood Cliffs, N.J.: Prentice-Hall, 1969).
   James S. Smith, *A Critical Approach to Children's Literature* (New York: McGraw-Hill, 1967).
3. See Selma G. Lanes's extensive and affectionate monograph on Sendak, *The Art of Maurice Sendak* (New York: Abrams, 1980).

"Examples of Form and Expression," is to demonstrate in what ways the artist makes use of the elements at his disposal—line, shape, color, texture, size—to create the composition and structure through which he expresses himself, and how he deploys visual forces to make his point and communicate his intentions. For this close look into the artist's workshop we have selected a number of diverse topics: each substantiates the principle of interdependence between the formal devices chosen by the artist and the expressive use to which he puts them.

"Variations on a Theme," comprising chapters 9 to 12, treats the illustrator's interpretative powers to influence moods and attitudes. The subject is introduced in chapter 9 and then treated in detail in chapters 10 to 12, by comparison of several editions of a fairy tale, a social utopia, and a myth.

Chapters 13 and 14 treat humanistic responsibilities. Chapter 13 presents a very specific theme, the animated machine, and shows, continuing a line of thought already noticeable in the two previous chapters, how children's literature is intrinsically bound up with moral issues.

In contrast to chapter 13, with its emphasis on the dangers of dehumanization, chapter 14 takes up the issue of the illustration's humanizing force, pulls together the examples and discussion, and winds up the argument by focusing on the ways in which the superior illustrator contributes to children's aesthetic and humanistic growth and maturation.

The emphasis throughout is on close inquiry: from analyzing individual illustrations in the early chapters we turn to examining motifs and then, in the later chapters, books and the work of single and singular artists.

In the same manner, we progress from the analysis of formal design to questions of composition and, toward the end, find ourselves involved with ways of interpretation touching upon aesthetic and educational values.

Our focus will shift as we turn our attention to different matters. Emphasis on aesthetic structural analysis will alternate with psychological and educational points of view.

The method of examination will vary with the topic. In chapter 4 the attempt is made to propose comprehensive categories for understanding the ways in which the metaphor is incorporated into the illustration, while in chapter 5, on the landscape, we are content with adducing a small number of categories; in this case, completeness is unnecessary and would be tedious. Chapter 10 is based on a random sample of editions, whereas chapter 11 examines all the editions that existed at the time, and chapter 12 considers an arbitrary selection of editions which seem to be relevant to the point we wish to make. Also, the number of illustrations reproduced varies with each chapter. In some cases the need for support of the text by pictorial evidence was felt to be greater than in others. Two chapters, 8 and 13, explore subject matter whose value we contest, and include no pictures at all.

Our objective is to enhance awareness of the ways of the illustrator through careful examination of specific themes, motifs, and contexts.

We see the illustrated book for children as both a meta-national and an international pattern. We are convinced that this is the only way of looking at it that can lead us to really understand its workings. It is meta-national in the sense that the illustration, as much of contemporary pure and applied art, is inspired and guided by trends issuing from academies, galleries, and schools of art linking New York to Paris to Prague to Tokyo to Rio de Janeiro. There exist regional distinctions characterizing nations and civilizations. For example, motifs of history and folklore abound in Lithuanian and Rumanian illustrations; surrealism is felt in France; some Japanese illustrators apply techniques and projections of their traditional theater to pictures. But the influence of the great art centers is considerable and often overriding. It is fortunately true, though, that as in all good art the universal significance found in the most excellent examples arises from a background with a strong local flavor: at the end of the last chapter we present a number of exemplary works that show Keats as urban American, Rettich as German North Sea Coast, and Brooks as rural Australian as can be.

The illustration is international in the sense that by means of translation, adaptation, the swapping of whole series of pictures to be reused within a new context, with both desirable and undesirable effects adhering to these activities, children everywhere are face to face with books originating in different countries. They and the adults who provide these books have frequently little reason to be aware of this fact on grounds of graphic styles and techniques. More than this, the most typical Dutch landscape might be found in a picture book created in America; the most exuberant Neapolitan family mood in a Swedish one. A French and a Japanese surrealist's style differ from each other mainly by the shape of the hero's eyes. But then a French artist illustrates a Japanese folktale, drawing eyes that have the correct shape and the book is translated into Japanese. And so on.

In keeping with this, in our view, exhilarating conviction that the illustrated book is to be studied as an emerging branch of art developing on a worldwide scale, we have drawn our examples from contemporary books published in a large number of countries and languages. These books exhibit a profusion of approaches and styles and levels; but at the same time it is almost immediately strikingly manifest that we are in the presence of artists whose work is inspired and nourished by, and in turn influences, the patterns and fashions and techniques of a common art form.

A point we wish to stress is that the accent will be on fiction: with few exceptions the books we have examined include stories and poems. It is as a companion of literature, we believe, that the illustrator attains his genuine stature and fully applies his creative vision.

Here we should also point out that a number of topics will be touched upon, when the occasion arises, but not developed systematically.

We shall not include another attempt to discern and classify types of picture books and illustrated books. This has been done a number of times, with varying success, according to various criteria. But changes happening in this field are so swift and far-reaching that any such classification will not hold its ground for more than a few years. Equally, there is the matter of age group suitability. A great many useful lists have been compiled, arranging children's books according to what is proposed for every age group. Here, too, the practical validity of such statements is doubtful. In any case, neither issue applies unequivocally to the illustration. It is probably correct that pictures for very small children have a simpler composition than those for older ones. But this is as much as can be said. One could make a case for the illustration becoming more intricate gradually, as the age level for books rises. The good artist uses complex means in this work for any age.

Something similar is also true for styles of art: style is a crucially important element in a children's book, as in any medium; we shall refer to it on frequent occasions. But style has no absolute value—there are no styles preferable to others as such, as is suggested sometimes. This also goes for questions like the similarity or dissimilarity of the writer's and the artist's style and their respective quality. All these issues acquire their substance in the contexts created by specific pictures and words.

We shall make sparing use of the term "education." We share Alderson's vein of skepticism about whether the illustration "educates."[4] Education is a systematic undertaking. The picture in the children's book should not be used systematically. It should be enjoyed leisurely, at random. However, it should be a naturally constant part of the environment the child grows in. If it is, the cumulative effect on the individual aesthetic and humanistic development of the child can be substantial, valuable, or otherwise. This is why the quality of illustrated books is an educational responsibility.

This is also the reason why children's taste in illustrated books cannot be a measure of quality. A considerable amount of reception research has been done in several countries, with the intention of finding out what children prefer and why.[5] Knowing *what* does not solve the question *why*. It is hard to believe that the *why*, the long-range, in-depth and partly unconscious influence, which is in the nature of art and literature, can be detected and gauged by children's responses to questionnaires or open-ended interrogation.

Of course, there cannot be the slightest doubt that we have to listen to and look at children's reactions, find out about their preferences and let them choose, to a large extent, what they wish to have. But their taste cannot be, as some would have it, an important criterion for creating, publishing, and distributing books and offering them to children. This is an adult responsibility, not to be delegated to children. They need aesthetic guidance. This is the reason we have to look at the illustrator's work in a very open-minded way, sustained by flexible judgments, but definitely with the aim of merging educational with aesthetic measures of evaluation.

---

4. Brian Alderson, "A View from the Island: European Picture Books, 1967–1976," in Kingman et al., eds., *Illustrators of Children's Books, 1967–1976*, pp. 20–43.

5. Little of this is convincing. One excellent example is Denise Escarpit, "l'image et l'enfant," in Anne-Marie Thibault-Lalan, ed., *Image et Communication* (Paris: Editions universitaires, 1972), pp. 75–105.

In the persistent confusion of visual and verbal-visual messages reaching the child the illustrated book is one of the most sensible and valuable ingredients. Many people seem to be cognizant of this, but in too vague a fashion. In an age to which Arnheim has offered his comprehensive statement on the essentiality of visual thinking,[6] and Gardner his passionate appeal for the recognition of art as the royal road to the mature personality,[7] there are still many adults, even those whose concern is with the child, who are visually and aesthetically illiterate.

In practice, the territory of the illustrated children's book stretches today from the low level of a commodity boasting its marketability, to the high level of an expanding art form reverberating and slightly inebriated with the sense of its powerfulness and its extending literary and artistic limits.

This book intends to contribute a share toward a growing critical and evaluative perceptiveness by offering an open-ended introduction to a rich and surprising art form.

6. Rudolf Arnheim, *Visual Thinking* (Berkeley: Univ. of California Pr., 1971).
7. Howard Gardner, *The Arts and Human Development: A Psychological Study of the Artistic Process* (New York: Wiley, 1973).

2

Relationships between Text and Illustration

Civilization began long ago to develop means of expression and communication based on the combination or fusion of different media. Specifically, language and the picture have always fulfilled, and fulfil today, a variety of common functions so essential to our culture that we could not imagine existing without them.

The alliance between the verbal and the visual modes is not achieved easily. Language discloses its contents *in time*; written language, ever since alphabets were invented, adds to this a fixed direction: we comprehend as we read along lines whose meanings we decipher in *linear progression*. The picture, on the other hand, confronts the viewer all at once, as *a surface*, an expanse; we see its contents *simultaneously*, as an immediate whole.

But as we read, we also connect in our mind the partial contents which we assemble as we go along, with the intention of understanding them as a whole (the page, the story, the chapter, etc.). We do so by partly reversing the linear progress, remembering *simultaneously* what we have read consecutively. Similarly, it is also true that soon after we have taken in the first overall impression of a picture, our eyes begin to meander, to linger over some spots in the picture and hurry past others, detecting certain connections between areas and shapes and colors. This is a process *in time* in the course of which we pay attention to parts of the picture with varying focus, and then usually return to look at the whole. Following an illustrated text is, then, a complex activity.

It is characteristic of the flexibility of the human mind that, even though the combination of the two media, each with its range of possibilities and its limitations, is an involved affair, humanity has developed a host of means of communications based on just this weaving together of linguistic and visual materials. It is as remarkable that children (to whom the verbal text comes at first through the sonorities and inflections of the adult voice) are impressed by combined verbal and visual messages so early in their lives, learn so soon to manipulate and appreciate them, to choose and reject and, above all, want to have ever more of them. The contemporary story-book-with-pictures, though its appearance is friendly, colorful, frank, open-faced, often trivial, is, as we shall see, a provocative, sophisticated, cultural product.

The text and the picture in the illustrated children's book enter into a variety of relationships, with the illustration fulfilling many functions within the shared framework. The clarification of a few basic issues pertaining to these relationships constitutes a point of departure for the discussion of the subjects to be dealt with presently.

We shall propose a number of categories and criteria and clarify them with specific examples. However, it is important to bear in mind that the criteria and categories to be adduced can, at best, only be approximations for guidelines which may serve for the understanding of illustrations in relation to texts. They are by no means accurate and absolute definitions. The reasons for this are quite clear. It is always hazardous to generalize on matters of symbolic and especially aesthetic communication. Both language and graphic expression include more than can be detected in them by the single reader and viewer; they can be understood on different levels and looked at from different angles. Any valuable verbal or visual message contains rich overtones beyond the intentions of the author and the artist, and may have more than one meaning. Besides, the combination of the verbal with the visual never means that contents and meanings may be translated from one medium to the other. It is always a matter of transfer, of transformation: no communication in any medium is ever exactly translatable into any other. Therefore, there will be no sharp lines. Categories are to be applied in an open-minded fashion; they are apt to overlap. Criteria will need revision at a future point. The field of illustrated children's books is both too vivacious and too intricate to be generalized easily.

Additionally, we have to be aware that our subject exists and develops as just one branch of the whole large area of verbal-visual communication. In other words, some of the issues are far beyond the scope of this book.

We might also add that none of the books and papers which we consulted in the course of preparing this chapter, and which constitute research in either the illustration as art or the specific issue of the illustration for children, has offered a comprehensive solution. We, too, can only hope to add a number of significant elements to the clarification of the issue.

With these limitations in mind, let us look at the functional relationships between the two media.

THE QUANTITATIVE ASPECT

Historically, there has been a rapid development in the last few decades for children's books to include more pictures proportionately to the space occupied by the text. Differences between books, publishers, countries, etc., are great, for reasons of contents, style, age group suitability, and budget. But the general trend is toward more space to be allotted to pictures in books for ever higher age groups. Today it would be easy to place books for any given age group on a sort of sliding scale, beginning with books having only one illustration on the dust jacket or the cover through books having a number of illustrations, getting to books where more space is given to pictures than to the text and ending up with wordless picture books.

These drily stated quantitative proportions have qualitative importance. Quite early when, moving on that sliding scale, we come to a point where a book has, say, six to ten illustrations, the illustrator begins to influence the effect a book may have, because by working in a certain style, repeatedly depicting the hero as a certain personality, and supporting and reinforcing certain events and situations (and not others), he creates a continuum. In this case the illustrations are more than a decorative item or a mere extension of the text. The text, to be sure, dictates the framework, guides the illustrator and limits him to an extent, but the illustrator is quite free to interfere where and how he wishes to do so. The text suggests ways of treatment but, as we shall see in later chapters, the illustrator's range of choice is broad.[1]

The more pictures there are in proportion to the text, the more the illustrator becomes involved in his partnership with the written word until, in the profusely illustrated book and the picture story book, we speak of composite verbal-visual narration, to which we shall refer presently.

But first we should look at the other end of the sliding scale, at the wordless book. The term is often used as if it covered a very simple phenomenon. The truth is that this type of "visual literature" has now branched into several directions.

There are funny wordless books for smaller children, such as Mercer Mayer's Frog books (one of which includes, by the way, the caption "Fancy Restaurant") and serious ones for older children, like Lynd Ward's *The Silver Pony* (eighty pages). There are simple ones like Mitschgut's *In Our Village*, more complex ones like *The Snowman* by Briggs and quite demanding ones like the Rettichs's *New Stories of the Hare and the Hedgehog* (fig.1).

Still more important, consider the effects created by: a Frog book, where consecutive whole pages pleasantly urge us forward; the dignity of *The Silver Pony*, where every picture is a whole page, but facing an empty white page, and inviting the viewer to meditate, to associate and imagine, or even write down his text; *In Our Village*, each page of which is dedicated to a different corner in the village, crammed with dynamic activities, but also is intended to be read and looked at in any order one wishes; *The Snowman*, whose doings have to be contemplated consecutively more than once to be perceived in detail, because some of the pictures are intricate and there are quick changes in size, corresponding to the viewing speed suggested by the artist; the sophistication of *New Stories of the Hare and the Hedgehog*, where each double page presents a single animal parable presented in six to eleven pictures, with the layout and design of each story differing from the rest and where the aesthetically appealing pictures also require a salutary intellectual effort to decipher the meaning of the stories—that of visual thinking.

---

1. See, in this respect, especially chapters 4 and 11.

Die Geschichte von der Libelle

Fig. 1. Rolf Rettich, "The Story of the Dragonfly"
From *Neues von Hase und Igel* by Rolf and Margret Rettich, published by Otto Maier Verlag Ravensburg © 1979.

In wordless books we move from the functions of the illustration to the message of the picture: the written word has vanished from inside the book; it appears sparingly, but is not to be overlooked, on the title page or as the caption of the story and thus forms part of the context. But many wordless books can be enjoyed and understood without their titles.

SPATIAL RELATIONSHIPS

In the past the illustration was usually neatly separated from the text and allotted a page or half a page in a certain order kept throughout the book. Vignettes, initials, and other decorative devices added some spice. But by the end of the nineteenth-century artists like Walter Crane and I. A. Bylibyn and many others experimented with the division of space between words and pictures. The classic arrangement is still found frequently; however, today anything goes. The fashion in which illustration and text combine, intertwine, and divide the pages between them, the way pictures break out of their frames, roam over the page, partly incorporate the text or swallow it up, is extremely varied. Illustrators make a point of inventing new arrangements, as one expression of their personal style, so that the reader-viewer has to be ready to encounter an unfamiliar design every time he opens a book.

This development has an interesting effect: the more vivid the interplay between the two media becomes, and the more fluent and flexible layout and compositions and proportions are, the more dominant the picture becomes in relation to the text; for the simple reason that the simultaneous visual impressions are more attractive than the linear textual progress. (Attention naturally also depends on quality: large trite pictures will not attract the child much if the accompanying story is better.)

Especially intriguing in this respect are books whose layout fluctuates considerably from one page to the next, creating a dynamic, arousing, sometimes hectic atmosphere. One has to leaf through books like McKee's *The Magician and the Sorcerer*, Pushkin's *Story of the Golden Cock*, with illustrations by Zotov, Janikovszky-Réber's books, for instance, *Something Always Happens to Me* (fig. 2), or Bechtel's *Lancelot the Ocelot*, to see how the illustrator evokes everchanging scenes composed of multiple pictures and how the text is moved around and has to accommodate itself to the requirements of the visual patterns.

Fig. 2. László Réber, *Something Always Happens to Me*
From *Velem mindig történik valami*, by Éva Janikovszky, illustrated by László Réber, published by Móra, Budapest, 1972.

COMPOSITE NARRATION

In the picture story book, and in all books whose story is accompanied by illustrations throughout, word and picture form a composite text.[2] One might compare it to what happens in other media; to an orchestra playing a piece of music, where single instruments and whole instrument groups combine to achieve the effect desired by the composer, each one offering and adding its special contribution, each one vying for the attention of the listener; or to dance where two different media, music and movement, together create acoustic-kinetic-visual patterns and rhythms. In these cases the media participate in a concerted effort to accomplish something that

2. I owe the term to E. Breitinger.

could not be accomplished by each medium itself. It also means that different voices, groups, etc., assume dominance, to be relieved presently by others; that the attention of the reader, the listener, the viewer, wanders in his or her search for enjoyment, understanding, and appreciation.

The book that is illustrated from cover to cover is a lively complex phenomenon. Complex because of the integration of text and picture to the point of interdependence; lively because of the diversity of styles, designs, compositions, etc., of which we have just spoken and which suggests to the child that he be flexible enough to want this diversity (this is true to a greater extent of good books; the run-of-the-mill ones are more redundant). This blending of two components forming the score (in the sense of a musical score) is intriguing because each is a rich system of expression and communication, including numerous elements, the linear one, language with its vocabulary, grammar, syntax and the simultaneous one, the picture, with contour, size, shape, color, texture, etc., to mention but the simplest ones. When the two systems work together, the distinction between the temporal and the spatial factors disappears to some extent; the pages of the book are perceived as temporal-spatial entities with the eye ranging about the page and the fingers turning each one.

SOME FUNCTIONS OF THE ILLUSTRATION

In this mutual game where words and pictures play together, the illustration fulfills a number of functions that tend to recur frequently and ubiquitously:

Congruency

When the text says "Yesterday the girl drew a white fence," "Then she drew a little girl," "Today she draws a ball," and so on, and accompanying illustrations faithfully show this activity and its results, with very little background added, the pictures simply double or parallel what is said in the text. But this is not all: in fact the picture tells us what the girl looks like, which the text does not. There is never complete redundancy because the picture is more concrete than the word. Now it is not a girl anymore, to be imagined as one wishes, but one having a recognizable shape. The general has become specific. Even if the illustrator makes an effort only to inform, to explain visually the contents of a textual passage, he does more than this, for his medium forces him to it. Hermerén, writing on the illustration in art, defines the dilemma and thereby also gives an example of how difficult it is to be precise about categories. The artist, he says, omits part of what is found in the text (in our example, the illustrator omits the "yesterday" and "today"); so he simplifies. But, without wishing to do so, he also adds to, elaborates the texts: stories do not usually mention that people have ears, fingers, a nose, and so on; but the artist will show these parts.[3]

3. Göran Hermerén, "Two Concepts of Illustration," *Representation and Meaning in the Visual Arts*. Lund Studies in Philosophy (Copenhagen, Oslo, Lund: Scandinavian University Books, 1969), p. 59.

But here and there we do find simplification to the point of *reduction*. Dick Bruna's illustrations of fairy tales are an extreme example. Cutting out background and action, he creates stark, static, alienated "portraits" of the persons in the stories.

Elaboration is one of the main functions of the illustration. It may achieve a number of different effects: When the text in Lasker's *The Boy Who Loved Music* tells us that Prince Nicolas did not condone trespassing his hunting reserve, and (the text) pities the countryman who dared do so, the picture *specifies* by depicting a man hanging from a tree.

In Anno's *The King's Flower*, the king's dentist orders the blacksmith to make a gigantic pair of pincers to pull the royal tooth; the picture temporarily stops the continuation of the main plot by *amplifying* the stages of making the pincers: the preparatory drawing, the parts being heated on coals, the parts being hammered into shape.

Iwasaki's *Staying Home Alone on a Rainy Day* is about a little girl who gets apprehensive when mother does not return soon, as she promised. Suddenly the phone rings. The girl tells us that she is afraid. The text also elaborates that the telephone rang and rang and that the girl did not answer it. The illustration *extends the situation* still further. The text describes the girl as passive—she did not answer the phone. The picture shows that she did act: she backed away from the phone and hid behind the window curtains.

In these examples the illustrations *complement* what the text really means, as understood and interpreted by the illustrator.

Sometimes the illustration complements by running ahead of the text and pushing the action forward. In Watts's *While the Horses Galloped to London* the text relates how the passengers of the stagecoach bicker about minor things, but Mayer's illustration suddenly sweeps us off and away—now we are looking down, together with the wicked highwayman, on the coach approaching the hill on which we stand, before the text gets there.

This last example is quite close to *alternate progress*, a device noted first by Baumgärtner.[4] It refers to text and picture taking turns in continuing the story, with some of the steps in the plot presented only once, by either of the two. At the end of Rachel Isadora's *Ben's Trumpet*, the trumpeter takes the boy, whose glowing dream is to play the trumpet, to the jazz club and promises to see what they can do. The illustration jumps ahead: we see the trumpeter teaching Ben, who finally holds a real trumpet in his hands.

The story of *Till and the Teddy Bear* by Max Kruse begins with the panoramic picture of a city. The text coming after that barely refers to it; instead, it describes in detail the market where the story is to happen but the market is not illustrated. In the next picture we see a small corner of it, but there stands a man who will figure prominently in the events to be told. He is not referred to in the text which follows. So the story develops, partly by paralleling, partly by alternation.

---

4. Alfred Baumgärtner, "Erzählung und Abbild," in Baumgärtner, ed., *Aspekte der gemalten Welt* (Weinheim: Beltz, 1968), pp. 71–73.

In these examples the two media function together, page by page, like links in a chain. In other cases alternation extends over longer stretches. We have always been accustomed to a story continuing verbally over a number of pages, uninterrupted by pictures. But in modern books it happens that the text disappears temporarily, pictures take over and carry the story along. A very well-known example of this is Sendak's *Where the Wild Things Are*. When the wild rumpus starts, three double pages present the hilarious liberating abandon—words are superfluous.

Bolliger's *Tiny One* is a boy who is mocked and rejected in school, because he is small for his age. He gets into trouble and is expelled from the classroom. While he is sitting on the stairs by himself, examining some of the treasures in his pocket, a nut, a feather, and more, an angel appears and puts stories in his heart, seven stories, one for each of his treasures. Up to this point black-and-white pictures accompany the text. Now the text disappears and seven wordless pages tell the wondrous tales. Then the spell is over, text and black-and-white illustrations recombine to conclude the realistic plot, leading to Tiny One being accepted by all and everybody.

In both these examples the visual takes over when the story arrives at a turning point, the intense experience that opens the way toward the solution of the conflict.

Deviation

There is what has variously been called the deviation of the illustration from the text, or *inspiration* instead of illustration. Both these terms refer to illustrations which are initiated by the textual framework but veer away from it due to the illustrator's own associations and ideas. Joan Anglund, in *Spring Is a New Beginning*, devotes a page to praising the delight of hunting strawberries and picking flowers. Illustrating her own lines, she draws some girls looking for flowers. But in the back stands a boy who cares neither for flowers nor girls. He is spellbound by the boat sailing in the bay.

Others, notably Tomi Ungerer, develop inspiration by spiting, and thus spicing, the text, sometimes to the point of *opposing and alienating* it. *Das Grosse Liederbuch*, edited by Anna Dieckmann and illustrated by Ungerer, includes a number of crisp examples. A song whose words extol the hunter's joys is accompanied by a boar pursuing the terrified hunter. Another song, about some little ducklings swimming peacefully in the lake, their heads in the water, their tails held up high, is portrayed this way: a painter sits in front of his easel, painting a stork. Two ducks squat nearby (no swimming for them) and a wicked boy with a frightening look in his eyes squeezes paint from tubes and feeds it to the ducks who take it to be worms. The boy wears a sailor's suit and a cap with "Speer" inscribed on it, probably to arouse political associations (fig. 3).

Here the illustration, though deviating from the text and really negating it, still depends on it, for it is the mood of the song the artist wishes to contradict. Other artists, especially writer-illustrators, inventively develop

Fig. 3. Tomi Ungerer, "All My Little Ducklings"

deviation still further, until text and illustration *counterpoint* each other. The text of *Rosie's Walk* by Pat Hutchins portrays Rosie the hen as she innocently walks across the yard and gets back in time for dinner. The illustrations, on the other hand, depict the indefatigable and frustrating efforts of the fox to catch her, until the bees finally drive him off. These are, in fact, two entirely separate stories. One, the verbal text, is peaceful, uneventful, boring. The other one, in pictures, relates the terrible dangers to which Rosie is exposed again and the fox's repeated failures. This is a perfectly understandable wordless story, with some tension and some fun, but of no great interest. However, when the two stories are brought together, an additional dimension appears: as the illustrations give to Rosie's walk a mood and meaning totally opposite to those found in the text, our fun and satisfaction arise from the fact that *we* know what the poor hen does not, for the pictures let us in on the secret.

Counterpointing has been developed to great depth by John Burningham in his Shirley books. They are moving stories, because on one level they are simply funny; on another, they exhibit the tragic lack of communication between parents and their children. Again, there are two separate stories. Left-hand pages show Shirley's mother (in the bathroom), or both parents (on the beach) and their tedious cautionary well-meaning patter. Right-hand pages show Shirley, wrapped up in her imagination, going off and getting involved, in fantasy or in fierce dramas like fighting pirates or joining feudal knights. The text to the left is just a wearisome rustle of words. The wordless story to the right tells a not-too-absorbing adventure. When the two are juxtaposed, they document the hermetic isolation of the child's fantasy world from the adults' reality. Again we are let in on a secret—how little parents seem to know about their children (fig. 4).

Fig. 4. John Burningham, *Time to Get Out of the Bath, Shirley*

Illustrations from *Time to Get Out of the Bath, Shirley*, written and illustrated by John Burningham. Copyright © 1978 by John Burningham. By permission of Thomas Y. Crowell, Publishers, and Jonathan Cape Ltd., Publishers.

NEW HORIZONS

How impracticable it would be to expect precision and finality in clarifying these functions and relationships can convincingly be demonstrated by the fact that every few years there appears a book whose illustrator creates something quite new, thereby expanding the range of expressiveness of children's literature and offering a model to be emulated. *Where the Wild Things Are* was an event in the development of the children's book not only because of its strange beauty and its uncanny meaningfulness, but also from the formal point of view: we have already mentioned the device of the pictures temporarily carrying the story along without words. There also is the compositional rhythm of the expanding visual space as Max withdraws from reality and arrives, in fantasy, at omnipotence and then returns to reality, with the pictures contracting again, and a blank page on which the story ends.

Thirteen, by Charlip and Joiner, offers a novel pattern of design and narration. There are thirteen stories running side by side on each of the thirteen pages of the book. Each story is represented on every page by one rather compact picture, and continued on the next one. Every page also includes a reduced reproduction of the previous page, including a still smaller reproduction of the page before that one. Some stories are wordless, others have brief texts. Most of them are based on slow visual transformations. Their vertiginous charm stimulates visual thinking.

Well, I must say! by Roswitha Fröhlich is a volume for children of eight and above of humoristic verses and pictures connected rather loosely. Some of the pictures illustrate events and themes brought up in verses on the opposite page. Other pages where verses and pictures face each other suggest associations. On still others there is no apparent link between the two. It is all quick and open-ended and very much up to the child who reads and looks to trace the connections.

Shenhav's *The Uproarious Book* is a fully illustrated adventure story where linear progress is scrambled. On every page we are told where to turn next, from page 14 to 47 and so on throughout the book (this also results in facing pages which do not belong together).

There is also the device of the *multipurpose* illustration, a fashion becoming popular in volumes of poetry. Here, one picture serves more than one poem. There are numerous such pages, done by several illustrators, in *Poems and Rhymes*. One landscape frames two poems on morning and on afternoon on the hill. Another picture comes with three rhymes on moving to a new neighborhood. A photograph of a train serves four poems on trains.[5]

Similar illustrations appear in *Once upon a Time, Children . . .*, edited by Jacques Charpentreau. For example, one seascape supports two poems on the common theme of little girls and their mothers.

The significant point arising from the multipurpose illustration is that one picture means different things in different contexts.

These are observations on the relationships between the text and the illustration.[6] They constitute guidelines for understanding the basic conditions arising when the two media mix and cooperate. The illustrator utilizes these conditions when he does his work, joining the text with his lines and colors and shapes and textures, and fulfills his two essential tasks, contributing aesthetically valuable creations and interpreting the mood and meaning of the verbal contents.

The superior illustrator, who is a genuine artist creating for children, will charge his pictures with variegated functions, employing a wide range of possible constellations they are likely to enter in with the written word.

5. See also page 45, ''Clouds,'' ''Brooms,'' ''Garment.''
6. Additional facets of the relationship between the text and illustration—differences in the styles of writer and artist, differences in the relative quality of their work and age group suitability—have been mentioned in the introduction and will again be referred to in several places.

CHILDREN'S WORKS CITED

ANGLUND, JOAN. *Spring Is a New Beginning*. New York: Harcourt, Brace, 1963.

ANNO, MITSUMASA. *The King's Flower*. New York: Collins, 1979.

BECHTEL, BEVERLEY. *Lancelot the Ocelot*. Illus. by Laurel Horvat. Minneapolis: Carolrhoda Books, 1972.

BOLLIGER, MAX. *Knirps*. Illus. by Klaus Brunner. Winterthur: Comenius, 1961.

BRIGGS, RAYMOND. *The Snowman*. New York: Random House, 1978.

BURNINGHAM, JOHN. *Come Away from the Water, Shirley!* London: Cape, 1977.

———. *Time to Get Out of the Bath, Shirley*. London: Cape, 1978.

CHARLIP, REMY, and JERRY JOINER. *Thirteen*. New York: Parents Magazine Press, 1975.

CHARPENTREAU, JACQUES, ed. *Il était une fois, les enfants* . . . . Illus. by Danielle Avezard. Paris: Éditions la Farandole, 1980.

DIECKMANN, ANNA, and WILLI GOHL, eds. *Das grosse Liederbuch*. Illus. by Tomi Ungerer. Zurich: Diogenes, 1975.

FRÖHLICH, ROSWITHA. *Na hör mal!* Illus. by Marie Marcks. Ravensburg: Otto Maier, 1980.

HUTCHINS, PAT. *Rosie's Walk*. New York: Macmillan, 1971.

ISADORA, RACHEL. *Ben's Trumpet*. New York: Greenwillow Books, 1979.

IWASAKI, CHIHIRO. *Staying Home Alone on a Rainy Day*. New York: McGraw-Hill, 1969.

JANIKOVSZKY, ÉVA. *Velem mindig történik valami*. Illus. by László Réber. Budapest: Móra, 1972.

KRUSE, MAX. *Till und der Teddybär*. Illus. by Lea Auvo. München: Betz, 1963.

LASKER, DAVID. *The Boy Who Loved Music*. Illus by Joe Lasker. New York: Viking, 1979.

MAYER, MERCER. *Frog Goes to Dinner*. New York: Dial Press, 1974.

———. *Frog, Where Are You?* New York: Dial Press, 1977.

MCKEE, DAVID. *The Magician and the Sorcerer*. New York: Parents Magazine Press, 1974.

MITSCHGUT, ALI. *Bei uns im Dorf*. Ravensburg: Otto Maier, 1970.

Poems and Rhymes. Childcraft—The How and Why Library, vol. 1. Chicago: World Book–Childcraft International, 1980.

PUSHKIN, ALEXANDER. *Skazka a zolotom petushke*. Illus. by Oleg Zotov. Moskva: Malysh, 1976.

RETTICH, ROLF, and MARGRET RETTICH. *Neues von Hase und Igel*. Ravensburg: Otto Maier, 1979.

SENDAK, MAURICE. *Where the Wild Things Are*. New York: Harper & Row, 1963.

SHENHAV, HAYA. *Hasefer hamishtollel*. Illus. by Giora Carmi. Tel Aviv: Am Oved, 1979.

WARD, LYND. *The Silver Pony: A Story in Pictures*. Boston: Houghton Mifflin, 1973.

WATTS, MABEL. *While the Horses Galloped to London*. Illus. by Mercer Mayer. New York: Parents Magazine Press, 1973.

Part 1

Examples of
Form and Expression

3

The "Continuous Narrative" Illustration

Ever since the visual arts came into existence artists have striven to exploit to the full the potential of their media and to stretch the limits of expression.

One of the perpetual challenges to static or "immobile" art has always been the representation of motion.[1] The artist uses static elements to produce a dynamic effect, an illusion of motion. Any movement consists of a chain of transitory states forming a continuum; yet the artist has to choose single states, particular points in the continuum, and to depict them in such a way as to create the semblance of continuous action taking place.

Creating the illusion of motion also entails the representation of time, because motion means both progress in space and progress in time. The artist's challenge, then, is to arrest and capture the fleeting movement and, by use of the same devices, create the illusion of time passing before the viewer's eyes.

Many techniques have been devised to create this effect. These have always been essential for the artist who took upon himself the task of illustrating literary narratives; for the illustration accompanies, we remember, a linear and consequently mobile verbal text which flows naturally, even unavoidably, in time; complex relationships are created between the picture and the written language that give rise to intriguing problems and ingenious solutions.

The illustrator of children's books has to be especially inventive in representing motion and the passage of time because kinetic experiences are vital for children at all ages and, consequently, an emphasis on action-in-time characterizes the literature created for them.

The simplest way to achieve the effect of movement-in-time is, of course, by a series of pictures representing the stages of an ongoing action in chronological order. However, art has developed various sophisticated

This chapter has been reprinted with changes from Geoff Fox and Graham Hammond, eds., *Responses to Children's Literature* (New York: K.G. Saur, 1980). Copyright 1980 by the International Research Society for Children's Literature. All rights reserved.

1. See Rudolf Arnheim, "Dynamics," *Art and Visual Perception: A Psychology of the Creative Eye* (Berkeley: Univ. of California Pr., 1974), pp. 410–40.

means to represent movement in one single picture. We shall focus on one such technique that has been called *continuous narration* or *continuous narrative*.[2]

Its essence lies in the fact that the protagonist of the story being illustrated (or any other figure) appears two or more times at different places in one and the same picture, while the background and the other elements of the picture remain more or less unchanged. This repetition of the figure indicates motion from one point to another and also the passing of time.

The continuous narrative is an ancient technique in art. The Italian painter Sassetta (fifteenth century), for instance, applies it in *St. Paul Meeting St. Anthony*; the pilgrim saint appears three times in the picture and is depicted in larger size as he comes from afar until he reaches St. Paul's cave.

A very famous example is, of course, Michelangelo's *The Original Sin and the Expulsion from Paradise* in the Sistine Chapel in Rome. The painting represents, on the left, Adam and Eve taking the forbidden fruit from the serpent and, on the right, their banishment from the Garden of Eden as a continuous action, taking place in a continuous landscape. As De Tolnay has pointed out,[3] Michelangelo takes liberties with the Biblical text—he shows Adam together with Eve receiving the fruit from the serpent and omits the sinners' confrontation with God, with the obvious intention of accelerating the action and increasing its visual power.

This specific technique implies what might be called the linearization of the visual text: while in any picture visual elements and forces vie with each other for the attention of the viewer, he is at liberty to concentrate on the whole or parts of it, or on various aspects of content and structure in any order he wishes. But the continuous narrative demands to be read, so to speak, in a certain direction, the one that indicates progress, in space and time, of the recurring figure. Only when this direction is accepted by the viewer can the picture be perceived and understood correctly.

Illustrators of children's books make extensive use of this technique, alternating it with other devices for the representation of motion and time, even in the same book.[4] A comprehensive analysis of illustrations of this type in children's literature reveals that two main applications of the continuous narrative can be discerned:

The representation of epic time spans
The representation of vivid, sudden events occurring in very brief time spans.

Do in the Red Boots by Herzka and Steiner is an excellent example of the representation of epic time spans. It tells of a girl's journeys into the magic

2. Göran Hermerén, "Two Concepts of Illustration," p. 58; Donald L. Weismann, *The Visual Arts as Human Experience* (Englewood Cliffs, N.J.: Prentice Hall, n.d.), p. 226.

3. C. De Tolnay, *Michelangelo*, vol. 2, *The Sistine Ceiling* (Princeton, N.J.: Princeton Univ. Pr., 1969), pp. 31–32.

4. Baumgärtner has analyzed the continuous narrative in illustrations for children, calling it simultaneous representation, from a different and very interesting angle (*Aspekte*, pp. 65–81).

country of nature. Each day's solitary adventures take Do into the woods, up the mountain and so on, and get her acquainted with many kinds of animals. Each trip is portrayed on a double page that contains the text and one large picture. On the first day, for instance, Do sets out on the wings of a large white bird, flies past the moon and the sun, glides down the steep mountain on a spider's threads and returns home on the back of a snail (fig. 5).

The journeys, seven in all, are narrated in a gentle, serene tone; even in moments of danger Do never loses her poise; her eyes are wide open to catch the wonder and excitement around her; mythical overtones can be felt throughout the simple tales; the cyclical pattern of setting out, getting involved with the elements and forces of nature, and returning home suggests the diurnal cycle.

The book is an exceptionally beautiful demonstration of the forcefulness with which the continuous narrative can be used to create an effect of "time on our hands." Each tale is illustrated by one picture in which the different episodes of each trip are indicated by the recurring figure of Do moving from place to place on the unchanging background. The six or seven or even ten "Dos" that are found on any one page roughly form a circle representing the cyclical nature of the tales.

Fig. 5. Heiri Steiner, *Do in the Red Boots*

From *Do in den roten Stiefeln*, by Heinz Stefan Herzka and Heiri Steiner, artist designer, A.G.I., published by Artemis-Verlag, Zurich.

The text has an epic quality, symbolizing a period in the development of a young girl; the illustrations give congenial expression to the intense and yet leisurely way in which Do is initiated into the mysteries of nature.

Another example: Ezra Jack Keats uses the continuous narrative for a somewhat different purpose in *Whistle for Willie*. Peter, the hero of the story, wants to learn to whistle so he can call his dog, just as the big boys do. But in spite of much practicing, "still no whistle." So Peter walks out of the house and into the street,

First he walked along a crack in the sidewalk. Then he tried to run away from his shadow.

The episode has a transitional character; Peter tries to overcome his sense of failure by skipping and jumping along the sidewalk, trying out various games. Soon he will have gathered energy and will surprise his dog Willie with a real whistle.

The illustration accompanying this phase in the story (fig. 6) emphasizes that it takes some time for Peter to work off his frustration. The sidewalk and the wall along which Peter progresses stretch out and recede into the distance. Peter appears twice: as a larger figure, to the left, and as a smaller one to the right, wandering away from our view, lost in his fantasies.

Fig. 6. Ezra Jack Keats, "Willie on the sidewalk"
From *Whistle for Willie* by Ezra Jack Keats. Copyright © 1964 by Ezra Jack Keats. Reprinted by permission of Viking Penguin Inc.

A still different application of the continuous narrative can be found in the illustration to a poem by Ayin Hillel,[5] about little Yossi who is mommy's darling. Whenever she asks him to run to the grocery and get some milk and bread or olives he returns, smiling radiantly, with a toy or a flower for

5. Ayin Hillel, "Yossi Yeled Mootzlah Sheli," in *Bulbul Lamah Kakhah*; illus. by Shmuel Katz (Tel Aviv: Massada, 1973).

mother instead; she receives it lovingly and sends him off once more. In the picture (fig. 7) Yossi appears twice; once facing the viewer, approaching him; then, to the left, he is seen from the back, moving away. Between the two figures stands a tree, and the viewer is induced to draw an imaginary circular line all around. This conveys, graphically, the idea of Yossi coming and going, again and again and again, the repetitive pattern of the plot.

Though they serve various purposes, these three illustrations demonstrate the application of the continuous narrative technique in representing extended, drawn-out stretches of time.

However, the technique may serve just as well to produce the illusion of an action taking place swiftly and rapidly, to represent vivid, sudden events occurring in very brief time spans.

When the pony in *Pony* by Ruck-Pauquét and Heuck breaks loose from his confinement one day, his escape into the wide open spaces is abruptly held up by traffic in the city. He is frightened, but only for a moment, then he races across the street and is off again. The illustration shows the pony twice, before and after the crossing, thus telescoping the sudden change of mind and position into one single picture.

Borchers's *The Red House in the Small Town* is a picture book that deals with a weighty subject. The mayor rules the town with a heavy hand and imposes

Fig. 7. Shmuel Katz, "Yossi, My Darling Child"
From *Bulbul Lamah Kakhah*, by A. Hillel, illustration by Shmuel Katz, by permission of Massada Publishers Ltd., Ramat Gan.

on the citizens a drab conformist way of life; they are commanded to be happy and satisfied; all houses have to be painted grey; no one may weep or say "no." One day the girl Mary cannot stand this any longer and, influenced by her, her father goes out and, by painting his house red, causes the uprising that brings about the mayor's downfall.

In the key scene (fig. 8) Mary sits in the corner and weeps—

> Why are you crying? asked her father.
> I am crying because I am forbidden to cry, said Mary.

Her father is jolted out of his complacency, his thoughts accelerate until he arrives at his dramatic decision:

> The father gazed at Mary's face and thought:
> What beautiful tears Mary has, round and brilliant.
> And he thought:
> Why is Mary forbidden to weep?
> Why are women forbidden to wear brightly
>   coloured dresses, and children, to wear
>   brightly coloured aprons?
> And he thought:
> Why does everyone say YES and why does nobody say NO?
> And he thought:
> I'll wait till nightfall . . .

Fig. 8. Günther Stiller, "What beautiful tears Mary has . . ."
From Günther Stiller/Elisabeth Borchers: *Das rote Haus in einer kleinen Stadt* © 1969 Verlag Heinrich Ellermann München.

In the illustration Mary's face is shown three times, growing in size from left to right, with more tears running down her cheek. The illustrator here is representing not movement—for the girl is sitting in the corner—but time, the short minutes during which her father finds himself all of a sudden confronted with his duty as both father and citizen. Mary's face(s) reflect(s) the growing intensity of *his* emotions, the increase in tension, until the conflict is resolved by his decision to stand up against the mayor.

In illustrations of this kind, then, the continuous narrative serves to create an impression of quick and, at times, fleeting action by telescoping, as it were, the recurring figures into one single picture.

At times illustrators make use of the continuous narrative to represent both the slow and the rapid passage of time. Blecher's *Where Is Wendelin?* includes several examples. When Wendelin enters the forest at night and gets lost, we are to understand that long hours go by while we detect him in different places, moving on beneath the trees. When, on the other hand, Wendelin is frightened by the ferocious dog who crosses his path and he thinks: "If only I were a lion!" only a few seconds elapse during his six-stage metamorphosis into the lion who drives the dog away (fig. 9).

The length of time or the speed with which it passes is not always clearly implied. An interesting case of ambiguity is a double page in Sendak's *In the Night Kitchen.* When Mickey flies up over the Milky Way into the Night Kitchen to bring milk for the cake, Sendak uses the continuous narrative with some hesitation. The giddy flight is depicted in a set of four illustrations which are actually one, for the background is continuous; it would seem that the division into four frames serves to increase the sense of urgency in the viewer's mind, or else simply to make it easier for him to grasp the illustrator's intention. But then we find still another ambiguous element. Both the

Fig. 9. Wilfried Blecher, "If only I were a lion!"

From *Wo ist Wendelin?* written and illustrated by Wilfried Blecher © 1965 Beltz Verlag Weinheim und Basel, Programm Beltz & Gelberg.

written text and the picture suggest very clearly that Mickey's flight in the night skies is speedy and short. Yet the picture also shows, four times, the course of the setting moon, thus indicating that a considerable part of the night passes while Mickey is away. A contrast exists, as it were, between Mickey's subjective sense of time and objective time (fig. 10). The complex combination of elements turns this illustration into a sophisticated example of telescoped narrative.

We noted above that the continuous narrative causes the visual text to become linear to some extent, which means that there is one logical direction in which the eye must follow the imaginary movements of the recurring figure, if the picture's meaning is to be revealed. It is therefore natural that the direction of the action represented will usually be from the left to right, in accordance with the flow of the linear verbal text. This is true of all the examples adduced here (except for *Do*, because of its cyclical character). It also means, of course, that in Semitic languages whose script reads from right to left this will also have to be the direction of the continuous narrative illustration. A simple example is *The Giraffe Has a Sore Throat*, Arieh Navon's poem in Hebrew: The poor animal, shown six times for six days of illness, gets better as the bandage around its throat slowly disappears toward the left.

By the same token a book written in Latin script that is translated into a Semitic language has to have its illustrations turned about. The Israeli edition of one of Tison and Taylor's Barbapapa books, *Barbapapa's Journey*, shows the space-flight as a continuous narrative from right to left, conforming to the Hebrew text; by an oversight the Latin inscription on the spacecraft has not been changed on this page; it appears in reverse, indicating the original "Latin course" of events.

At this point we might well ask where the psychological basis for the continuous narrative type of illustration is to be found. What justification does the illustrator have for his assumption that by applying this specific device he will succeed in having his picture perceived and understood in a manner consistent with his intentions?

We have to assume that the artist relies, consciously or unconsciously, on phenomena characterizing the operation of the human mind. Two of these seem to be particularly relevant to our topic.

Studies in the psychology of visual perception have shown the tendency of the perceiver to join together objects and elements which are found in the visual field and to combine them into patterns and configurations, especially if these objects are relatively close to each other. This is understood as "Gestalt closure" by most writers on the subject,[6] though others would explain it differently. Gregory speaks of the assumption that illusory data can be created simply by setting up sufficiently high probabilities that they

6. See, for instance, Edmund B. Feldman, "Perceiving the Elements: Aesthetics," *Art as Image and Idea* (Englewood Cliffs, N.J.: Prentice-Hall, 1967), p. 291 ff.

Fig. 10. Maurice Sendak, "And up and up and over the top"

Illustrations from *In the Night Kitchen*, written and illustrated by Maurice Sendak. Copyright © 1970 by Maurice Sendak. By permission of Harper & Row, Publishers, Inc. *In the Night Kitchen*, by Maurice Sendak, is published in the United Kingdom by The Bodley Head.

should be present, and states that this is essential for graphic art to be possible.[7] Experimental psychologists know that illusory movement can be created experimentally by identical stimuli that are very close to each other.[8]

We may accept as probable that the recurring figures in the continuous narrative picture constitute such identical stimuli. Though they are not absolutely identical, they bear sufficient common marks of identity and are perceived in an appropriate time interval to give rise to an imaginary line of movement and an illusory perception of action performed by one person.[9]

In this connection we might also refer to Michael Polanyi's[10] concepts on how a picture is viewed. He distinguishes between focal awareness and subsidiary awareness: to look at the parts of a painting separately is to see them focally, while to see them together forming a whole is to be aware of them subsidiarily. Now, in the special case of the continuous narrative it seems that in order to understand the illustration we have to look first at the "movement" of the recurring figure with focal awareness, detaching it from the rest of the picture, and only then to see it with subsidiary awareness as

7. R. L. Gregory, "The Confounded Eye," in Richard L. Gregory and Ernest H. Gombrich, eds., *Illusion in Nature and Art* (London: Duckworth, 1973), pp. 49–96.

8. See, for instance, K. V. Smith and M. E. Smith, *Psychology: An Introduction to Behavior Science* (New York: Little, Brown, 1973), pp. 14–15, 79.

9. Certain concepts developed by artists like Marcel Duchamp and Balla as well as some of their paintings would also be relevant to our discussion.

10. Michael Polanyi, "What Is a Painting?" *The American Scholar* 39, no. 4: 655–69 (1970).

aspects of a whole. Expressed differently, in this case the background becomes a stage on which the recurring figure acts in illusory space and time.

The other phenomenon facilitating the perception of the continuous
narrative is found in the cognitive area. Ernest Gombrich, for one, has
several times called attention to the importance of the context, situational,
sociocultural and verbal, in which a work of art or any other visual object is
placed in order to understand its meaning.[11] In the case of the illustration
whose function it is to accompany a verbal text, this dependence is clearly
felt; knowledge of the verbal text will make it easier to grasp the visual
message. After all, even the two paintings by Michelangelo and Sassetta are
in the widest sense illustrations, illuminations of stories told. Whoever
knows the title of Michelangelo's work and remembers the relevant chapter
in Genesis, will be in an easier position to recognize the figures on both sides
of the tree as the recurring dramatis personae of a violent action. The child
who hears Wendelin's cry "if only I were a lion!" will more readily identify
(and identify with) the transformation.

Though the verbal-visual context clearly facilitates perception and understanding, it does not constitute a condition to that effect; for, as was said
above, the recurring figures creates a perceptual attraction so that the eye is
easily persuaded to grasp the seven figures of the child-turning-into-lion as
one and the same Wendelin.

However, it happens quite often that the continuous narrative represents
an instance of ambiguous visual codification and creates intriguing perceptual problems: how and why is the viewer to decide that he sees a number of
similar figures, or just one figure repeated? To give two examples: why are
we supposed to see, on the pages of Milne and Shepard's "Hoppity,"[12]
repeated three times the *one* and *same* Christopher Robin who cannot stop
hopping, and not *three* children skipping together (fig. 11), while in Shlon-

Fig. 11. E. H. Shepard, "Hoppity"

From *When We Were Very Young* by A. A. Milne, illustrated by Ernest H. Shepard. Illustrations copyright © E. H. Shepard. By permission of Curtis Brown Limited. *When We Were Very Young* is published in Hebrew by Macberot Lesifrut, Tel Aviv.

11. Ernest H. Gombrich, "The Visual Image," *Scientific American*, Sept. 1972, pp. 82–96.
12. A. A. Milne, "Hoppity," *When We Were Very Young*; illus. by Ernest H. Shepard (London: Methuen, 1943), pp. 60–61.

sky and Navon's picture of an animal choir in *Mickey-Mahu's Adventures*, we discern three upright frogs and not one frog moving to and fro as he sings? (fig. 12)—why not vice versa? In such moments, only the text will guide us.

We may therefore conclude that the communication of meaning in the continuous narrative rests mainly with two factors: the aesthetic quality, the degree of excellence, by which the illustrator convinces us that we look at imaginary movement, and the verbal-visual context in which the illustration appears.

Fig. 12. Arieh Navon, "Frogs' Trio"
From *Sefer Allilot Mickey-Mahu*, by Avraham Shlonsky, illustrated by Arieh Navon. By permission of Sifriat Po'alim Workers' Book-Guild (Hashomer Hatzair) Ltd., Tel Aviv.

CHILDREN'S WORKS CITED

BLECHER, WILFRIED. *Wo ist Wendelin?* Weinheim: Beltz, 1965.
BORCHERS, ELISABETH. *Das rote Haus in einer Kleinen Stadt.* Illus. by Günther Stiller. München: Ellermann, 1969.
HERZKA, HEINZ, and HEIRI STEINER. *Do in den roten Stiefeln.* Zurich: Artemis, 1969.
HILLEL, AYIN. *Bulbul Lamah Kakhah.* Illus. by Shmuel Katz. Tel Aviv: Massada, 1973.
KEATS, EZRA JACK. *Whistle for Willie.* New York: Viking, 1964.
MILNE, A. A. *When We Were Very Young.* Illus. by E. H. Shepard. London: Methuen, 1943.
NAVON, ARIEH. *La Giraffa Ke'ev Garon.* Merhavia, Tel Aviv: Sifriat Po'alim, n.d.
RUCK-PAUQUÉT, GINA, and SIGRID HEUCK. *Pony.* Zurich, Freiburg: Atlantis, 1961.
SENDAK, MAURICE. *In the Night Kitchen.* New York: Harper & Row, 1970.
SHLONSKY, AVRAHAM. *Sefer Allilot Mickey-Mahu.* Illus. by Arieh Navon. Merhavia, Tel Aviv: Sifriat Po'alim, 1952.
TISON, ANETTE, and TALUS TAYLOR. *Massa'o shel Barba-abba.* Trans. by Uri Sela. Tel Aviv: Zmora-Bitan-Modan, 1977.

4

Interplay of the Literal and the Figurative

VERBAL METAPHOR AND THE ILLUSTRATOR

Figurative language is one of the basic modes of human expression and communication. We will, then, expect that it also occurs in the literature written for children.

A growing proportion of children's literature is accompanied ever more profusely by illustrations; so an intriguing question arises—how does the illustrator render figurative and especially metaphorical speech found in the texts that he is involved with? The question intrigues us because metaphor is very much an idiosyncratic way of expression, peculiar to an author and/or a language. In a way, illustrating may be compared to translating. Yet, whereas in verbal translation it is both very important and difficult to find equivalents for the original expression, the visual artist is in a somewhat different situation. For illustrating a text is, in an even wider sense than verbally translating it, a matter of interpreting and commenting on it. Coming upon a metaphor in a text he is about to illustrate, the artist has a wide range of possibilities; he chooses contents and meanings and transfers them to his pictures, depending on the nature and limitations of his medium.

Assuming that the most engaging instances of metaphorical language would particularly, if by no means only, be found in poems written for children we leafed through a large number of poetry books for children in several languages. We especially looked for poems in which the metaphorical expression plays a rather significant role in creating mood and meaning and which are accompanied by an illustration. In what ways, we asked ourselves, do illustrators convey these expressions from the verbal source language to the visual target language.[1]

CATEGORIES OF METAPHORS

First, while attempting not to get lost in the intricate terminologies of the metaphor (for that is not our subject), we would like to note some of the

---

This chapter has been reprinted with changes by permission of Beltz Verlag.

1. For the terms *source language* and *target language*, see M. B. Dagut, "Can 'Metaphor' Be Translated?" *Babel: International Journal of Translation* 22, no. 1, pp. 533–37 (1976).

categories we found in poems for children, and in a few prose texts. The accent is on content, not on formal semantic elements.

Metaphors and Similes

PERSONIFICATION:
> The school yearns for us . . .
>   the chalk waits impatiently . . .
>   they are bored without us . . .[2]

> The moon kissed her[3]

> The moon refreshes his bright face in the river[4]

> The clouds weave a shawl . . . for the sky to put on[5]

DEHUMANIZATION:
> I'd like to be a lighthouse . . . to keep my eye on everything . . . with the ships all watching me[6]

> My father's hand is a roadmap[7]

THERIOMORPHIZATION (object compared to animal):
> The fog comes on little cat feet . . .[8]

> A troop of horses races across the sky[9]

> A train is a dragon . . . he wriggles his tail[10]

OBJECT COMPARED TO OBJECT:
> Snow flakes like goose feathers[11]

> The sea is an orchestra[12]

> . . . taxis green or blue . . .
> they roll along the avenue . . .
> like spools of colored thread[13]

Extended Metaphor (poetic image dominating the poem)

> Sleep has bound me to the night by my head . . .
> Sleep has not yet finished sleeping me . . .[14]

> The noonday train's whistle . . . blows a hole in
> (the owl's) dream[15]

2. Jerzy Ludwig Kern, "Przed pierwszym dzwonkiem," *Nasze Podwórko*; illus. by Jozef Wilkoń (Warzawa: Nasza Księgarnia, 1975).
3. Fanya Bergstein, *Vayehee Erev*; illus. by H. Hausmann (Tel Aviv: Hakibbutz Hame'uhad, 1948).
4. Mírko Hanák and Ljuba Štíplová, "Byla hluboká a chladná řeka," *Co sí povídají zvířátka v noci* (Praha: Albatros, 1976).
5. Langston Hughes, "Garment"; illus. by Angela Adams, in *Childcraft*, vol. 1 (Chicago: World Book–Childcraft, 1980), pp. 86–87.
6. Rachel Field, "I'd Like to Be a Lighthouse"; illus. by S. Fleishmann, in *ibid.*, p. 210.
7. Armand Van Assche, "De hand van mijn vader," *De Zee is een Orkest*; illus. by Gijs Mertens (Gottmer, Haarlem: Altiora Averbode, 1978).
8. Carl Sandburg, "Fog"; illus. by Dick Smith, in *Childcraft*, vol. 1, p. 100.
9. Leopold Staff, "Kwiecien," *Szum Drzew*; illus. by Jozef Wilkoń (Warzawa: Nasza Księgarnia, 1961).
10. Rowena B. Bennett, "A Modern Dragon"; illus. by Farrell Grehan, in *Childcraft*, vol. 1, pp. 206–7.
11. Ivy O. Eastwick, "From the Sky"; illus. by Rosi Marie Bednarik-Gaigg., in *Childcraft*, vol. 1, pp. 88–89.
12. Armand Van Assche, "De Zee is een Orkest," *De Zee*.
13. Rachel Field, "Taxis"; illus. by Hope Taylor, in *Childcraft*, vol. 1, pp. 200–1.
14. Nurit Zarhi, *Yashnoonah*; illus. by Ruth Tsarfati (Jerusalem: Keter, 1978).
15. F. Du Plessis and Katrine Harries, "Ou Uil," *Rympieboek vir Kinders* (Kaapstad: Tafelberg, 1963).

And the bygone days would suddenly return if
the merry-go-round started turning backwards . . .
But when I come to think, I even get afraid . . .
Turn, merry-go-round, in the usual direction[16]

Water is a Mirror[17]

Idiom

Bookworm[18]

She gets on his nerves[19]

A fat father crocodile weeps . . .
crocodile tears . . . because he has eaten . . .
three nice little ducks . . .[20]

APPROACHES AND SOLUTIONS

When the illustrator is confronted with metaphorical language, several approaches are open to him.

He may simply, and legitimately, *ignore the metaphorical component in the text on hand and concentrate on other parts.* In "Reflection in the Water" the artist is interested in the main poetic image, water as a mirror, and neglects the metaphor:

The light paints on the water
it scurries over it like over a piano[21]

The illustrator may present the metaphor realistically, without any visual reference to its figurative intention. When "Taxis" rolling along the avenue are compared to spools of colored thread, the cars in the picture are painted in many colors, but the idea of swift passage that blurs their form is not represented.[22]

The same author's poem expresses a child's wish "to be a lighthouse" and to have the ships all watching him, but the lighthouse in the picture is drawn very realistically with no hint of personification about it.[23]

"What the lightning rod tells" the child is that he will always protect and save him but what we see in the illustration (fig. 13) is heavy rainclouds and a house with a small lightning rod just being struck by lightning.[24]

16. Vytantas Rudokas, "Ir prabėgė dienos grįžtu vel staiga," *Kai Ženie potekės arba laiškāi į ateítį;* illus. by Aruydas Každailis (Vilnius: Vaga, 1967).
17. Mílena Lukešová, "Odraz ve Voďe," *Bačkůrky z Mechu;* illus. by Mírko Hanák (Praha: Státní Naklada Telstri Detské Knihy, 1968).
18. Horst Kunze and Heinz Wegehaupt, "Bücher-Wurm," in Kunze and Wegehaupt, eds., *Für Kinder gemalt. Buchillustratoren der DDR.* (Berlin: Der Kinderbuchverlag, 1970).
19. Uri Orlev, *Meshaga'at Pilim;* illus. by Orah Eitan (Jerusalem: Keter, 1977).
20. Raymond Lichet, "Les Larmes de Crocodile," *Galipettes—Comptines de R.L.;* illus. by Colette de Gaillarbois (Paris: L'école des loisirs, 1971).
21. Lukešová, *Bačkůrky.*
22. Field, *Childcraft,* vol. 1, pp. 200–1.
23. *Ibid.,* p. 210.
24. Hans Baumann, "Was der Blitzableiter sagt," *Wer Flügel hat kann fliegen;* illus. by Wanda Zacharias (Reutlingen: Ensslin und Laiblin, 1966).

Was der Blitzableiter sagt

Am Haus bin ich ganz oben,
drum soll mich jeder loben,
bin ich auch schrecklich spitz.
Denn ich, ich fang den Blitz,
damit er mich, nur mich, durchsaust
und keinem, der im Hause haust,
den kleinsten Schaden tut.
Gehört dazu kein Mut?
Mir, einer Eisenstange,
macht kein Gewitter bange,
drum brauchen Mädchen nicht und Knaben
und auch nicht Katzen Angst zu haben,
wenn's in den Wolken kracht.
Ich wach bei Tag und Nacht,
geb jeden Blitz mit Eilpost weiter,
ich, euer alter Blitzableiter.

Fig. 13. Wanda Zacharias, ''What the Lightning Rod Tells''
From *Wer Flügel hat kann fliegen,* by Hans Baumann, illustrated by Wanda Zacharias, Ensslin und Laiblin Verlag, Reutlingen.

The child who is on his way to school before the bell rings for the first time this school year, ''Before the First Bell Rings,'' imagines that the school and everything in it—benches, chairs, the teacher's desk, the armorial white eagle, the chalk, etc.—are all yearning and impatiently waiting for him and his fellow students. The illustration gives visual form to some of these items, as stemming from the child's imagination, but again quite concretely without any attempt at personification.[25]

25. Kern, *Nasze.*

Illustrators who create purely realistic pictures like these refrain from interfering with, or offering support to, the child's imagination, except that they present to her or him the object about which the metaphor is being spun.

He may also represent the metaphor as if it were meant literally. This is a very old device in art. Shapiro tells of the habit of medieval artists to represent textual metaphors purely descriptively. He adduces the example of the Utrecht Psalter where the invocation "Awake, why sleepest thou, O Lord" (Psalm 44) is rendered pictorially by the figure of God lying in bed and being awakened by angels.[26]

The moon who "kisses the little girl" literally fastens his mouth to the back of her head while her father kisses her on her face.[27]

In "Ride in the Clouds" by Josef Guggenmos the boy imagines that he sees a white horse in the clouds and wishes to ride off on it: on a soft cloudscape the illustrator superimposes a horse, done in a firmer line; it does not really grow out of the cloudy shapes.

The poet has the child muse "On the inside my father's hand is a roadmap," and the picture shows the outlines of a hand with outstretched fingers, with topographical symbols inscribed on it.[28]

This descriptive approach offers some support to the child's mind: though the illustration does not represent the sense of the metaphor, it implies, by depicting it literally, how absurd or unrealistic, and thus often humorous, it becomes when taken literally. On the other hand, this is a narrow interpretation; it neglects the essential ambiguity of the metaphor and presents itself as an accurate piece of information, having an exact meaning and consequently an exact visual counterpart (semantic information in the sense the term is used by Moles[29]).

Sometimes illustrations of the descriptive kind acquire a distinctively didactic character. The illustrator takes up the metaphor, often an idiom, and explicates it; usually he does this in a humorous vein. Yet the inclination to teach in a playful way is unmistakable; in some cases the explication is carried on over a number of pictures.

"The Book-Worm" winding its way through a book and looking at us with its smiley face is one such example.[30]

Another one is Van Assche's "The Sea Is an Orchestra." The poem is an extended metaphor; the sea with its waves and winds reminds the author of the instruments, voices, and players in an orchestra. The illustrator makes use of the fact that the title of the poem also is that of the book. On the cover appears a picture of the undulating sea with an outsize shell riding on it. On the inside cover the sea has quietened down and the shell has become even

26. Meyer Shapiro, *Words and Pictures: On the Literal and the Symbolic in the Illustration of a Text* (The Hague, Paris: Mouton, 1973), p. 14. See also Hanns Swarzenski, *Monuments of Romanesque Art: The Art of Church Treasures in North-Western Europe*, 2nd ed. (Chicago: Univ. of Chicago Pr., 1967), plates 2, 3.

27. Bergstein, *Vayehe.*

28. Van Assche, "De hand van mijn vader," *De Zee.*

29. A. A. Moles, *Information Theory and Aesthetic Perception*; trans. by J. E. Cohen (Urbana: Univ. of Illinois Pr., 1968).

30. Kunze and Wegehaupt, *Für Kinder.*

larger and musical staves and notes are issuing from it; the third picture (fig. 14), accompanying the poem itself, responds to its opening sentence

> When it rains
> the sea is a big drum

and shows two large drumsticks beating on the rainswept gales. In the course of looking at the three pictures in the correct sequence we are led from a rather implied representation to a concrete one.

De zee is een orkest

Als het regent
is de zee een grote trommel
en de steeltjes van de regen
slaan erop. Spatten bonzen.

Dan komt de zon. Die blaast hoog
van de toren, in de wolken

een warme hoorn, tussen wangen als
sinaasappels.

En de golven met strijklicht,
violen die rood worden
tot achter hun oren. Ze duiken
kopje onder, zwieren en wiegen
als meeuwevleugels.

In het orkest van de zee
laat ik me drijven op de rug
als een noot tussen de notenbalk

tot het licht uitgaat. Kijk
daar krult nog wat schuim. Dat zijn
de witte hemdsboorden
van de zwartgeklede muzikanten.

Fig. 14. Gijs Mertens, "When it rains / The sea is a big drum"
From *De Zee is een Orkest* by A. Van Assche, illustrated by Gijs Mertens. By permission of Uitgeverij Altiora n.v., Averbode.

In Orlev's book called *She Drives Elephants Crazy*, after an idiom meaning "she drives people crazy," author and illustrator combine to play with idiomatic expressions. A little girl relates how her parents get angry at her because she stops talking to them—

> Father says . . .
> That girl drives elephants crazy

and the illustration depicts the parents' exaggerated gesture of despair—

> But I lie in bed alone
> I don't weep, for I have got an idea
> I am thinking of a troop of elephants
> that I am driving crazy very easily.
> They stand on their heads
> They stand up and fall down . . .

and a number of pictures show the elephants in all kinds of tricky poses.

Another simple device is used in the same book. The idiom "to leave the dishes" or lose one's cool is explicated in the text:

> And I would really like to see
> How father leaves the dishes
> surges up from the plate
> or comes out of the bottles . . .

The picture shows father coming out of six different kitchen utensils simultaneously (fig. 15); the expression cannot, therefore, be taken literally. This reminds us of what Binkley calls excavation,[31] that is, digging up, visually in our case, the true meaning hidden in the verbal expression, namely that father has lost his patience with his daughter.

Fig. 15. Orah Eitan, "How father leaves the dishes"
From *Meshaga'at Pilim* by Uri Orlev, illustrated by Orah Eitan. By permission of Keter Publishing House, Jerusalem.

Here, too, belongs "The Pikefish" by Robert Desnos. It relates the terrestrial adventures of a French fish. One sequence called Pike of Fortune (in the sense of soldier of fortune, someone who tries his luck and depends on it)

31. Timothy Binkley, "On the Truth and Probity of Metaphor," *The Journal of Aesthetics and Art Criticism* (Winter 1974), p. 175.

explicates the idiom in three pictures: in the first one the fish is standing proudly at the roadside in plain sunlight flashing a placard that says "To the Moon" at passing cars. In the second picture, toward evening, with only one car left on the road, the fish has a worried look and the placard says "To Italy." In the last one, deep in the night, the lonely fish collapses on his suitcase and the placard reads "To the Loire" (a river in France): the growing despair and the successively more modest requests clarify the meaning of Pike-of-Fortune and demonstrate what happens when luck runs out.

These didactic illustrations, then, are intended to please and instruct by being rather drily descriptive and often funny. Yet they view the metaphor as if it were denotative.

There exist more refined and complex ways of interpreting the metaphor in visual terms. One of them is *recreating or supporting the mood of the verbal image without actually representing it.*

In "May Rain" the poet exclaims

> Sparks, pearls and diamonds
> Drop from the smiling cloud.
> These are jewels, not rains . . .[32]

Nothing in the adjoining illustration is explicitly reminiscent of the comparison; yet with bright streaks and drops of rain on a sombre background the artist echoes, in a subdued manner, the lyrical mood.

Similarly, in "There Was a Deep Cold River"

> . . . When the moon comes
> To refresh his bright face in the river
> The goldfish sparkles
> Like the morningstar in the water

the illustrator conjures up, in sepia colors, the darkness of the night river and the fish that will shortly shine in the light of the moon.[33]

Many illustrations of this kind have a poetic quality which suggests why a metaphor should come into being at all.

In "Old Owl"

> The noonday train's whistle
> Blows a hole in (the owl's) dream.[34]

There is, in the illustration (fig. 16), something about the owl sleeping in the willow tree and the far-off train, which recreates the impression or mood that gave rise to the metaphor.

In "Sunrise" the sun

> Soft-touched by birds' wings in her head
> Her feet caressed by trees
> . . . strides to meet the day.[35]

32. Staff, "Deszcs Majowy," *Szum Drzew.*
33. Hanák amd Štíplová, *Co sí povídají.*
34. Du Plessis and Harries, *Rympieboek.*
35. Katharina Kosmak, "Sunrise"; illus. by Nicolas Mordvinoff, in *Childcraft*, vol. 1, p. 78.

Ou Uil

Ou Uil slaap langs die spruitjie
in die wilgerboom
Die middagtrein se fluitjie
blaas gate in sy droom

Fig. 16. Katrine Harries, "Old Owl"

From *Rympieboek vir Kinders* by F. Du Plessis, illustrated by Katrine Harries. By permission of Tafelberg-Uitgewers Beperk, Cape Town, South Africa.

The illustrator refrains from personifying the sun; but the branch of the tree and the bird sitting on it with outstretched wings, cutting across the red-hot sun, reflect the glowing daybreak which inspired the personification.

In "Winternight" by Christian Morgenstern:

> The bell sounded . . .
> and a snowflake
> fell with it like in a dream . . .
> it fell so silently
> like some angels' feathers
>
> . . .
>
> and when many thousands have fallen
> the earth will be white as if with angels'
> down.

The red-brown tints of the illustration (fig. 17) sustain the dreaminess of the night-bound town; there is no suggestion of angels' feathers in the picture. Its vertical panels indicate the passage of time, from left to right, the bell, a single snowflake, and the heavy snowfall covering the roofs and ground. Infinite softness and silence are conveyed. Moreover, the tall panels create a subtle sense of earth and sky, earth and heaven, being open and connected.

These illustrations outline, or mold, the frame or state of mind in which the metaphorical association could conceivably occur.

Fig. 17. Horst Lemke, "Winternight"
From *Kindergedichte* by Christian Morgenstern, illustrated by Horst Lemke. By permission of Carl Ueberreuter Verlag, Vienna.

The photograph illustrating "Fog" (fig. 18) does more; while alluringly reflecting the poem's mood:

> The fog comes
> . . . on little cat feet
> . . . sits . . . on silent haunches
> and then moves on[36]

36. Sandburg, in *Childcraft*, vol. 1, p. 100.

The fog comes
on little cat feet.
It sits looking
over harbor and city
on silent haunches
and then moves on.

CARL SANDBURG

Fig. 18. Dick Smith, "Fog"

it also moves much closer to the metaphor. In the mist small boats become visible, the shadows of their thin masts rippled by the almost silent waters. The row of boats points diagonally toward some large black poles; there is a sense of slow movement, of direction, in the picture. Here we have the double referential focus that does justice to the metaphor, the hint of an illusion.[37] Do we see only boats in the fog, or is there the trace of a supple beast moving toward us?

37. M. B. Dagut, personal communication (1979).

There exist ways of rendering metaphorical language in visual terms and retaining the dynamic power of the verbal expression, thus suggesting to the child how he might grasp and enjoy the open oscillating nature of the metaphor.

This can be done very simply, for instance, by the device of one illustration (fig. 19) being juxtaposed to, and serving, three poems: "Clouds" where clouds are compared to white sheep; "Garment" where clouds weave a shawl for the sky to put on; "Brooms" where the trees sweep the sky blue again.[38] Together with the children in the illustration who point at the sky, the child who reads the poem or has it read to him or her is challenged to try out different viewpoints: are the clouds busy weavers or slow sheep or just rubbish to be brushed off?

CLOUDS

White sheep, white sheep,
On a blue hill,
When the wind stops
You all stand still.
When the wind blows
You walk away slow.
White sheep, white sheep,
Where do you go?

CHRISTINA ROSSETTI

BROOMS

On stormy days
When the wind is high
Tall trees are brooms
Sweeping the sky.

They swish their branches
In buckets of rain,
And swash and sweep it
Blue again.

DOROTHY ALDIS

GARMENT

The clouds weave a shawl
Of downy plaid
For the sky to put on
When the weather's bad.

LANGSTON HUGHES

Fig. 19. Angela Adams, "Clouds," "Garment," "Brooms"

In *Sleepy One* the poet urges the small girl:

> Come out of sleep
> Sleepy one
> Get up and dress

38. *Childcraft*, vol. 1, p. 86.

and the girl replies

> How—?
> Sleep has bound me
> To the night by my head

and then again

> Sleep has not yet finished
> Sleeping me[39]

The illustrator refrains from personification (fig. 20); instead she paints several faces, partly overlapping: the girl trying to get up and falling back again, numb and dizzy with sleep, bound by sleep—three mouths but two (or three?) pairs of eyes, a situation real and unreal at one and the same time. When we compare this illustration with, say, "The moon kissed her," we have a demonstration of what Binkley means when he states that we have to distinguish between the literal reading of the words of a metaphor (compare the illustration to "The moon kissed her") and a literal translation of the sense of a metaphor (the illustration for "Sleep has bound me").[40]

"April," a poem about a rainstorm, begins and ends with the metaphor

> A troop of horses races across the sky.[41]

The dark heavy clouds in the illustration are suggestive of beasts. This is a faithful rendering of the metaphor: the child's associations may move to and fro—the ambiguous shapes in the sky, whether clouds or animals, are symbols of power. This is aesthetic information in Moles's sense, open to various interpretations, reminiscent of the indecisive shapes in the Rorschach test.

The illustrator for Lina Schwarz's "Clouds" treats the subject similarly. The poem relates that in a "sky that is a vast blue meadow" clouds move toward the sun; now one of them is a flower; now it dissolves in the heat of the sun—"a sigh . . . and it's gone." The cloud in the picture suggests the changing form of a flower, but not too explicitly.

In Prassinos's poem, a girl turns to her mother:

> In your eyes there is the sea.
> In the sea there is a storm,
> In the storm: a boat.
> In the boat: a little girl.
> In the little girl there is your child
> and I am going to drown myself mummy
> if you don't stop scolding

The urgency of the girl's threat and plea, clad in a concise poetic image, is rendered well by the illustrator (fig. 21) by the ambiguity of the eye in the storm, swaying, in abeyance, in the stylized stormy sea and the storm

---

39. Zarhi, *Yashnoonah.*
40. Binkley, "On the Truth and Probity of Metaphor," p. 176.
41. Staff, "Kwiecien," *Szum Drzew.*

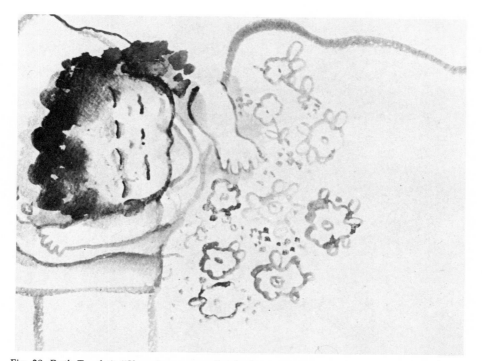

Fig. 20. Ruth Tsarfati, "Sleep has not yet finished / sleeping me"
From *Yashnoonah* by Nurit Zarhi, illustrated by Ruth Tsarfati. By permission of Keter Publishing House, Jerusalem.

within the eye, with the dark clouds of mother's anger moving above it all. The dramatic confrontation is represented effectively. The artist is less sensitive to the girl's desperate appeal for warmth and protection and her unconscious wish to identify with her mother. The stress is interpreted, but not its psychological roots.

Rudokas's poem "And the Bygone Days," too, is based on a poetic image,

> And the bygone days would suddenly return
> If the merry-go-round started turning backwards . . .

But in the next moment the child becomes afraid of his own wish; what would happen to his development and his growing sense of responsibility toward parents and homeland? He would be unable to fulfill them if he were to stay a small child. And so he concludes:

> Turn, merry-go-round, in the usual direction . . .

The illustrator (fig. 22) seizes the child's momentary dream, the wish to return to the earlier days that is expressed by the image of the merry-go-round turning the other way. He draws an impressive surrealistic fantasy: a clock in the center, its hands flying off into space. The moon above the horizon and the sun and a star below it add to the sense of disorder: time and space are out of joint. Only the seesaw stands steady.

Dans tes yeux il y a la mer.
Sur la mer il y a la tempête.
Dans la tempête : une barque.
Dans la barque : une petite fille.
Dans la petite fille il y a ton enfant
et je vais me noyer maman
si tu ne cesses de gronder.

Gisèle Prassinos

Fig. 21. Danielle Avezard, "In Your Eyes There Is the Sea"
"Dans tes yeux il y a la mèr," by Gisèle Prassinos. From *Il était une fois, les enfants . . .*, edited by J. Charpentreau, illustrated by Danielle Avezard. By permission of Editions La Farandole, Paris.

Ir prabėgę dienos grįžtų vėl staiga.
Jeigu karuselė suktųsi atgal...

Bet kai pagalvoju, daros net baisu:
Aš juk likčiau mažas, kaip dabar esu.

O širdis man tuksi, rodosi, girdžiu:
„Niekad nepasiektum tolimų žvaigždžių.

Ir tave pranoktų sodo obelis...
Būtum pionierius šimtmečius kelis.''

Iš tiesų, kiek Žemėj atvirų kelių,
Kiek nepastatyta miestų didelių.

Kiek Tėvynei reikia rankų šilumos,
Kiek šviesos dar trūksta kiekvienuos namuo

Ne, nenoriu būti aš našta tėvams, —
Tokią karuselę skirčiau tinginiams.

Tegu peteliškių gaudyt eis kiti...
Sukis, karusele, įprasta kryptim!

Fig. 22. Aruydas Každailis, "If the merry-go-round started turning backwards . . ."
Reproduced from *Kai Ženie potekės arba laiškai į ateitį*, by Vytantas Rudokas. Vaga Publishers, 1967.

Yet the illustration is an open one and so it is open to interpretation: does the illustrator by way of his haunting picture sympathize with the child's dream and widen its scope, or else caution him against the awesome disruption of order; does he, in other words, counteract the cautionary text or support it?[42]

This last group of illustrations convincingly demonstrates that the connotative dynamics of verbal metaphor can certainly be rendered in visual images, even in illustrations for children.

VISUALIZATION OF FIGURATIVE LANGUAGE AND THE MIND OF A CHILD

Our subject is the interpretation of figurative and especially metaphorical speech in visual terms. We cannot, however, express an opinion on the educational function and value of the artist's approach to his work without saying a few words about metaphor and the child.

Arbuthnot wrote long ago that to her mind figurative speech in poems for children is hazardous and even harmful: the child is literal-minded and tends to misinterpret figures of speech; these are more likely to muddle than to inspire the young (even sixth-graders); many figures of speech are platitudinous; less and simpler figurative speech is better for the child.[43]

Arbuthnot's misgivings were and still are justified; about that time attention began to focus on the culturally deprived child and the problems he faces in his language development, even on the level of literal communication. For the fifties and sixties the endeavor to increase the child's ability for denotative expression and understanding became an overriding concern; and of course it is true that the understanding of figurative speech presupposes the understanding of the literal meanings of words and phrases that make up a figure of speech.

Yet it is no less true that purely literal speech is not only dull but practically nonexistent. Man naturally introduces figures of speech in his most prosaic communications; he is unable to refrain from doing so. More than that; as Dagut has put it:

Metaphor is perhaps the greatest life-giving force in language. For it is certainly through the individual speaker's capacity for, and receptivity to, metaphor that language is endowed with the absolutely vital potential for semantic expansion.[44]

In other words, figurative language is part of the human heritage of symbolic communication and no child should be deprived of the opportunity to learn to use and to enjoy this aspect of it. Obviously this has to be accomplished tastefully and with circumspection. One should also remember that the work of Piaget and his disciples, while emphasizing rational cognitive

---

42. See Hans A. Halbey, "Die offene und geschlossene Form im Bilderbuch," *Festschrift für Horst Kunze: Buch-Bibliothek-Leser* (Berlin: Akademie Verlag, 1969), pp. 533–37.
43. May H. Arbuthnot, *Children and Books*, 1st ed. (Chicago: Scott, Foresman, 1947), p. 196.
44. Dagut, "Can Metaphor Be Translated?" *Babel*, p. 23.

processes, has also made us more aware of the child mind's proclivity for personification and anthropomorphization.

What is the illustration's share in all this? What does the fact that there exist different ways of rendering a metaphor visually mean in this context? Mainly, that the illustration, by commenting on the figure of speech, is likely to aid the child to understand it better and to derive more and richer pleasure from both the illustrated text and the illustration, or else to effect the opposite, to impede such an experience from taking place.

It also means that the types of treatment we found fulfill various functions.

What we have called realistic presentation, the lightning rod, the teacher's desk, etc., that are personified in the text but shown as inanimate objects functioning in their environment, is in fact a rather exact description of physical appearance. The illustrator wishes to help the child by clarifying what the subject of the text "really" looks like. He leaves it entirely to the author to draw the child into his game of "as if" or into his daydream; he just supplies basic information. This is rather important for those children who have to be helped to understand the meaning of concepts; but it has little or no aesthetic potential. There is a gap between the poet who presents the object not as it really is, but with an imaginative purpose, and the illustrator who stays aloof. The child's imagination has to operate somewhere in between the two.

Literal, or descriptive, representation differs very much from realistic presentation. Here, too, the illustrator professes to offer accurate information: the horse galloping in the sky, the drumsticks beating on the sea, and other metaphors are drawn with precision and it is just this precision which is apt to introduce the child, as we said above, to one facet of the metaphor. Taken literally it becomes impossible or ridiculous; it has, therefore, to be understood "as if." Then it becomes a game. This is useful information that is able to help the child to grasp something of the nature of figurative language. Still, it treats the metaphor as if it were a riddle with a single solution to it; as if it had a closed single focus[45] one is supposed to aim at. It supports the imagination and restrains it at the same time. Illustrations of this kind, and especially the didactic ones, are often charming or full of humor. Yet at some point the information they offer becomes inaccurate because it is denotative and seemingly so practical. It tends to be visual demonstration rather than art. When the moon comes physically close to the girl and gives her a kiss, what is lost is the impression of intense light enwrapping her that the poet had in mind.

Art happens when the child's imagination is offered stimulation and support but also some freedom for its search for pleasure and meaning; when the opportunity is created for what Arnheim has called the stirring participation that distinguishes artistic experience from the detached accept-

45. Dagut, personal communication (1979).

ance of information.[46] Such occasions may arise within the range of the child's capacities, with the last two types of illustration.

When the illustrator succeeds in creating a picture which somehow resounds with the mood that gave rise to the metaphor in the first place, even without rendering the verbal image at all, he is asking the child to join him at a point in time *before* this image was coined or applied, the point at which the poet was inspired by a landscape or a state of mind, etc., and reacted by expressing and interpreting it. The vagueness of the aesthetic information included in the illustration implies an open invitation to the child to experience some empathy with the author.

Finally, there are the illustrations which are analogues of the verbal image. Though an aesthetic message cannot ever be really translated into another medium, an illustration by using its own elements in a similarly ambiguous way, confirms the openness of the verbal metaphor and intensifies it by transforming it into a visual metaphor. This blending of media is likely to enrich children's interest in, and potential for, aesthetic experiences.

TWO MORE QUESTIONS

There are at least two more questions which are relevant to the issue of the illustrator's approach to figurative speech and to which we ought to refer briefly.

One is the age of the child. It will be correct to assume that we find more realistic and literal rendering of metaphors accompanying poems for younger children and the more complex type in those for the older ones. But distinctions are not very clear-cut: *Sleepy One* was surely written for more or less the same age group as *She Drives Elephants Crazy*; the same is probably true of "To Be a Lighthouse," and "Winternight," and "Clouds." In addition, individual differences in the capabilities of children of the same age are certainly considerable in this respect; so it seems one should not expect too much correlation between age and type of illustration.

The other question is that of artistic quality. It is important to note and to bear in mind that illustrations of one and the same type differ very much in aesthetic level and excellence of execution: "Before the First Bell Rings" has a more stimulating structure than "What the Lightning Rod Tells"; "Father Leaves the Dishes" has a humorous appeal that is lacking in "The Pikefish"; "Winternight" and "Old Owl" are delicate in a way "May Rain" is not; "Fog," and "In Your Eyes There Is the Sea," and "And the Bygone Days" are sophisticated and intricate to a degree not achieved by many illustrators.

The well-illustrated poem opens various avenues for developing the child's power to operate with, and to derive satisfaction from, the connota-

46. Rudolf Arnheim, *Art and Visual Perception* (Berkeley: Univ. of California Pr., 1974), p. 460.

tive and the figurative modes of human communication which are characteristic of art.

FROM LITERAL TEXT TO VISUAL METAPHOR

As a kind of last thought we may note that at times the illustrator takes up a
literal text and transforms it into a pictorial metaphor. This, too, is a device
found not infrequently in art. The best known example is probably Michelangelo's painting of the *Creation of Adam* in the Sistine Chapel in Rome. The
first chapters of the book of Genesis relate how God created man in his own
image, breathing the spirit of life into the body molded of the dust of the
earth. This biblical account is originally intended to be taken literally. Michelangelo renders the scene by picturing the Creator's finger reaching out
toward Adam, transmitting to him the spark of life. Arnheim has stressed
that the artist chose to introduce a change in the scene so as to make it more
effective pictorially: transmitting a spark, Arnheim shows, is visually more
dynamic and expressive than breathing into a lifeless body.[47] We can add
that by doing so, Michelangelo also substitutes a visual metaphor, one
fitting the spirit of the original, for the literal text.

In a similar way, in Miyoshi's adaptation for children of the story of the
prophet Jonah, a voice speaks to the young man telling him to get up and go
to Nineveh. Jonah thinks that God has spoken to him. This is a cautious but
still literal rendering of the biblical text, which simply says that God spoke to
Jonah. However, the illustration (fig. 64) represents the event, God address-
ing Jonah, by replacing direct speech with a festive yellow veil, a solemn
emanation descending upon Jonah from above, encompassing him and
detaching him from the everyday commonplace world. God's personal
verbal message is converted into a visual metaphor of divine, numinous
presence. The transformation results in a representation more dignified and
universally expressive than the attempt to depict God.

These two pictures, Michelangelo's painting and Miyoshi's illustration,
are worlds apart artistically, but they share a common approach: a literal text
is "metaphorized" by the artist to facilitate the transmission of a fun-
damentalist religious message.

"Skyscraper," by Hans Stempel and Martin Ripkins, is a poem with an
ideological message.[48] A skyscraper dominates the town, dwarfing the old
beautiful buildings. This is a pity because the skyscraper offers no joy to
anyone. It is just an office building, empty after 5:00 P.M.

The illustrator intensifies the message. In her drawing, the skyscraper is
an enormous typewriter. A tiny cathedral and more diminutive historic
buildings squat around it. By using a visual metaphor, in this case a part
standing for the whole, the typewriter representing the bleak functionality

---

47. *Ibid.*, pp. 458–60.
48. "Wolkenkratzer," *Purzelbaum: Verse für Kinder*; illus. by Ulrike Enders (München: Ellermann, 1972).

of the office building, she exaggerates and drives home the intention of the poem, creating an effect that is at once dramatic and funny.

Visual hyperbole, an exaggeration not to be taken literally, is also used to humorous effect by Margret Rettich, the illustrator of "It Rains," an anonymous rhyme telling us that it rains day and night and then it will stop.[49] The poem does not use figurative language, except for the idiom (or "fossil" metaphor) that the sun will smile again. The illustration depicts a rainstorm sweeping up people armed with umbrellas high into the sky (fig. 23).

Fig. 23. Margret Rettich, "It Rains"
From *Kindergedichte*, illustrated by Margret Rettich, selected by Edith Harries, published by Otto Maier Verlag Ravensburg © 1978.

The concept of a part standing for the whole is put to impressive tragicomic use by Delessert. When, in Ionesco's *Tale Number 1*, little Josette talks nonsense and all the people in the grocery turn around and look at her with heavy frightened eyes, the illustrator turns this into one large eye, with people's legs visible behind it.

We said before that one should not expect too much correlation between types of illustrations and the ages of the children for whom they are intended. The present example is a case in point. The figurative eye, a quite demanding metaphor, appears in a book which has, according to its subtitle, been created for very small children.

49. Anonymous, "Es regnet," in Edith Harries, ed., *Kindergedichte*; illus. by Margret Rettich (Ravensburg: Otto Maier, 1978).

In Ionesco-Delessert's *Tale Number 2* there is another interesting instance of metaphorizing the literal. When Josette's father quarrels with the maid, Josette ends the squabble remarking, simply, that both say the same things.

The illustration shows Josette, flag in hand, sitting high up above the adults' heads, on a huge white dove; the dove carries an olive twig in her beak. Behind Josette two rainbows cross the sky. This allusion to Noah and the great Flood, after which God made peace with humanity, is a detailed metaphor of Josette's feeling of omnipotence. It is quite an amusing figurative statement of the child's aggrandized feelings of his or her importance in the scheme of things. It conforms to and illustrates very well Piaget's concepts on the child's modes of thought (on which the two tales, *Number 1* and *Number 2*, are based). However, the allusion to Noah may please and amuse the older child and the adult who are aware of the connection. It cannot possibly make sense to the very young child for whom the illustration has been painted.

These examples demonstrate that illustrators will apply visual metaphor to literal texts mainly with the intention of increasing their impact and frequently also in order to make an abstract idea more concrete.

CHILDREN'S WORKS CITED

BAUMANN, HANS. *Wer Flügel hat kann fliegen*. Illus. by Wanda Zacharias. Reutlingen: Ensslin & Laiblin, 1966.

BERGSTEIN, FANYA. *Vayehee Erev*. Illus. by H. Hausmann. Tel Aviv: Hakibbutz Hame'uhad, 1948.

CHARPENTREAU, JACQUES, ed. *Il était une fois, les enfants . . . .* Illus. by Danielle Avezard. Paris: Éditions la Farandole, 1980.

DESNOS, ROBERT. "Brochet de Fortune." In *Le brochet*. Paris: Éditions la Farandole, 1971.

DU PLESSIS, F., and KATRINE HARRIES. *Rympieboek vir Kinders*. Kaapstad: Tafelberg, 1963, 1970.

GUGGENMOS, JOSEF. "Wolkenritt." In *Mutze Butz*. Illus. by Emanuela Delignon. Recklinghausen: Bitter, 1977.

HANÁK, MÍRKO, and LJUBA ŠTÍPLOVÁ. *Co sí povídají zvířátka v noci*. Praha: Albatros, 1976.

IONESCO, ÉUGENE. *Conte, Numéro 1. Pour enfants de moins de trois ans*. Illus. by Étienne Delessert. Paris: Harlin Quist, 1969.

———. *Conte, Numéro 2. Pour enfants de moins de trois ans*. Illus. by Étienne Delessert. Paris: Harlin Quist, 1970.

KERN, JERZY LUDWIG. *Nasze Podwórko*. Illus. by Josef Wilkoń. Warzawa: Nasza Księgarnia, 1975.

LICHET, RAYMOND. *Galipettes—Comptines de R.L.* Illus. by Colette de Gaillarbois. Paris: L'école des loisirs, 1971.

LUKEŠOVÁ, MÍLENA. *Bačkůrky z Mechu*. Illus. by Mírko Hanák. Praha: Státní Naklada Telstri Detské Knihy, 1968.

MIYOSHI, SEKIYA. *Jonah*. Tokyo: Shiko-Sha, 1977.

MORGENSTERN, CHRISTIAN. *Kindergedichte*. Illus. by Horst Lemke. Wien, Heidelberg: Ueberreuter, 1966.

ORLEV, URI. *Mishaga'at Pilim*. Illus. by Orah Eitan. Jerusalem: Keter, 1977.

Poems and Rhymes. Childcraft—The How and Why Library, vol. 1. Chicago: World Book–Childcraft International, 1980.

RUDOKAS, VYTANTAS. *Kai Ženie potekės arba laiškai į atéitį*. Illus. by Aruydas Každailis. Vilnius: Vaga, 1967.

SCHWARZ, LINA. *Ancora . . . e poi basta*. Illus. by Maria Enrica Agostinelli. Milano: Mursia, 1965.

STAFF, LEOPOLD. *Szum Drzew*. Illus. by Jozef Wilkoń. Warzawa: Nasza Księgarnia, 1961.

STEMPEL, HANS, and MARTIN RIPKINS. "Wolkenkratzer." In *Purzelbaum: Verse für Kinder*. Illus. by Ulrike Enders. München: Ellermann, 1972.

VAN ASSCHE, ARMAND. *De Zee is een Orkest*. Illus. by Gijs Mertens. Gottmer, Haarlem: Altiora Averbode, 1978.

ZARHI, NURIT. *Yashnoonah*. Illus. by Ruth Tsarfati. Jerusalem: Keter, 1978.

5

The Roles of Natural Landscape

With the exception of a few eras and a small number of schools, the landscape has always been an element of pictorial art—be it as the subject of paintings dedicated to the presentation and celebration of its beauty or its sinister power, its eternal glory or changing moods, or else as part of the composition, constituting the environment where events take place.

Nature is represented in art in many different ways and is used to represent many different things. All art is an abstraction; it is, as Kenneth Clark has written in his book *Landscape into Art*, to some degree symbolic;[1] this is why the viewer of an art work depicting a landscape is wont to search for moods and meanings. While it is true, as Susanne Langer has emphasized,[2] that the landscape does not express a mood, it has a mood. The artist who creates a picture of a landscape wishes to express a mood or at least the background for one. More than this, there exists a certain interdependence between natural landscape and pictured landscape. Much as the latter is influenced by the appearance of the former, countless people have gained access to nature, have acquired a relationship to their neighborhood, their country, and the wide world through the mediation of visual art. Our appreciation of nature depends more than we know on the eyes of artists who create the shapes and symbols which we accept and apply to our own vision.[3]

So, too, natural landscapes in the illustrations in children's books are an important symbolic means of expression. They offer depth to children's imaginary experience; they strengthen their sense of beauty, belonging, and identification with their small intimate world; beckon to them in the shape of landscapes presented as ideal or open for them the liberating vistas of faraway sceneries where elemental forces range. They may serve as symbols for abstractions such as tension and direction (flowing water), rhythms of change (the sea, the seasons), and for the seemingly eternal (mountain ranges, the desert). However, landscapes in children's books are not usually

---

1. Kenneth Clark, *Landscape into Art* (Harmondsworth: Penguin Books, 1949, 1961), p. 18.
2. Susanne K. Langer, *Feeling and Form: A Theory of Art* (New York: Scribner's, 1953), p. 19.
3. See Ernest H. Gombrich, *Art and Illusion* (New York: Pantheon Books, 1960).

the subject of pictures; they represent the imaginary space where the protagonists—children, adults, animals—live, move, suffer, set out for adventures, discover new realms of danger and grandeur.

Within this framework, illustrators assign various roles to the landscape
in their pictures. Frequently indeed, they use it just to mark the environment, to indicate the factual background where certain stages of the plot
develop. In *The Golden Axe*, edited by Chu Yang, the mountainous environment illustrated helps us to better understand how hard Cheng Ping, the
brave boy, has to work, chopping firewood and carrying water, to satisfy the
wicked landlord. In Mitschgut's books without words, *In Our Village*, nature
appears as the colorful background for the manifold lively activities of
children and adults alike; the illustrator makes it perfectly clear through his
slightly naive and yet sophisticatedly humorous pictures that he wishes to
help the child recognize and get acquainted with his environment by way of
getting involved with the numerous people milling around on these pages,
working and playing and moving about with joyful alacrity. Similar
approaches are found in other German books which appeared in the seven-
ties. Fuchshuber's *Come and Spend the Vacation with Us*, also without words,
whisks groups of children through a continuous panorama of regions. In
Animals around Us, Fechner creates peaceful backgrounds for the various
animals which she depicts for the child to recognize and learn to relate to.
Zimnik's *Bill's Balloon Trip* uses wide sweeps of pastures, forests, and
mountains to reinforce our impression of Bill's vertiginous adventure.

In these books the landscape is depicted without any special emphasis.
But factually, as it were, it is shown to be bright, open, beautiful, inviting: an
important environmental message issues from these pictures.

However, many illustrators use nature to accentuate the mood of the
story. One outstandingly beautiful example is the double page in *The Snowy
Day*, by Ezra Jack Keats (fig. 24), where we are told how Peter, who the day
before had spent many hours playing in the newly fallen snow all by
himself, now calls to his friend, after breakfast; they go out together into the
deep, deep snow. The illustration which Keats creates around the text
shows the two very small boys walking in the towering snow that shines in
pastel colors, with a V-shaped, deep-blue open sky above them, and,
joining the tactile experience to the visual one, large sparkling snow crystals
drift, to be touched, all over the picture. An expression of deep satisfaction
reigns as Peter steps out to immerse himself, together with his friend, in the
snow, a mood of happiness and togetherness.

In Starshinov's *That's the Way It Can Be* there is a poem on a cloud:
grandmother wakes up to lament the drought. Dust lies on the dry fields
and lanes. The flowers dream of rain. A cloud passes in the sky and, taking
pity, drops its tears onto the land. The rain gets stronger. Yet the illustrator
wanders away from the text. He mentions, visually, the cloud bursting with
rain over the horizon, but the mood arising from the illustration is one of

After breakfast he called to his friend from across the hall, and they went out together into the deep, deep snow.

Fig. 24. Ezra Jack Keats, *The Snowy Day*
From *The Snowy Day* by Ezra Jack Keats. Copyright © 1962 by Ezra Jack Keats. Reprinted by permission of Viking Penguin Inc.

lyric praise of the beauty of nature. The small figure of the man fishing in the brook is surrounded by tall trees that watch over his peaceful seclusion.

In Talmi's short poem, *Spring Has Come*, which speaks of the fragrant air, the green meadows, the blue sky, and the golden sun above, a double illustration heightens the gay mood: to the right, in simple black and white lines, a girl picks flowers while she advances into the picture on the left, an innocent lyric presentation, in soft colors, of ideal spring.

Many landscape illustrations that vibrate somehow between just being backgrounds and yet calling forth, evoking a mood, are found everywhere; but it seems they abound especially in Russian books for children. There they figure prominently, being painted in warm colors and easy structures and styles. They reflect a firm empathy with the places and regions and seasons portrayed, a constant love for the countryside that is presented as captivating the children's attention and arousing their sense of beauty.

Often the landscape serves to visualize an *idea*, a concept. The frontispiece of Ivitch's *How to Harness Rivers* shows a waterfall cutting deeply into huge looming rocks; even more than the illustration depicts a corner in the faraway mountains it intends to convey, by exaggerating shapes and perspective in an expressionistic vein, the idea of the powerfulness of water.

Or *Pony*, by Ruck-Pauquét and Heuck, the story of a horse who breaks out of his confinement in a backyard in the big city: all of a sudden he stands still, the last smokestacks have fallen behind, around him bright green meadows spread far over the mountain slopes toward the high horizon, an ideal landscape that stands for freedom and fulfillment (fig. 25).

French's *Huni* is a young Egyptian prince who embarks on a fearsome journey through the dark underworld to prove that he is brave enough to be

Fig. 25. Sigrid Heuck, "The city was far behind him"
From *Pony* by Gina Ruck-Pauquét and Sigrid Heuck. Atlantis Verlag Zurich and Freiburg Br., 1961.

the next pharaoh. When day comes at last and he has shown himself to be worthy of the crown, a bird tells him to watch the lotus flower; its pointed petals are reddened by the first rays of light; but, in the next illustration (fig. 26), the sunlight bursts through the petals as they grow, showing Huni that they are really the mountains of Egypt. The background of the picture becomes an abstract pattern of rhythmically repeated red petal-mountains, an emblem symbolizing the Egypt Huni has won for himself.

Fig. 26. Fiona French, "The mountains of Egypt"
From *Huni*, written and illustrated by Fiona French. By permission of the publisher, Oxford University Press.

The biblical account of life in paradise and the expulsion from it is retold and elaborated in Omer's *Adam and Eve*. The artist who illustrated the story worked with large areas of pure red, white, and black to signify bliss, danger, sin, shame, and God's wrath; only the final picture, the closed gate of paradise, the angel's sword guarding it, a bleak stony, almost abstract landscape, is done in anticlimactic shades of grey, symbolizing the concept of man's unsheltered raw future. Only a small row of schematic trees, like red swords, shows the way out, adding a final accent to the drama that has just come to a close. Adam and Eve are not seen anymore; they are already on their way to their earthly existence.

We have looked at Herzka and Steiner's *Do in the Red Boots*, the story of a girl's seven cyclical journeys through nature, in the chapter on the continuous narrative. There we examined its technique. Here we want to add that the book is also a movingly beautiful example of natural landscape used to illustrate an idea: far beyond the detailed description of the corners and trails and the times of day and night where and when Do roves and strays, gets involved in subtle adventures, acquainted with the large and small miracles she finds out there, and returns home at the end of each journey enriched by the experience—beyond these concrete accounts it is clear from the overtones in both text and illustration that they intend to convey, and gracefully do, the *idea of wisdom* found in nature, in its rhythmical patterns of living change.

Fascinating in their own special way are illustrations where nature, its shapes and forces, represent aspects of the protagonist's state of mind; where, in other words, emotions are projected onto the landscape, and expressed visually.

In Carigiet's *Maurus and Madleina*, Maurus the village boy sets out to visit his girl cousin in the city, has to cross white rocks and a very steep mountain slope, where he has to proceed on a narrow, partly decayed path, keeping close to the rocks. While the illustration includes realistic elements, its force lies in the strongly marked, scraggy, nervous lines of the almost perpendicular threatening slope, reinforced by a few broken trees, the only horizontal line being the thread-like meandering path on which the boy wearily advances. Thus expression is given to the anxiety and dynamic tension gripping him. Yet the triangle formed by his body and by the stick he supports himself with, introduces an element of balance, of decision.

Another remarkable sample of this is Haacken's opening picture in Prokofiev's *Peter and the Wolf*. It shows, to the left, Peter who has opened the garden gate and is walking on the grass. The picture is composed in white, green and black; white appears mainly behind Peter, with black shapes looming large as he resolutely advances toward the right: Peter starts his day courageously but the composition of the picture intimates that some hidden anxiety, some inkling of the dangers that lie ahead, occupies the boy's mind. The picture is much more than just an illustration of how the day begins. For in the text everything is as yet calm and gay as the meticulously etched grass over which Peter walks. But the distribution of colors and the marked diagonal perspective build a dramatic effect that hints at his as yet unconscious forebodings of things to come.

One outstanding example, glowing with dramatic and yet graceful beauty, is Mayer's illustrations in *Beauty and the Beast*. In this version, romantic landscapes continually accompany and signify feelings and thoughts that are projected onto nature, in pictures whose elegance does not impair their emotional impact. When decisiveness reigns in the hearts of the actors in the story, the trees are stable and the mountains in the background have solid lines. When, in her dream and then later on actually, Beauty is united with her prince, nature bursts out in bloom. When Beauty speeds home to be with her father again, the branches of the trees visually echo the motion of the galloping horse's legs, in a gesture of empathy with the urgency that grips Beauty (fig. 27).

Fig. 27. Mercer Mayer, "Beauty riding back home"
Reprinted by permission of Four Winds Press, a division of Scholastic Inc., from *Beauty and the Beast* by Marianna and Mercer Mayer. Copyright © 1978 by Marianna Mayer. Illustrations copyright © 1978 by Mercer Mayer.

Illustration styles like these enrich, as Hearne has said of Mayer's *Beauty*,[4] the symbolism of the stories while at the same time making them more accessible to children on an emotional level.

Occasionally nature is the real protagonist of a story. In Fletcher's *I Saw* the author-illustrator aims at having the child experience the ever-new

4. Betsy Hearne, reviews, "Mayer, Marianna: Beauty and the Beast" and "Goode, Diana: Beauty and the Beast," *Booklist* (Sept. 15, 1978), pp. 217, 223.

charm inherent in nature, as day and night and the seasons go by. He creates a twofold situation, within a recurring, slightly forced but still aesthetically attractive pattern: a child standing at his window and looking out at the landscape appears in most of the pictures. At the same time the child seems to identify with the blackbird that flies through the sky, again in almost all of the illustrations, seeing and experiencing nature's transformations from above. The appearance of the landscape changes as new shapes and colors introduce flamboyant views. The composition of the book is based on a double viewpoint, the child's at his window, and the child's again through his empathy with the roving blackbird. There are two observers, a static and a dynamic one. However, the real emphasis is on the varying images of nature; nature is the hero of the story.

Sometimes, illustrators work wonders by using only single natural elements as expressive motifs. The lucidity of the evening sky becomes obscured by somber velvety swirls during the night but becomes clear again as morning arrives in Keats's *Dreams*, adding depth to Roberto's dramatic experience of how his paper mouse saved his friend Archie's cat. So, too, in an edition of Hans Christian Andersen's *The Tinderbox* the illustrator uses, in three consecutive pictures, the shapes and colors of clouds. When the magic dog carries the princess through the night to the lucky soldier's room, the clouds echo in outline and partly in color the dog's shape, and so add to the impression of speed. In the following illustration, when the suspicious governess detects, to her surprise, that the princess really has been carried off on a dog, the clouds are blue-grey with black rims, suggesting danger; when the soldier is imprisoned for his daring, light-yellow clouds passing by his barred window express freedom lost, to be regained at any price.

Not all illustrators take the representation of nature seriously. There are too many books in which nature is treated and presented in a purely decorative way, like a stage set, two-dimensional and artificial. When we compare these books with those having aesthetically valuable illustrations, it will strike us forcibly to what extent flat, schematic, negligible cardboard landscapes, lacking in grace, intimacy, and depth, mar the child's experience, though they may be stylistically pleasant. The difference is easily demonstrated, for instance, by two versions of the Russian folktale *The Frostman*, as retold by Aleksei Tolstoi. A girl is expelled from her home by her stepmother into the wintry forest. The frostman appears and after he puts her to tests of endurance, he richly rewards her. In the first one of the two books the crushing and yet majestic might of northern winter is given authentic expression, with some pictures composed of large white-grey-blue shapes of trees and snow (fig. 28). In the second book, though it is pleasing to the eye and true to Russian style in many details of dress and utensils, the attributes of winter produce a not-so-convincing stage effect.

This artificiality is characteristic of many illustrations created for fables and parables. The following are two examples of animal fables. In Aardema's *Why Mosquitoes Buzz in People's Ears*, a retelling of a West African tale,

Девушка сидит под елью, дрожит, озноб её пробирает. Вдруг слышит — невдалеке Морозко по ёлкам потрескивает, с ёлки на ёлку поскакивает, пощёлкивает. Очутился на той ели, под которой девица сидит, и сверху её спрашивает:
— Тепло ли тебе, девица?
— Тепло, Морозушко, тепло, батюшка.
Морозко стал ниже спускаться, сильнее потрескивает, пощёлкивает:
— Тепло ли тебе, девица? Тепло ли тебе, красная?
Она чуть дух переводит:

— Тепло, Морозушко, тепло, батюшка.
Морозко ещё ниже спустился, пуще затрещал, сильнее защёлкал:
— Тепло ли тебе, девица? Тепло ли тебе, красная? Тепло ли тебе, лапушка?
Девица окостеневать стала, чуть-чуть языком шевелит:
— Ой, тепло, голубчик Морозушко!
Тут Морозко сжалился над девицей, окутал её тёплыми шубами, отогрел пуховыми одеялами.

Fig. 28. A. Pakhomov, *The Frostman*
From *Morozko*, retold by Aleksei Tolstoi; illustrated by A. Pakhomov. Izdatelstvo Detsakaya Literatura, 1966.

the actors are all the animals of the forest and are portrayed quite elaborately in a stylized fashion; the forest is repeatedly represented only by a few cut-out schematic trees. In *The Fox Plays a Hoax on the Bear*, by Ion Creangă, the bear and the fox are treated quite realistically with a slant toward comics; yet the very conspicuous vegetation of the places where the story takes place is painted in stylized shapes, although in autumn colors harmonizing with the bear's and the fox's furs (fig. 29). The reason why fables are so often accompanied by artificial representations of nature is quite obvious: the illustrator of a fable is aware that the plot is an allegory; the actors, too, are usually described schematically in the text. Emotional depth is, in the fable, secondary to rational enlightenment, and generality of instruction to individuality. Decorative token landscape fits the literary genre.

The aesthetically sensitive and authentic treatment of natural landscape may, we believe, further the child's development: his sense of beauty and love for his own environment; his understanding of natural forces and phenomena outside himself and beyond his pale; his grasp of the greatness and variability of nature and the place of man in the grand scheme of things. The thoughtful and intuitively excellent illustrator achieves his or her effect in many different ways. As we have seen, meaningfulness may adhere to the illustration whatever various symbolic roles and functions the artist charges it with: except for one or two remarks we have not, in this chapter, touched on the question of style in art. There is no perfect correlation between the mode, impressionist, realistic, or fantastic, etc., of the illustrator's work, and the role he assigns to his illustration. The visual message is

Atunci vulpea rînji dinții și zise: «Alei, cumătre! da' nu știi că nevoia te duce pe unde nu-ți
e voia și te-nvață ce nici gîndești? Ascultă,
cumătre: vrei să mănînci pește? Du-te desară
la băltoaga cea din marginea pădurei, vîri-ți
coada-n apă și stăi pe loc, fără să te miști,
pînă despre ziuă; atunci smucește vîrtos spre
mal și ai să scoți o mulțime de pește, poate
îndoit și-ntreit de cît am scos eu.».
Ursul, nemaizicînd nici o vorbă, aleargă-n
fuga mare la băltoaga din marginea pădurei
și-și vîră-n apă toată coada!...

14

Fig. 29. Ileana Ceaușu-Pandele, *The Fox Plays a Hoax on the Bear*
From *Ursul Păcălit De Vulpe*, by Ion Creangă, illustrated by Ileana Ceaușu-Pandele. Editura Ion Creangă, București, 1975.

not unequivocally or necessarily dependent on style. It is this freedom of choice which widens the artist's range of possibilities of how to enrich the holistic experience of the child.

CHILDREN'S WORKS CITED

AARDEMA, VERNA. *Why Mosquitoes Buzz in People's Ears*. Illus. by Leo and Diana Dillon. New York: Dial, 1975.

ANDERSEN, HANS CHRISTIAN. *Ognivo*. Trans. by A. Ganzen. Illus. by U. Tchizhikov. Moskva: Izdatelstvo Malysh, 1973.

CARIGIET, ALOIS. *Maurus und Madleina*. Zurich: Schweizer Spiegel Verlag, 1969.

CREANGĂ, ION. *Ursul Păcălit De Vulpe*. Illus. by Ileana Ceausu-Pandele. București: Editura Ion Creangă, 1975.

FECHNER, AMREI, and CHRISTINE ADRIAN. *Tiere bei uns*. Ravensburg: Otto Maier, 1979.

FLETCHER, ALAN. *Was ich sah*. Hamburg: Friedrich Oetinger, 1967.

FRENCH, FIONA. *Huni*. London: Oxford Univ. Pr., 1971.

FUCHSHUBER, ANNEGERT. *Fahr mit in die Ferien*. Freising: Sellier, 1977.

HERZKA, HEINZ, and HEIRI STEINER. *Do in der roten Stiefeln*. Zurich, Stuttgart: Artemis, 1969.

IVITCH, ALEKSANDR. *Kak zapregli reki*. Illus. by V. V. Kulkov. Moskva: Izdatelstvo Detskii Mir, 1962.

KEATS, EZRA JACK. *Dreams*. New York: Macmillan, 1974.

———. *The Snowy Day*. New York: Viking, 1962.

MAYER, MARIANNA. *Beauty and the Beast*. Illus. by Mercer Mayer. New York: Four Winds Press, 1978.

MITSCHGUT, ALI. *Bei uns im Dorf*. Ravensburg: Otto Maier, 1970.

OMER, DVORAH. *Adam Vehavah*. Uriel Ofek, ed. Illus. by Ruth Tsarfati. Tel Aviv: Levin-Epstein-Modan, n.d.

PROKOFIEV, SERGEJ S. *Peter und der Wolf*. Illus. by Frans Haacken. München: Parabel, 1958.

RUCK-PAUQUÉT, GINA, and SIGRID HEUCK. *Pony*. Zurich, Freiburg: Atlantis, 1961.

STARSHINOV, NIKOLAI K. "Tutcha." In *Vot kak byvaet*. Illus. by V. Kulkov. Moskva: Izdatelstvo Malysh, 1973.

TALMI, EFRAIM. *Tiyool shel Hofesh*. Illus. by Tirtzah. Ramat Gan: Massadah, n.d.

TOLSTOI, ALEKSEI. *Morozko*. Illus. by A. Pakhomov. Leningrad: Izdatelstvo Detskaya Literatura, 1966.

———. ———. Illus. by T. Shevariov. Moskva: Izdatelstvo Malysh, 1967.

YANG, CHU, ed. *The Golden Axe*. Illus. by Li Tien-hsin. Peking: Foreign Languages Press, 1959.

ZIMNIK, REINER. *Bills Ballonfahrt*. Zurich: Diogenes, 1972.

6

The Letter and the Written Word as Visual Elements

In all civilizations there runs an age-old fascination with the visual aspects of the written word. Of course, in a very elementary sense writing is visual communication. But although many writing systems probably start as pictorial representations of reality, they later become sets of more or less arbitrary signs. The importance of the written word lies in the contents it signifies or symbolizes, contents which we perceive through a process we call reading and which takes place by linear progress of our eyes along fixed lines in a certain direction. But the surface of the written and the printed word and the visual stimula hidden there have always fulfilled various functions. Relative sizes, ways of placing and arranging words and sentences on a page, the choice of scripts for special occasions and messages (such as a wedding announcement) are habitual means of communication. Man is very adept at discovering ever new ways of turning written verbal messages into simultaneous visual messages and even art. In this respect, civilizations differ; Chinese is said to be far richer in its possibilities than languages whose writing systems are based on alphabets. But some of the games seem to recur, over the ages, in many places.

One of them is embellishing initials until they become pictures. Often these pictures tell something about the text which they accompany.

Another quite serious game is what has variously been called visual poetry, pattern poetry, or emblematic poetry; what it comes to is that a poem is written and printed so that the typographical arrangement displays the visual shape of the theme or subject of the poem. Visual poetry is probably as old as Greek civilization. About 300 b.c. Simmias of Rhodes wrote poems in shapes allusive of their contents: wings, an egg, an axe. Emblematic poetry, mainly religious, flowered in England in the sixteenth and the seventeenth centuries (Herbert's well-known altar poem) and in France, where it was especially used for satire until the eighteenth century. Poems and liturgic texts arranged in decorative patterns were very popular in the Middle Ages and later in two civilizations whose orthodoxies frowned upon the pictorial representation of reality, Judaism and Islam. Both developed a very strong affection for their alphabets in some historical periods even to the point of ascribing to them mystical qualities. The decorative use of letters and words including pattern poetry is very widespread in Arabic, traditional Turkish and Persian literature (all using the Arabic alphabet) and in Hebrew.[1] In the twentieth century visual poetry has been rediscovered and regenerated by the French poet Apollinaire who wrote what he called calligrammes, figure poems such as "The Tie" and "The Watch," printed in these shapes, "It Rains" in the form of lines of words streaming over the page, and more.[2] Then there exists today the genre of concrete poetry which is again based, with some difference, on the precept that the poet should create a simultaneity of the semantic and the aesthetic function of words.[3] In a lighter vein, patterned texts appear nowadays in satire and in advertising in any imaginable shape.[4]

Then there are the devices through which single words become expressive of their contexts. The most perfect and famous example is an Islamic confession of faith in God and his prophet, in Arabic, written so that it may be read both from right to left and from left to right. At the same time the letters and words represent the seven minarets and domes of the mosque in Mecca.[5]

This device of turning whole words or letters within words into expressions or descriptions of themselves has become a captivating fashion. The capital *A* in the word Paris assumes the shape of the Eiffel Tower; the *t* in television is an aerial; suddenly the *o* in Newton is an apple dropping down, out of the word, reminiscent of the way the great scientist is supposed to have discovered gravity; the *g* in Louis Armstrong's name turns into a large, blaring trumpet. Magazines like *Mad* and *Playboy* cultivate the game. For instance, in an announcement by a hotel that its swimming pool is now open, the words are shown gliding into the water.

In art, especially cubists, futurists, and pop artists have, in widely different ways, blended letters, words, printed pages, walls covered with prints, etc., into their pictures, utilizing written material for the visual messages that may be detected in it.

Many more games have been and are being invented; there are puzzles like the rebus; and there is the ubiquitous and quite inventive visual use the written word is put to in the cartoon, in comics, and in advertising. It goes without saying that a phenomenon of such universal occurrence will also appear in children's books. Indeed, examples abound. All we have to do is

1. See John Hollander, "The Poem in the Eye," in *Vision and Resonance: Two Senses of Poetic Form* (New York: Oxford Univ. Pr., 1975), p. 245ff.; A. L. Korn, "Puttenham and the Oriental Pattern-Poem," *Comparative Literature* 6, no. 4: 289–303 (Fall 1954).

2. See Guilliaume Apollinaire, *Calligrammes: Poèmes de la Paix et de la Guerre (1913–1916)*; Preface by Michel Butor (Paris: Gallimard, N.R.F., 1925).

3. See Max Bense, in M. E. Solt, ed., *Concrete Poetry: A World View* (Bloomington: Indiana Univ. Pr., 1970), p. 75.

4. See Robert Massin, *La lettre et l'image. Du signe à la lettre et de la lettre au signe* (Paris: Gallimard, 1970), p. 27. This entire work is a comprehensive and at the same time delightful treatment of the subject from both the historical and the contemporary point of view.

5. *Ibid.*, p. 175.

to collect some of them and sort them out in order to discover a few of the visual games the written language plays with children.

RELATIVE SIZE, INTERVALS, AND DIRECTION OF TYPE

A simple and convincing example of this is Milne's poem, "Politeness." The first ten lines, printed regularly, one below the other, tell about what Christopher Robin is supposed to think of being polite. Then comes what he really thinks: a line left empty; then two words in larger print—a larger interval—two words in smaller print moved over to the right—one more large empty interval—and three words in very small print near the lower right-hand corner of the page. The effect is reinforced by the visual treatment.

A sentence relating that someone has to walk uphill may be printed as a rising diagonal.[6] In Kush's *Shmulikipod* when the hedgehog who comforted the sick boy finally leaves him, the progressively tinier repetition of the phrase "Went away, went away . . . ," in Hebrew letters, accentuates the mood of departure. When the crocodile in Fröhlich's *Well, I Must Say!* swallows its *r*, the *r* is printed rushing down through the German word until it disappears. In a poem about children sliding in the snow, the words are printed sliding down the page.[7] Then there is the classic example of Virginia Burton's *Choo Choo*: when the young engine that has run away gets dizzy from speed and indecision about which track to take, the text doubles the winding lines of the railway tracks in the illustrations (fig. 30).

PATTERNED TEXTS

These appear in a great variety of shapes, such as title pages in a number of French books. In Hélène Tersac's *The Story of a Tree*, the title of the book and the names of author and illustrator form a tree. In *The Growing Fish*, by Paula Delsol, all the important information about the book is included in a fish with large fins, formed by words. The title of *The Gang of the Red Caterpillars*, by Maymat and Deneux, winds its way over the page just like some caterpillars.

A German alphabet poem is accompanied by two funny faces formed with the help of letters[8] (fig. 31). A nonsense rhyme about a sinking ship takes on the shape of a towering wave in Charlip's *Arm in Arm*. A German illustrator of children's books gives some autobiographical information in a

---

6. Terry Southern, *Thin Wisdom*; illus. by Larry Rivers (Long Island: Universal Limited Art Editions, 1968–76).

7. Myra Cohn Livingston, "Sliding"; illus. by Mary Miller Salem. In *Childcraft*, vol. 1, p. 97.

8. Josef Guggenmos, "Das ABC im Rückwärtsgang," in Edith Harries, ed., *Kindergedichte*; illus. by Margret Rettich (Ravensburg: Otto Maier, 1978).

At last they came
to the place where
the tracks divided.
They didn't know
which way to go
now. While they
were deciding an
old man, who used
to be an engineer
when he was young,
called out to them,
"If you're looking
for a runaway en-
gine she's right up
that track there. And
she won't be far as
it's an old track
which hasn't been
used for well nigh
forty years."

Fig. 30. Virginia Lee Burton, *Choo Choo*

From *Choo Choo* by Virginia Lee Burton, published by Houghton Mifflin Company. Copyright 1937, by Virginia Lee Burton. Reprinted by permission.

L   mag ihn gern leiden,
M   muß stets ihn meiden,
N   will sich den halben nehmen,
O   sagt: O du mußt dich schämen,
P   will ihn gleich packen,
Q   fängt an zu quaken,
R   fängt an zu rufen,
S   beginnt zu suchen,
T   darf ihn dann tragen,
U   will ihn umrennen,
V   ihn verbrennen,
W   will das nicht wagen.
Schließlich aber tragen
Ihn auf einem Kuchenbrett
XYZ.   *Unbekannter Verfasser*

Das ABC im Rückwärtsgang

Kennst du das
ZYX?
Für den Könner
ist das nix.

WVU,
TSRQ.
Siehst du wohl,
das geht im Nu.

PONM,
LKJI.
Aufgepaßt!
Das schadet nie.

Noch mal Gas,
dann sind wir da:
HGFE,
DCBA.   *Josef Guggenmos*

Fig. 31. Margret Rettich, "The Alphabet in Reverse"

From *Kindergedichte*, illustrated by Margret Rettich, selected by Edith Harries, published by Otto Maier Verlag Ravensburg © 1978.

CHI DONDOLA?

La bimba che culla la bambola
il bimbo a cavallo sul dondolo
la nonna su e giù sulla seggiola
il ticchete-tàc della pendola
la gente che in treno s'appisola
e insieme sussulta col capo che ciondola
la martinella che squilla
la ballerina che oscilla
l'altalena nell'aria
e la luna sull'onda
e la foglia che vola
e la piuma che plana
la campana che suona
ora lenta ora vana
e dondola dòn dòn
dondola
dondola dondola
dòn · · ·
dòn · · ·
· · · dòn

Fig. 32. Mario Faustinelli, ''The Seesaw''
From *Le rime-figure*, written and illustrated by Mario Faustinelli. © 1973 Ugo Mursia Editore, Milan.

number of sentences arranged in the shape of a snail, adding that the similarity is not accidental.[9] In a Hebrew version of the story of Noah and the great flood, the page picturing the torrential rains is filled with straight diagonal lines made up of the word for rain repeated endlessly in tiny letters.[10] Faustinelli has taken up the idea of the calligrammes and has written and illustrated a whole volume of figure rhymes for children in Italian (fig. 32). The book consists of amusing and pleasing poems, frankly imitating Apollinaire, but adapted to the interest level of children. In varying configurations, shapes and contents appear twice, as a pattern rhyme and as an illustration: parallels and railway tracks; the serpentine and skying; rain—diagonals, for sure; an especially beautiful poem about fireworks, and more. Apart from offering pleasant experiences, this book also

9. Renate Jessel, in Horst Kunze and Heinz Wegehaupt, eds., *Für Kinder gemalt* (Berlin: Der Kinderbuchverlag, 1970).
10. Michael Flanders, *Noah, Hamabbul Veteyvat Hahayoth*; illus. by Harold King (Tel Aviv: Am Oved, 1977). Originally published as *Captain Noah and His Floating Zoo* (Twickenham, Eng.: Felix Gluck Pr., 1972).

cautiously introduces to the child some of the secrets of signifying and of symbolizing in language and in art.

Then there is the famous example of the mouse's tale in *Alice's Adventures in Wonderland*, which appears in any translation of the book. For instance, comparison of an Estonian version with the original English shape proves that the two are not identical typographically; but the main pattern is there, the meandering line getting smaller until it almost vanishes.

PERSONIFIED LETTERS

In a Croatian book called *The Crazy Ones*, a collection of very short absurd tales, there is one tale about the letters of the alphabet taking pity on the boy who had to read whole stories; so they run away from the book to make it easier for him. Then, of course, he is afraid because he will have to learn all the empty pages. The illustration shows the letters scampering off.[11] A German fantasy tells of a boy who had difficulties in learning to write. In his desperation he writes his name on the wall of his school building. At night, in a dream, the capital *I* appears and takes him to meet all the letters and their king, capital *A* (fig. 33). There he is praised for the beautiful writing on the school wall. When he goes to school the next day, writing is much easier. Fortunately, the illustrator of this didactic dream creates some droll animal shapes for the letters.[12] A most ambitious personification of a letter is *The Story of Capital A*, a German book by James Krüss. A red-colored solitary *A* wanders through the land. It has no place to go; no one knows it; nobody needs it. Not even the bright neon lights in the city. Finally it achieves social adjustment by turning into the roof of an old castle. The illustrations vividly picture the *A*'s vicissitudes and emotions. The story seems to be overdoing a good thing. An abstract, functional sign does not impress us as being a suitable vehicle for confronting children with issues like the search for identity and how to become useful in society.

WORDS REPRESENTING THEMSELVES

In an old book of Swiss children's songs we found a musical notation to reflect the theme of any particular song: the notes are drawn in the shape of clocks, or ships, or flowers or whatever the subject of the song is. In a collection of German stories and pictures we found the word for *bee* being changed, in two steps, into an insect's shape.[13] In an Israeli story, in Hebrew, about a boy who turns into a bulldozer, the word for bulldozer assumes the

11. Zvonimir Balog, *Šašavi*; illus. by Miroslav Šutej (Zagreb: Naprijed, 1975).
12. Eveline Hasler, *Der Buchstabenkönig und die Hexe Lakritze*; illus. by Peter Sís (Zurich: Benziger, 1977).
13. "Biene"; illus. by Helga Gebert, in Hans-Joachim Gelberg, ed., *Das achte Weltwunder* (Weinheim: Beltz Gelberg, 1979).

Fig. 33. Peter Sís, "Max and Capital I"
From *Der Buchstabenkönig und die Hexe Lakritze* by Eveline Hasler, illustrated by Peter Sís, Benziger Verlag Zurich, Köln 1977.

shape of the machine.[14] In a Lebanese book in Arabic, *Our Language*, where there are many different visual ideas used to good effect, we find, for instance, two words portraying themselves: the word meaning to *break*—shown to be rent by repeated lines crossing the word; the word meaning to *shake*—formed by trembling lines.[15]

WORDS AS THREE-DIMENSIONAL OBJECTS

Illustrators frequently like to use this device for titles or whole title pages. In a Russian children's magazine (fig. 34) the little bear sits snugly, smiling on

14. Hava Avi-Yonah, *Esther Hamalkah Vehadahpor* (Tel Aviv: Am Hassefer, n.d.).
15. A. D. Damashqia, *Luġatina*; illus. by Nabil Taġ (Beirut: Dar Al-Fata Al-Arabi. n.d.).

Fig. 34. V. Dmitryuk, "8th of March"

From *Murzilka*, no. 3, March 1976. Illustration by V. Dmitryuk. By permission of VAAP, the copyright agency of the USSR, on behalf of the illustrator.

the printed words for "8th of March" (Women's Day in Russia).[16] The cover of a German collection of stories for the beginning reader has a capital *L* produced by a wavy line (fig. 35); an elephant is sitting in it, a seesaw is suspended from it, and children look at us from behind it.[17] A similar Israeli book has spelled out on its cover the name of the first letter in the Hebrew alphabet, with children climbing up and down, and the name of the last letter on the back cover.[18] An animal story from Bangla Desh, in Bengali, shows a large bird resting on the printed title of the book.[19] The idea of combining both the front and the back cover of a book for the letter game is used in a pleasant way in the German version of *The Tree*.[20] The title is presented as two large words, with children jumping about between the letters, and the back cover as its mirror image. The cover of *Patatrac*, a French picture book without words, by Jean Jacques Loup, is especially effective

16. Illus. by V. Dmitryuk. *Murzilka* no. 3 (March 1976).
17. Cover illus. by Dieter Wiesmüller; Ute Andresen, ed., *Das andere grosse L.* (Ravensburg: Otto Maier, 1980).
18. Levin Kipnis, *Alef*; illus. by Isa (Tel Aviv: Karni, 1958).
19. Rokanuzzaman Khan, *Hat tima tim*; illus. by Hashem Khan. the page is reproduced in Heinz Wegehaupt, ed., *Das schöne Kinderbuch* (Berlin: Der Kinderbuchverlag, 1977).
20. Eleonore Schmid, *Der Baum* (Zurich: Benziger, 1969). Originally published as *The Tree* (New York: Harlin Quist, 1966).

Fig. 35. Dieter Wiesmüller, *The Other Capital L*
From *Das Andere Grosse L*, published by Otto Maier Verlag Ravensburg 1980. Cover by Dieter Wiesmüller after illustrations by Helen Oxenbury, Jack Kent, and Nancy Winslow Parker.

and charming (fig. 36). The hero is a sort of goblin who is prone to getting involved in accidents and catastrophes—derailed trains, fires, foundering ships, crashing rockets. The cover signifies this single motif of the book with visual conciseness: all the other goblins are standing up behind a high wall while only Patatrac falls off it, crashing into the middle *T* of his name and dislodging it downward. He is, as ever, ready to move in when a calamity offers itself.

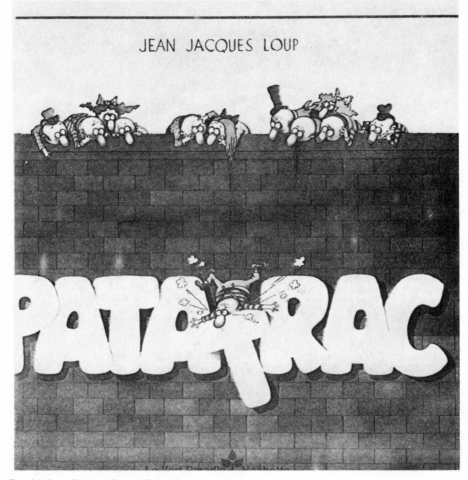

Fig. 36. Jean Jacques Loup, *Patatrac*
From *Patatrac* by Jean Jacques Loup, Hachette International, Paris, 1975. By permission of Emme Edizioni, S.p.A., Milan.

TEXTS AS PART OF THE CITYSCAPE

Torn newspapers, announcements, and grafitti are sometimes used to underline the mood of downtown areas in a fashion inspired by cubism and pop art. Ezra Jack Keats's collages are a good example of this, especially in *Louie* (see also fig. 6).

DECORATIVE USES OF WRITING

Especially in books printed in Arabic characters, one may find words and phrases developed into decorative patterns. Some Iranian religious texts for children are fine examples of this, for instance, *The Mother of the Prophet*, where the title evolves into an ornamental motif embellishing the pages of the book.[21]

ALPHABET BOOKS

For a long time now there have been books made up of figures or objects, usually belonging to one category, human figures, animals, flowers, etc., which take on, consecutively, the shapes of all the letters constituting the alphabet.[22] We will not treat them here. It is true that these collections, compiled in any language and any imaginable alphabet, and generally set out in such a way that each letter figures as the creature or object whose word begins with this letter, fulfill an important function as a pleasant and stimulating teaching aid. Many alphabet books are tasteful and humorous and have been conceived and carried out with care. On the whole, though, they appear to be somewhat contrived and redundant. Anyhow, to split a hair, while this chapter presents instances where letters turn into pictures, alphabet books are, in fact, pictures turned into letters.

Has this amusing and lighthearted flirt with the visual expressiveness of the written word an underlying significance? Humanity has always liked to play more or less serious games with its media of expression and communication. It has also ever harbored a profound admiration, even a kind of awe, for its own invention, language, and for the magic inherent in its written signifiers.

In our age written and printed language has become practically ubiquitous, and in any given society more and more children have to learn that visible words are very powerful when it comes to comprehending the world around or communicating with others. So many media (the magazine, propaganda poster, television, and advertising, etc.) increasingly utilize the visual aspects of the printed word. So it is only natural that children's books and their illustrators will be looking for opportunities to introduce the letter and the word to the child in a playful fashion. They also wish and hope thereby to ease some of the anxiety many children experience when they first confront these forbidding signs and symbols. Playing games takes off some of the pressure and adds to the fascination.

21. Bint Al-Shati, *Madar-e paiambar*; illus. by Ali Akbar Sadiqi (Teheran: Institute for the Intellectual Development of Children and Young Adults, 1974).
22. It is also an adult game. See Massin, *La lettre*, p. 75.

CHILDREN'S WORKS CITED

ANDRESEN, UTE, ed. *Das andere grosse L.* Ravensburg: Otto Maier, 1980.

AVI-YONAH, HAVA. *Esther Hamalkah Vehadahpor.* Tel Aviv: Am Hassefer, n.d.

AL-SHATI, BINT. *Madar-e paiambar.* Illus. by Ali Akbar Sadiqi. Teheran: Institute for the Intellectual Development of Children and Young Adults, 1974.

BALOG, ZVONIMIR. *Šašavi.* Illus. by Miroslav Šutej. Zagreb: Naprijed, 1975.

BURTON, VIRGINIA L. *Choo Choo: The Story of a Little Engine Who Ran Away.* Boston: Houghton Mifflin, 1937.

CHARLIP, REMY. *Arm in Arm.* New York: Parents Magazine Press, 1964.

CARROLL, LEWIS. *Alice Imedemaal.* Trans. by Jaan Kross. Illus. by Vive Tolli. Tallinn: Eesi Ramaat, 1971.

———. *Alice in Wonderland and Through the Looking Glass.* Illus. by John Tenniel. New York: Heritage Press-Macy, 1941.

DAMASHQIA, A. D. *Luġatina.* Illus. by Nabil Taġ. Beirut: Dar Al-Fata Al-Arabi, n.d.

DELSOL, PAULA. *Le poisson qui grandissait.* Illus. by Arnaud Laval. Paris: Editions G.P. Paris, 1973.

FAUSTINELLI, MARIO. *Le rime-figure.* Milan: Ugo Mursia, 1973.

FLANDERS, MICHAEL. *Noah, Hamabbul Veteyvat Hahayoth.* Illus. by Harold King. Tel Aviv: Am Oved, 1977.

FRÖHLICH, ROSWITHA. *Na hör mal!* Illus. by Marie Marcks. Ravensburg: Otto Maier: 1980.

GELBERG, HANS JOACHIM, ed. *Das achte Weltwunder.* Weinheim: Beltz-Gelberg, 1979.

HARRIES, EDITH, ed. *Kindergedichte.* Illus. by Margret Rettich. Ravensburg: Otto Maier, 1978.

HASLER, EVELINE. *Der Buchstabenkönig und die Hexe Lakritze.* Illus. by Peter Sís. Zurich: Benziger, 1977.

KEATS, EZRA JACK. *Louie.* New York: Greenwillow Books, 1975.

KIPNIS, LEVIN. *Alef.* Illus. by Isa. Tel Aviv: Karni, 1958.

KRÜSS, JAMES. *Die Geschichte vom grossen A.* Illus. by Eleonore Schmid. Stuttgart: Thienemann, 1972.

KUSH. *Shmulikipod.* Merhavia, Tel Aviv: Sifriat Poalim, 1964.

LOUP, JEAN JACQUES. *Patatrac.* Paris: Hachette, 1975.

MAYMAT, NICOLE, and YOLAINE DENEUX. *Le gang des chenilles rouges.* Moulins: Éditions Ipomée, 1976.

Murzilka no. 3 (March 1976).

MILNE, A. A. *The World of Christopher Robin.* Illus. by E. H. Shepard. New York: Dutton, 1958.

Poems and Rhymes. Childcraft—The How and Why Library, vol. 1. Chicago: World Book–Childcraft International, 1980.

TERSAC, HÉLÈNE. *Histoire d'un arbre.* Illus. by Renate Magnier. Bruxelles: Éditions de la Marelle, 1979.

7

Visible Sound

We shall treat this game briefly. For visible sound—the attempt to represent pictorially various aspects of sound, and especially letters, words and music notes signifying sound—is a mainstay of the comics code, apart from being widely used in cartoons and in advertising, and is to be systematically treated in that connection. Also, the remarks made in the previous chapter about humanity's relationships with its media, and its inclination to mix them, are true here too, and do not have to be repeated. On the other hand, illustrators do play the game quite successfully and, at times, with meaningful intentions; so it is worthwhile having a look at it.

What happens is that graphic shapes, signs and symbols, represent aural, acoustic sensory perceptions received by our ears: spoken language, voices singing, music issuing from instruments, noises caused by creatures or objects. The illustrator's intention is that these visual configurations be transformed again by the viewer into acoustic impressions or associations. This is quite an intriguing instance of the degree of intricacy human communication may arrive at.

Visible sound is, as was said above, ubiquitous in the lower arts, and frequently used in modern art altogether. From among the many kinds of messages containing visible sound that are created for adults, we shall refer only to one, that found in the work of the great cartoon artist, Saul Steinberg. Representations of visible sound recur in his drawings in changing fashions over the years: be it a woman swathing the man sitting opposite her in clouds of speech issuing from her mouth; an impossible dialogue between a little girl "talking" flowers, birds, cats, etc., and a stern adult crossing out everything she says by replying in no-nonsense black lines, or other expressions of typically anti-communicative "mumblified" speech.[1] Or be it abstract ornaments, such as a cartoon on country noises, including a phone ringing, a dishwasher, a willow and many others.[2]

1. See, for instance, Harold Rosenberg, *Saul Steinberg* (New York: Knopf, Whitney Museum of American Art, 1978), p. 47.
2. Saul Steinberg, "Country Noises" (cartoon), *New Yorker*, Feb. 12, 1979, p. 29.

Here is a small sample of various ways in which illustrators visualize sound in children's books.

WORDS DESCRIBING THEMSELVES

In the Lebanese book adduced in the previous chapter there is a good example of this.[3] The middle consonant of the Arabic word for whistling, an *f*-sound, is pictured as an aperture, a mouth, from which three musical notes emerge in a speech balloon.

PITCH AND DEGREE OF LOUDNESS

Frequently, changes in the sizes of printed words are utilized to indicate alterations in the degree of loudness of speech. In the Russian versions of the tale *Goldilocks and the Three Bears*, by Lev Tolstoi, the questions exclaimed by the bear family returning home—who has been sitting on my chair? who has eaten from my porridge? etc.—are printed in large letters for father bear's deep loud voice, in ordinary ones for mother bear's more delicate tone of voice, and in very small ones for little bear. At the beginning of Sendak's *In The Night Kitchen*, when Mickey is annoyed by a noise (in his parents' bedroom?), his shouting is pictured in very large print (fig. 37). When a girl wakes up and reacts to everyone being cross with her—nothing she does today seems to be right—the long poem is printed so that the verses become successively larger and the final decision, to stay in bed this day, is impressively distinct indeed: the girl's monologue increases in emotional quality and in sound level toward the climax.[4]

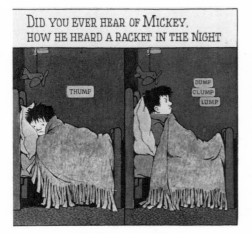 

Fig. 37. Maurice Sendak, "Quiet down there"

Illustrations from *In the Night Kitchen*, written and illustrated by Maurice Sendak. Copyright © 1970 by Maurice Sendak. By permission of Harper & Row, Publishers, Inc. *In the Night Kitchen*, by Maurice Sendak, is published in the United Kingdom by The Bodley Head.

3. Damashqia, *Luġatina*.
4. Karla Kuskin, "I woke up this morning"; illus. by Maude Petersham, in *Childcraft*, vol. 1, pp. 146–47.

Fig. 38. Avi Margalith, ''A song that escaped''

From *Shirim lemi she'ohavim* by Mihal Snunith, illustrated by Avi Margalith. By permission of Sifriat Po'alim, Tel Aviv.

ABSTRACT FORMAL SHAPES

A poem, in Hebrew, by Mihal Snunith, tells of ''a song that escaped'' and swept down to the sea. The illustration (fig. 38) accompanying the fragile verses is done in a poetic vein, too: to the right there is the picture of an orange-colored background of houses lining a street from which a big, loosely fringed circle is missing, leaving behind a yellow afterglow. To the left, we find the orange circle again, covering the picture of the seashore. But now the illustrator adds a single large musical staff with notes and a clef, gliding elegantly, though probably less poetically, down and out of the street to the sea.

Borten, in *Do You Hear What I Hear?*, a book dedicated to the objective of developing the child's acoustic sensitivity, uses visible sound sparingly, once on the title page which has been decorated with colored ornaments of different designs, the ornamental rhythms imitating, more or less accurately, the physical shape of sound waves; and once more, when she introduces sounds so quiet that one can't hear them at all. The sound of the butterfly's wings beating against the air is pictured by an irregular spiraling line which represents both the butterfly's dance and the sound implied. It is proof of good taste that the author-illustrator refrained from abundantly using visible sound symbols; for, applied systematically, this would quickly have become redundant. Instead, she presents categories of sound by depicting the creatures or objects or processes that give rise to particular kinds of sounds or noises.

A complex and convincing example of the use of abstract shapes standing for sound is found in an Arabic, Tunisian book on language. In a manner reminiscent of Steinberg's mumblified speech it pictures two men belonging to different strata. One is a well-dressed bespectacled city-dweller, the other a barefoot villager. From the former's mouth issue rich flourishes of abstract speech; the latter ''speaks'' a single, simple, small, almost square shape:

different dialects and levels of expression make communication burdensome. Another picture, coming soon after the previous one, shows a more satisfactory situation. The speech balloons forming in the space between the fruit vendor and his customer contain legible sentences and have similar shapes: communication is taking place.[5]

ONOMATOPOETIC WORDS

These are words formed from sounds which resemble or imitate the sounds associated with object or action concerned. Such words are found in any language. In children's literature they are frequently formed on the spot, whenever they are needed, by writers and by illustrators. (Without onomatopoetic words comics would not be what they are.)

In a French nonsense verse, when the grasshopper who lives in a lemon on the bridge calls on the phone, the illustrator creates a funny picture, including a huge telephone; the ringing is indicated and imitated by the word *driiiing!* arching upwards and supported by visible sound-rays emerging from the phone.[6] When, in a German story, a chicken is born, the moment that he breaks the shell is indicated by the word *kling* (*klingen* means to sound, ring, tinkle), imitative, as the text says, of people clinking their glasses together in celebration.[7] When an Israeli child's building blocks fall down, the slanting Hebrew letters forming BOM! help us both to see and hear this happen.[8] The well-known Polish poet for children, Julian Tuwim, writes a poem about a steam-powered railway engine. The illustrator paints steam clouds all around the engine, but the effect of steaming heat and hard work done by pulling carriages and loads is reinforced by four, large red onomatopoetic expressions: BUCH-UCH-PUFF-UFF, *buch* being the Polish word for breathing hard.[9]

Burton's *Choo Choo*, again, is as expressive acoustically as it is visually (fig. 39). The poor tired little steam-driven engine with the onomatopoetic name, her energy spent, has come to a sad end. Changing letter sizes, fragmented words, and dotted lines—CHOO choo ch. . . . . ch. . . . ch. . . aa, and so on, "printpaint" a vivid picture of exhaustion, almost a piece of acoustic concrete poetry.

CONTINUOUS USE OF VISIBLE
SOUND REPRESENTATION

Burton's *Choo Choo* is apparently the earliest important children's book where printed language is consistently used for both visual and acoustic

5. Al-Tayyib Al-Ashash, *Alif*; illus. by Gawal Mikrili (Tunis: Dar Alif Lil-Nasr, 1979).
6. Jacqueline Held, Claude Held, and Yvan Pommaux, *lune vole* (Paris: L'école des loisirs, 1976).
7. Käta Steinitz and Kurt Schwitters, *Hahne Peter* (Hannover: Merz, n.d.).
8. Renanah Yellin-Kalai, "Kubioth," *Hineh ani*; illus. by Yehudith Yellin-Ginath (Tel Aviv: Massada, 1965).
9. Julian Tuwim, *Lokomotywa, Rzepka, Ptasie Radio*; illus. by Julitta Karwowska-Wnuczak (Warszawa: Nasza Księgarnia, 1977).

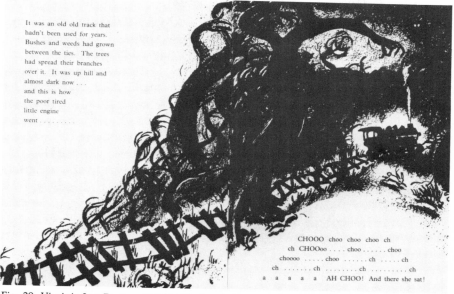

It was an old old track that
hadn't been used for years.
Bushes and weeds had grown
between the ties. The trees
had spread their branches
over it. It was up hill and
almost dark now . . .
and this is how
the poor tired
little engine
went . . . .

CHOOO choo choo choo ch
ch CHOOoo . . . . choo . . . . . . choo
choooo . . . . . choo . . . . . . ch . . . . . ch
ch . . . . ch . . . . ch . . . . ch
a a a a a   AH CHOO! And there she sat!

Fig. 39. Virginia Lee Burton, ''CHOOO choo''
From *Choo Choo* by Virginia Lee Burton, published by Houghton Mifflin Company. Copyright 1937, by Virginia Lee Burton.
Reprinted by permission.

purposes in a manner that pleasantly heightens the humor and the dynamic quality of the story. Three later books also demonstrate very creatively how effective the visual representation of sound can be when it appears not just incidentally but rather evolves into a substantial element of style.

The Hungarian book *If i were an ADULT* is one of many books created by a pair of artists, author Éva Janikovszky and illustrator László Réber. Janikovszky writes in an easy, amusing style and Réber is one of the few illustrators around who know how to arouse and cultivate the child's sense of humor without resorting to the grotesque or the techniques of comics. In this book a boy recounts his grievances against the adults who continually pursue him with their demands; yet even when he finally complies with their unreasonable ideas, they are not really satisfied. All the time, though, *they* do whatever they like to. The boy thinks: when I grow up I'll handle things quite differently.

The pages of the book are occupied by Réber's drawings, simple, humorous, and obviously somewhat inspired by children's art. The text is accommodated between the figures on the pages. But every now and then, whenever the adults' patience with the boy and the boy's frustration with their pursuit of him reach a limit, the printed word runs wild. When the so-kind-lady says, condescendingly, see, you can be a good boy, too, large elegant cursive letters tilt downward toward the little boy. When the strict male adult admonishes him, tell me, couldn't you have listened to me the first time? two still larger heavy square rows of words descend upon him. So it goes on. On some pages only the boy himself remains with a number of outstretched fingers warning him. Demands, commands, and reproaches rain down on him: wash your hands, put on your sweater, just look at your feet, don't bite nails, and a barrage of "How many times do I have to tell you?" in motley typographical arrangement. It all culminates on the page where four adults bear down on the boy exclaiming be-glad-you-are-still-a-child!, each type of person throwing in his or her own word in a different type of print (fig. 40).

The Polish book *If Tigers Ate Irises*, by Wanda Chotomska, tells how a popular song by that name was created: if tigers ate irises the world would not be wicked. The story presents to children, in a light vein, how this happened; how the poor melancholy composer invented a melody and the poet wrote the words; how they got in touch with the lady singer; how the small band practiced the song together with the singer until they were ready to record it and, finally, how the record was processed, ready to be sold and

Fig. 40. László Réber, *If i were an ADULT*

From *ha én FELNŐTT volnék* by Éva Janikovszky, illustrated by László Réber, published by Móra, Budapest, 1965.

sung by the whole town—including the mishaps that befell the participants in these activities. The illustrations are done in a combination of warm brown colors with black pen drawings. All the artists and their city, Warsaw, are pictured with affectionate humor; there is fun, too, as astounded lovable tigers stroll through the pages, the singer's family gets fed up with the song while she practices it, and the orchestra members are a difficult crowd to handle.

Beginning with the first page, visible sound plays a role. Throughout the book music notes float and soar over the pages, by themselves or on staves. They crowd about the composer's piano, invade trees, or rush out of old-fashioned gramophone loudspeakers. At first, when the composer and the poet talk over the nascent song, the notes form musical bunches of flowers. In the recording session onomatopoeia takes over: the orchestra sneezes—A, PSIK!—all over the page; a fly buzzes on the ceiling and the music instruments go after it, BZZZ-BZZYK-BZY (fig. 41); next, the violinist's knee creaks—STRZYK!! Visual shapes lay a sprightly, animated mesh of sounds, voices, and noises over the story and define its atmosphere.

The German story *The Red House in a Small Town*, by Borchers, puts the device to serious use. This is the story of a dictatorial mayor who systematically indoctrinates the people in his town toward drab conformist behavior until the day he is deposed.[10] Every few pages, important announcements to be heeded by every citizen are printed in large type. There are puffed-up

Fig. 41. Maria Uszacka, "BZZZ—BZZYK—BZY"

From *Gdyby Tygrysy Jadły Irysy* by Wanda Chotomska, illustrated by Maria Uszacka, Ruch, Warszawa, 1968. By permission of Maria Uszacka.

10. See also chapter 3.

speech balloons for the arrogant mayor's pronouncements. When he introduces the doctrine that Everything Is Fine The Way It Is and all the people, young and old, applaud and return to their homes and work happier than before, joyfully repeating the mayor's maxim, part of the space in the picture showing the people going about their business is filled with repetitions of that maxim printed in various directions.

But the most powerful visualization is the page of laughter (fig. 42). One day the mayor establishes that nobody will weep anymore. What use is a beautiful town if one man laughs and the other one weeps? So the people run home laughing: the illustration shows eight masklike faces lining the page above and below rows of laughter, the laughter represented by five rows of the word *ha-ha-ha* repeated twelve times and, in addition, printed in diagonally arranged series of three colors, red, yellow and blue. This results in an ornamental representation of the people laughing together, staccato, keeping time, the fearful visual symbol of an audible expression of mindless regimentation.

Fig. 42. Günther Stiller, "Ha ha ha"
From Günther Stiller/Elisabeth Borchers: *Das rote Haus in einer kleinen Stadt*. © 1969 Verlag Heinrich Ellermann München.

Another outstanding example of the consistent use of visible sound representation is Isadora's *Ben's Trumpet*, to which we shall return in chapter 14 (fig. 67).

Again, this is only a small sample of the many devices, some naive and some sophisticated and fraught with significance, that are being invented to signify or symbolize one sensory expanse by another.

CHILDREN'S WORKS CITED

AL-ASHASH, AL-TAYYIB. *Alif*. Illus. by Gawal Mikrili. Tunis: Dar Alif Lil-Nasr, 1979.

BORCHERS, ELISABETH. *Das rote Haus in einer kleinen Stadt*. Illus. by Günther Stiller. München: Ellermann, 1969.

BORTEN, HELEN. *Do You Hear What I Hear?* New York: Abelard-Schuman, 1960.

BURTON, VIRGINIA L. *Choo Choo: The Story of a Little Engine Who Ran Away*. Boston: Houghton Mifflin, 1937.

CHOTOMSKA, WANDA. *Gdyby Tygrysy Jadły Irisy*. Illus. by Maria Uszacka. Warszawa: Ruch, 1968.

DAMASHQUIA, A. D. *Lugatina*. Illus. by Nabil Taġ. Beirut: Dar al-Fata Al-Arabi, n.d.

HELD, JACQUELINE; HELD, CLAUDE; and POMMAUX, YVAN. *lune vole*. Paris: L'école des loisirs, 1976.

JANIKOVSZKY, ÉVA. *ha én FELNŐTT volnék*. Illus. by László Réber. Budapest: Móra, 1965.

Poems and Rhymes. *Childcraft—The How and Why Library*, vol. 1. Chicago: World Book–Childcraft International, 1980.

SENDAK, MAURICE. *In the Night Kitchen*. New York: Harper & Row, 1963.

SNUNITH, MIHAL. "Shir al shir shebarah," *Shirim lemi she' ohavim*. Illus. by Avi Margalith. Tel Aviv: Sifriat Poalim, 1971.

STEINITZ, KÄTA, and SCHWITTERS, KURT. *Hahne Peter*. Hannover: Merz, n.d.

TOLSTOI, LEV. *Tri Medvedya*. Illus. by V. Lebedev. Moskva: Detgis, 1956.

TUWIM, JULIAN. *Lokomotywa, Rzepka, Ptasie Radio*. Illus. by Julitta Karwowska-Wnuczak. Warszawa: Nasza Księgarnia, 1977.

YELLIN-KALAI, RENANAH. "Kubioth," *Hineh ani*. Illus. by Yehudith Yellin-Ginath. Tel Aviv: Massada, 1965.

8

Puppets and Dolls

There is one kind of illustrated book, the photographed story of puppets and dolls, which does not seem to arouse the interest of writers on literature and art for children. Very little has been written on them as a special phenomenon (Bader briefly refers to them).[1]

This is surprising because of the large number of such books that has been appearing ever since this has been technically feasible, and also because of the fact that from the aesthetic point of view they are quite intriguing and differ from the books which are illustrated by an artist's picture. The latter results from the cooperation of a writer and an artist. The responsibility for the former, on the other hand, rests with a whole team: the writer, the creator of the puppets or the dolls; the stage designer; the stage director who arranges the scenes; and the photographer who also decides on the lighting. The illustrations—their style, composition, pictorial continuum (what pictures and how many are to accompany the text), the way the action and the relationships between the actors in the story are represented, etc.—do not flow from the crayon or brush of one artist; they are compiled and edited by the combined efforts of a number of artists and artisans. Even if, as is often the case, one member of the team fulfills several of these tasks, he still serves in various capacities.

The painter evokes an illusion of space through his work on two-dimensional pages. The creators of the doll-stories place three-dimensional dolls on three-dimensional stages and then photograph them. This is, then, an art form which draws its inspiration mainly from the tradition of the stage arts, the puppet show, the marionette theater, and corresponding cinematic and video films. In fact, a large percentage of these stories have their source in plays or films; they are stills, selected to capture and arrest a number of instants out of the animated rush of events on stage or screen and arranged in the form of a book, with text added.

---

1. Bader, *American Picturebooks*, p. 100.

CHARACTERISTIC FEATURES

This origin of the illustrations explains some of their characteristics. Usually they convey the rather static impression of a collection of attentively taken photographs that succeed each other, rather than that of a close sequence of illustrations following each other and carrying the story along. The expression of immobility of the puppets is not easily overcome; it is too obvious that neither are living beings photographed in mid-movement nor did a painter's hand energize them; they are just puppets whose trunks and legs and heads are turned and bent in certain ways so as to indicate movement, mood, or mutual relationships. The facial expression of the dolls never changes throughout the story. The face and the eyes are painted on once and photographed that way in all illustrations. The actors have a stiff and often even vacuous look that lacks focus and never reveals any emotional secrets.

The designers of books of this genre are well aware of this; they find many ingenious and aesthetically pleasing ways to minimize or overcome the lack of ease of their subjects and to enrich the expressiveness of their pictures:

The scenes are composed or selected painstakingly from stills. Great care is taken to pose and juxtapose the actors so that the meaning of each scene is clear; much attention is paid to all those parts of the body, apart from the face, which are apt to carry expression: hands, arms, legs, head, and stance are employed in a very outspoken way, to the point of exaggeration. At times the hands and arms are relatively larger so as to be more conspicuous.

The stage sets, too, are designed elaborately and often exquisitely. The background, whether realistic or fantastic, historical or modern, is colorful, rich in details, and attractive. The same goes for the costumes. The lighting of the different scenes is flexible and dramatic.

The way the scenes are photographed also adds much to their expressive quality. A close-up coming immediately after a long shot makes for an impression of movement; well-chosen picture angles and viewpoints dramatize the action. So do surprising lighting angles: a good photographer may almost persuade us that the expression on a doll's face changes between scenes.

SUBTYPES

Many means are used to enliven the books. Actually, there exist various kinds of photographed puppet stories, differing in artistic approach and technique. It is quite a lively field, where new inventions and devices keep turning up.

Numerous books reproduce the very style of the puppet theater. Often the cast and the scenery are especially constructed for a story or a series of connected stories; or the books really are photographic essays on performances that took place in puppet theaters.

Some designers freely mix techniques and media. Photographs appear alternately with simple drawings so that the same events are depicted more than once: the action is offered to the viewer *twice*. Still other books go one step further and *alternately* illustrate the story with photographs and drawings so that they complement each other.

There are also those books which simply relate the adventures of a doll or a teddy bear; here the stiff photographs carry the expression of the toy that is the subject of the story.

LIMITATIONS OF THE GENRE

Puppet story books usually have a special charm. The actors are constructed well. They are elegant or quaint or clumsy in an obvious way that makes the child smile. Their costumes and the stage and its accessories are wrought thoughtfully. All sorts of tricks and inventions brighten up the pictures. Pleasing color schemes abound. A delicate sense of humor is reflected in the staging of the scenes and the layout of the book. Although there are some inane examples around, on the whole this is a genre which offers the child pleasant and tasteful stimulation of his aesthetic capabilities.

Still, books of this kind are reminiscent of expertly arranged displays. Their illustrations do not suggest the more continuous sweep found in a comparable number of pictures created by the pictorial artist. There is something artful about them, a lack of immediacy.

It has been said that the photographed puppet is especially close to the minds of children due to the intense emotional attachment they develop with their dolls and toy animals, and the many roles these fulfill in the child's play and fantasy. Yet there is some misunderstanding about this. The importance of the doll and toy animal arises from the child's play with them. *He* handles them, moves them about and puts them where he wants and needs them and thereby, in a way, animates them. In the minds of children dolls are not pictures.

This is also true, of course, of the hand puppet and the marionette in the puppet theater. There, too, as the great writer and playwright Heinrich von Kleist observed in his classic essay on the marionette theater, the charm and lively appeal of the dumb puppet remain *outside* of it. Its dynamic focus lies in the manipulative fingers of the puppeteer who animates them and calls them to life.[2] By contrast, when the puppets are photographed they become motionless and solid, probably also because of the very attempt of their makers to create them so lifelike and true to style. When the child sees the puppet in action, or plays with his or her own dolls, this solidity is obliterated. But stills have their limitations.

---

2. Heinrich von Kleist, "Ueber das Marionettentheater," *Saemtliche Werke*, vol. 3 (Leipzig: Max Hesses Verlag, n.d.), pp. 213–19.

The mixing of pictorial media we referred to above, the duplication of photographs by drawings, the succession of photographs and drawings by turns, probably is an admission of one such limitation. The designer seems to be aware that by adding drawings he injects liveliness into the visual message or clarifies it. What else could be the point of joining or alternating two techniques which don't have much in common, double rendering as a kind of double indemnity? When the photographs and the drawings are compared, it turns out that the figures appearing in both media resemble each other (themselves) only superficially. The child's perceptive powers are rather confounded than supported by the variation. Persons, objects, and backgrounds lose their convincing visual identity. Neither is the child's capacity to comprehend the blending of text and illustration furthered by this. The two kinds of illustration turn into mere, if often attractive, decoration. What would we say if a writer were to alternate from one style to a very different one every two pages for no discernible reason except diversity's sake? We would find this disturbing. This is also true on a visual level.

However, the most strongly felt limitation is the unchanging facial expression we alluded to before. One of the prominent elements in the child's human environment is the communicative message found in the scarcely perceptible movement of the eyes. One important example would be the well-known fact that the pupils dilate or contract according to changes in emotional states.[3] The shrewd illustrator intuitively guides the child in decoding and encoding these subtle messages, interpreting and applying them. The puppet is, by contrast, inarticulate.

The endeavor to create a specific genre of illustrated children's books by combining elements of the picture book and the stage results in an aesthetically and psychologically unsatisfactory pseudo-medium that renounces both the illusion of movement on the stage and the illusion flowing from the single artist's imagination. It is wanting in authenticity.

---

3. See Ian Hindmarch, "Eyes, Eye Spots and Pupil Dilation in Non-Verbal Communication," in Mario von Cranach and Ian Vine, eds., *Social Communication and Movement* (London: Academic Pr., 1974), pp. 299–321.

Part 2

*Variations
on a Theme*

9

Modes, Moods, and Attitudes

The point we wish to make in this chapter is introduced best by a double citation from two book reports by Hearne, on two books dedicated to the same subject, *Beauty and the Beast*.[1]

On Diana Goode:

A flexible but faithful translation of de Beaumont's French fairy tale carries the formal court style into a graphic interpretation entirely different from Mercer Mayer's (below), Goode's elegant line work, conscious architectural planes, sharpened color, and delicate, coiffured characters place the story clearly in the realm of magic. Poses are dramatic in the manner of an eighteenth-century royal play, and the discrete, structured tone of both art and language leaves much to the imagination. A worthwhile version that shows considerable care.

On Marianna and Mercer Mayer:

Marianna Mayer's adaption has dropped the distancing stylization of the original and picked up considerably on pace and simpler dialogue, lending an immediacy powerfully reflected in Mercer Mayer's art (which is developed here beyond any of his previous efforts); the relationship between Beauty and Beast is also imagined more fully. Mayer's graphic setting is wilder, with almost a baroque atmosphere, heightened tensions, and somber colors unleashed occasionally by an intense, startling blue. His beast has fearsomely expressive eyes and a magnificent presence only faintly reflected by the anticlimactic prince. Such warmly human, yet elaborately detailed illustrations facing every page of text enrich the symbolism of the story while at the same time making it more accessible to children on an emotional level.

These two passages succinctly and beautifully analyze some of the effects illustrations may have. In these two books they join the text and support and underline its specific approach to the ancient story: delicate structures versus dynamic tension; watching the action on stage from a distance versus being drawn into emotional involvement. The interdependence of word and picture creates the tone of the book.

This is not to say that the partnership between the verbal and the visual

---

1. Betsy Hearne, reviews, "Mayer, Marianna: Beauty and the Beast" and "Goode, Diana: Beauty and the Beast," *Booklist* (Sept. 15, 1978), pp. 217, 223.

will always be as close or as felicitous. For all the countless books in which the two media reinforce each other's message, there are possibly as many where this does not happen. But this is simplifying the issue. The essential fact is that the illustration cannot be what it is too often stated to be—a sort of beautification, an embellishment, a decoration harmonizing with the text or bringing harmony to the text, as a bunch of flowers decorates a room. Actually, any bunch of flowers will somehow affect the tone of the room it is put in. So, too, illustrations can never be a neutral delight for the eye. They constitute an additional medium that intervenes between the text and the reader; they upset any balance that might have been arrived at by adding weight to the scales; they represent a mode of communication, the visual one, and so they offer impressions and messages to the perception, cognition, and emotional power of the child. This interference and cooperation can take on numberless different forms. New ones are invented all the time, as illustrators relate to texts supporting or neglecting, intensifying or weakening, clarifying or impairing what the text says about the characters in the story, the course of the plot, the physical and social background, the atmosphere and ideas pervading it. Illustrations may mold the intentions of the author or detect aspects the author was never aware of. The illustrator locks his shapes and colors into the text and they shape and color the experience that may be derived from the page and the book.

There is nothing spectacularly new in what we have just said; the idea has been around ever since art appreciation and art criticism have come into existence. But in books and articles on children's literature it is usually treated slightly hazily, if at all (with notable exceptions like the passages cited above), and we wish to spell it out. The purpose is to show some of the ways in which the illustrator suggests to the child the moods, understandings, and attitudes that he, the artist, has found or wished to find in the poem, story, or book he has illustrated.

Let us start with small, or apparently small things. Venerable "Old King Cole," the merry old soul from Mother Goose, is usually portrayed as a jovial, portly gentleman (with his three fiddlers) and as a historical king (somewhere between Tudor and the Renaissance), as in a version published in 1976.[2] He also appears this way in an Italian version, with an archway and a stone wall added for ornateness.[3] But in yet another version, in 1978,[4] while the historical frame with the fiddlers is there, and even the king's ermine coat, Old King Cole has become a plump boy with a childish smile. We are not sure that this really makes sense; in any case it causes a shift in the possible meaning of the poem. The illustrations of the first two books lightly introduce the child to the pageantry which somehow clarifies the back-

2. "Old King Cole"; illus. by Linda Gist, in *Childcraft*, vol. 1, p. 42.
3. "Il vecchio Re Nicola"; illus. by Nicola Bayley, in *La scarpa in fondo al prato* (Milano: Emme Edizione, 1978).
4. "Old King Cole"; illus. by Bonnie and Bill Rutherford, in *Mother Goose* (Racine, Wis.: Western, Golden Press, 1978).

ground of the amusing rhyme. The third one explains that here children are playing at king-and-court.

Or take Milne's wonderfully philosophical poem about Christopher Robin, "Halfway Down." Christopher is sitting on the stairs and has all kinds of funny thoughts running around in his head, just because he is not at the bottom and not at the top. He decides that where he is isn't anywhere, but somewhere else instead. For a long time Milne's poems and stories "came together" with Shepard's drawings. It was one of those cases where the book seemed to have been cast in one inseparable shape. Yet they have occasionally been separated and it is interesting to compare at least one example of another illustrator's work with the original book.[5] In both pictures, of course, the children are sitting somewhere midway on the stairway. Both close their eyes, surely to avoid getting dizzy from not being at the bottom and not at the top, or else because they are concentrating so intensely on their doubts. There the similarity ends. Shepard's stairs are few and plain. Grant's staircase is taller and socially updated, with a staircover of richer material and elaborate banisters (fig. 43). Surprisingly, Grant's child is a girl. Why not? The poem says nothing of the small philosopher's sex. Why should not a girl think the same kinds of thoughts? Yet there is an essential difference; it lies in the fact that the original Milne-Shepard page forms part of ever-ruminating Christopher Robin's world. The Milne-Grant page has been taken out of this context; briefly we come upon an equally lovable child thinking equally wise thoughts, but the poem now stands by itself. There is one more small but significant detail. Christopher is sitting there all by himself—the teddy bear lies on the uppermost stair, craning his neck as if much offended. Have his thoughts gripped Christopher so terribly that he is able to abandon Winnie-the-Pooh? The girl tightly clasps a panda to herself—to help her solve the question? The verses have not changed, the poem has.

Other works where story and picture constitute a seamless classic creation are Lewis Carroll's Alice books, with John Tenniel's illustrations. Yet there exist many editions, especially of *Alice's Adventures in Wonderland*, both in English and other languages that have been illustrated by other artists.[6] Many illustrators, by the way, have the "classic" feeling that black-and-white illustrations suit Alice better than color. Maybe they are right, but in fact Sir John himself was the first illustrator who agreed to colored pictures when Carroll published, twenty-five years after the original book, an abridged version, *The Nursery Alice*.

It is impossible to relate here to the complexities of Alice—that book

5. A. A. Milne, "Halfway Down," *The World of Christopher Robin*; illus. by E. H. Shepard (New York: Dutton, 1958); idem, "Halfway Down"; illus. by Leigh Grant, in *Childcraft*, vol. 1, p. 172.
6. See Graham Ovenden, ed., *The Illustrators of Alice in Wonderland* (London: Academy Editions; New York: St. Martin's Press, 1972).

HALFWAY DOWN

Halfway down the stairs
Is a stair
Where I sit.
There isn't any
Other stair
Quite like
It.
I'm not at the bottom,
I'm not at the top;
So this is the stair
Where
I always
Stop.

Halfway up the stairs
Isn't up,
And isn't down.
It isn't in the nursery,
It isn't in the town.
And all sorts of funny thoughts
Run round my head:
"It isn't really
Anywhere!
It's somewhere else
Instead!"

A. A. MILNE

Fig. 43. Leigh Grant, "Halfway Down"
Illustration by Leigh Grant from Volume 1, *Childcraft—The How and Why Library*. © 1981 World Book–Childcraft International, Inc.

which has been characterized as intended to be a lighthearted excursion into nonsense[7] and has also been researched and analyzed from literary, philosophical, theological, and psychological points of view.[8] But it must surely be one of the main objectives, and also one of the vexing problems for the artist who takes on Alice, to convey the uncanniness and surreality of her

7. Arbuthnot, *Children*, 3rd ed., p. 340.
8. See, for instance, Robert Phillips, ed., *Aspects of Alice: Lewis Carroll's Dreamchild as Seen through the Critics' Looking Glass 1865–1971* (Harmondsworth, Eng.: Penguin, 1974).

adventures and at the same time communicate the humor inherent in these frightfully delightful experiences. It seems that in order to succeed in this, the artist has first of all to create a gripping Alice, one that the reader will be able to identify with because her appearance will allow him to believe that she was strong enough, and willing, to pass through all these surprising realms. Is not this the secret of Tenniel's achievement?

Two fairly recent editions of *Alice in Wonderland*, in translation, illustrated by artists who became genuinely involved with the story, may serve as examples of how wide a range of possibilities is at the illustrators' disposal.

One of the two books has been richly illustrated in black-and-white by Kalinovsky—over half the pages in the story bear illustrations. They reflect a profound grasp of the book. The crazy mood is sounded by the cover (fig. 44), where the letters forming the word ALICY get smaller as they move down the page (down into the rabbit hole); the large *A* especially represents a topsy-turvy world through which Alice wanders, appearing and reappearing in changing sizes and from changing angles. Then there are the chapter headings: frames in which seemingly three-dimensional letters and words

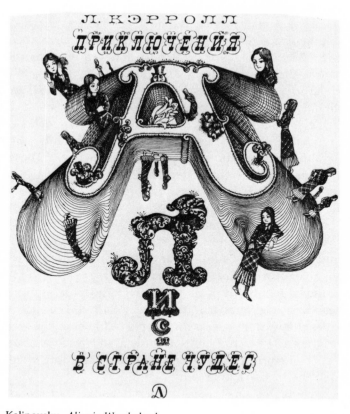

Fig. 44. H. Kalinovsky, *Alice in Wonderland*

From *Priklyutcheniya Alicy v Strane Chudes* by Lewis Carroll, illustrated by H. Kalinovsky, Detskaya Literatura, Moskva, 1977. By permission of VAAP, the copyright agency of the USSR, on behalf of the illustrator.

Fig. 45. H. Kalinovsky, "The letter of invitation"
From *Priklyutcheniya Alicy v Strane Chudes* by Lewis Carroll, illustrated by H. Kalinovsky, Detskaya Literatura, Moskva, 1977. By permission of VAAP, the copyright agency of the USSR, on behalf of the illustrator.

stomp and dance and fall over themselves.[9] The pictures in the book are drawn in a surrealistic manner (fig. 45). They present strange locations and scenes, all haunted, some sparse and others rich with exotic pageantry and romantic settings, replete with grotesque figures. Through these absurd spheres moves the one real figure, a tall Alice in her early 'teens, in a narrow checkered dress; she has long straight hair and lovely, intelligent eyes. She is meditative at times and then roguish or, rarely, frightened, and always curious to find out what all this is supposed to mean: she stands out as the one sane being in this rushing confusion. Kalinovsky creates an almost perfect fusion of realistic with surrealistic style elements out of deep empathy with the spirit of the story and with its heroine. These pictures appeal to the imagination of the older child.

The other example is illustrated even more lavishly—there are illustrations by Haacken on 136 of the 194 pages in the story. The pictures, pen drawings, and colors exhibit much creativity. The book's endpapers, for instance, present the well-known anecdote of how "Alice's Adventures Underground" came into being, when Carroll rowed the three Liddell sisters on the river on a summer day. In front we see Carroll and the girls in the boat. At the bottom of the page, underneath the river, appears, written in wavy lines, the text of the anecdote as told by Carroll. The endpaper at the back continues the text; however, the people in the boat have turned into characters in the story—Carroll himself is the Mad Hatter. Or, the mouse's tale, instead of being printed in ever smaller letters according to the original, is inscribed in the mouse's long tail.

But on the whole this version of Alice and her adventures is not success-

9. This is another example of playing with the visual properties of the written word—see the chapter on "The Letter and the Written Word as Visual Elements."

ful. Too many pictures of objects and small details lead us astray, too many close-ups of people milling around underground, and enough animal portraits to portray Wonderland as an animal reserve. Most pictures have no background; no magic world of Alice comes into being. They all wear slightly caricatured expressions, except for the Hatter, who has some of the patina of a crazy old man. Instead of the spell of an enigmatic happening we get the feeling of a gay outing not far beyond the neighbor's garden. Things are too natural, too tangible. Alice, on whom everything hinges, is a nice little girl, a bit supercilious, not one cut out for such baffling developments. Mood and meaning are lost. (This failure of a very gifted and experienced illustrator is surprising, given his extensive involvement with the story and the fact that Haacken was a master of suspense. His version of Prokofiev's *Peter and the Wolf*, done in black-and-white with sparing mixtures of color, achieves that rare masterly combination of the funny with the uncanny which is also so essential an element in Alice. In his last book, *Django*, the life story of a gipsy guitarist, black and white constitute a dramatic background for the characters painted in color.)

Contrasts in approach may be very pointed. *The Dragon in the Clock Box* by M. Jean Craig is about a boy's imaginary play. He takes possession of an empty clock box and keeps a dragon's egg in it for seven days, carrying the box with him wherever he goes. The dragon hatches and flies away; now the box will serve well to keep marbles in.

The story is written with delicate humor; we never quite know what taciturn Joshua really thinks when he reluctantly responds to his family's questions about the egg's progress. The story is really about how parents should relate to their children's fantasy play—interfering little and sympathetically. The illustrator joins the mood with pictures depicting affectionate, considerate parents, brothers and sisters, and a comfortable home where the boy moves around with his box (fig. 46). It is a pity that at one point he starts portraying the dragon baby, which is an unwonted interference with the imagination of the child reader.

When the book appears in a Hebrew translation, the new illustrator introduces a new mood (fig. 47). Sociologically, we find ourselves in a poorer environment, indicated by a few pieces of furniture and some walls in the house. Psychologically, the situation has changed drastically. Except for one picture in the beginning, Joshua's family does not appear in the book; the cautious active interest they take in his secretive doings is visually removed—though all the dialogues in the text are there—and thus the illustrator emphasizes that the daydream should be Joshua's alone. When he talks to his mother or brother, his head turns in a certain way, but his preoccupation sets him apart from them. The illustrator also refrains from depicting the dragon's shape. The mellowness of the original has gone; the atmosphere is rougher. For the environment he has stripped away, this illustrator substitutes a continuous red line that accompanies the black-and-

On Tuesday afternoon Joshua's mother went shopping and bought a new alarm clock. When she unwrapped it, Joshua asked her if he might have the box it came in.

"Of course, Josh, if you like. What are you going to do with it?"

Fig. 46. Kelly Oechsli, *The Dragon in the Clock Box*
From *The Dragon in the Clock Box* by M. Jean Craig, illustrated by Kelly Oechsli, Norton, New York, 1962. By permission of Kelly Oechsli.

ביום שלישי אחר הצהרים
הלכה אמא של יהושע הצעירה
וקנתה שעון מעורר.
כשהוציאה את השעון
מתוך הקפסה שבה היה ארוז,
שאל יהושע אם הוא יכול לקבל את הקפסה.

"אם אתה רוצה, בודאי."
אמרה אמא.
"מה תעשה בה?"
"עכשיו."
ענה יהושע. אבל בנימוס.

Fig. 47. Ari Ron, *The Dragon in the Clock Box*
From *Hadrakon bekufsat hasha'on* by M. Jean Craig, illustrated by Ari Ron, Am Oved Publishers, Tel Aviv, 1975.

white drawings and dominates the pages; it very aptly symbolizes Joshua's concentration on his imaginary pet. Needless to say, the two Joshuas are utterly dissimilar: the first one is a gentle dreamer; the other one is smart and prankish.

Either version is excellent in some respects and less so in others. But the main point we are concerned with here is that it is in the illustrators' power to shift accents and express opinions by what they draw, how they draw it by what they omit to draw.

Similarly, when *Oma*, a German story by Peter Härtling about a boy who is brought up by his grandmother, is published in America, subtle changes reflect attitudes. The original Oma is portrayed only once and she is a grave, slightly bent woman (fig. 48); the American granny is pictured time and again, mostly smilingly optimistic (fig. 49).

The illustrator conscious of his work takes care to announce his own accent on the cover of the book. Two Chilenian editions of Oscar Wilde's well-known *The Happy Prince* demonstrate this well. The cover of the first one shows the people of the town as they admire the huge statue from below; we see only the pedestal and the feet. This sets the tone for the whole series of pictures inside the book. Feet and pedestal accompany the many events which happen in the town; only rarely are we elevated to the Prince's and the swallow's angle of vision high in the sky. The illustrator chooses to depict the plot rather than to signify its emotional temper. The other book is an abbreviation of the story, concentrating on the main episodes. The cover is a resplendent Prince looking down on the night-bound town. This keys us to what will follow. We see little of the town. The pictures show, from above, the destitute souls to whom the swallow brings the Prince's gifts. It is night and romantic colors reign—except for the anticlimax, the bleak morning, when the dilapidated statue is pulled down. The choices indicated are, then, factual narration versus emotional appeal.

One problem illustrators have when they choose their own personal variations is how to break away from the commonplace, to avoid the self-evident, when they treat subjects that have already been illustrated a hundred times before.

For an example of the challenge of illustrating a well-known motif or situation beautifully and meaningfully, though not necessarily from a new angle or from a fresh point of view, let us look at what happens when illustrators approach the ending of *The Ugly Duckling*. We are all familiar with Andersen's moving autobiographical allegory. Its theme is achieving—or is it discovering?—identity. It has been praised for its symbolic quality and the way in which it leads us from hopelessness to serenity by Arbuthnot,[10] Hürlimann,[11] and others. Bettelheim rejects it for precisely that reason: the ugly duckling does not really have to accomplish anything. He does not mature; the hero's life is changed by fate, not by his own actions. This is, says Bettelheim, a depressive world view.[12]

However, the last scene in the story, when anguish dissolves and the duckling finds out who he has become and is accepted by his fellow swans and admired by children, is a moment of radiant happiness. How is this

10. Arbuthnot, *Children*, 3rd ed., p. 401.
11. Bettina Hürlimann, *Europäische Kinderbücher in drei Jahrhunderten* (Zürich: Atlantis, 1963), p. 109.
12. Bruno Bettelheim, *The Uses of Enchantment: The Meaning and Importance of Fairy Tales* (New York: Vintage-Random, 1977), pp. 104–5.

Fig. 48. Ingrid Mizsenko, *Oma*
Illustration by Ingrid Mizsenko from *Oma* by Peter Härtling, © Beltz Weinheim und Basel, Programm Beltz & Gelberg.

moment to be visualized? What sets of circumstances can illustrators create around the noble shape of the new swan? Choices seem to be limited: he may be pictured solitary, facing, as Narcissus does in the myth, his own image in the water; or together with the other swans; or with swans and people. What else can be imagined? But the choices have their significance for the child who looks at the illustrations. The swan alone with his image emphasizes pride in his own self; with the other swans, social acceptance is accented; if human beings, especially children, are included, the scene is seen through their eyes—a distancing effect is introduced at the last moment. The choices differ from each other in the degree to which we will focus on the happy swan.

We looked at thirty-four versions published in fifteen countries during

Fig. 49. Jutta Ash, *Oma*

Illustration by Jutta Ash from *Oma* by Peter Härtling, translated by Althea Bell. Copyright © 1975 by Beltz Verlag, Weinheim und Basel. By permission of Harper & Row, Publishers, Inc. and Andersen Press Ltd.

the last decades to find out how illustrators feel about this motif. Taking into consideration that a number of books have more than one illustration to jubilate with the swan, there were thirteen pictures of the swan by himself, eight of the swans among themselves, and seventeen of the swans being admired by children and adults. We would say that this last variant, which corresponds with Andersen's own choice of expertly conducting the tale back, as it were, to the child who listens to it or reads it, is also the most desirable one educationally.

To be sure, there are differences in the level of execution. Not a few illustrations are stereotyped portrayals of swans; these can be, in this case, quite satisfactory, because there is intrinsic beauty in the shape of the swan. Still, there exist many attractive pictures. There is Huens' lonely swan, already flying high above the village, far away from the crowd.[13] Then those of the swans by themselves: Brunovský's, reminiscent in its composition and mystical colors of a medieval miniature, showing the swans elegant in confrontation, from above;[14] Karma's, where, behind the new swan facing the older ones, two black ducklings take our thoughts further away, beyond the present moment (would Andersen want that?);[15] Bogdanovic's, where the new swan abruptly turns away from the others.[16] And the illustrators who include the human spectators: Schwarzer's wide-eyed children arriving on the riverbank,[17] Jensenius's classic family looking down the bridge,[18] Hložník's parents and children forming a frame through which we look at the swans out there, together with this family.[19] And one of the finest, Adams's sequence of three pictures: the three swans sizing up the new one, the children rushing to the river with the other swans bowing before the young one, and the new swan alone with his thoughts.[20] Few illustrators communicate so poignantly as Adams and Brunovský the feeling of triumph that is with the swan at this hour.

How many different associations the illustrator is capable of arousing in the child, in relation to the one ending the author wrote! Put simply this means that illustrating is not lacing or icing a text but adding a message. It means that aesthetic *modes* offer certain appeals, stimuli which represent psychological *moods* and social and ethical *attitudes*. The illustrator, consciously or unconsciously, tastefully or crudely, *interprets*. As Robert Motherwell once said of art in general, there is no work of art which is not a selection, an abstraction for the purposes of emphasis.[21] The illustrator of children's books, as any artist, suggests meanings which he recognizes in the text and wishes to communicate through the content and style of his work.[22]

In the following chapters we shall take up a number of variations on a number of themes and look at them closely.

13. Hans Christian Andersen, *O Patinho Feio e outros contos*; trans. by Herberto Helder; illus. by Jean-Léon Huens (Lisboa: Verbo, 1969).

14. Hans Christian Andersen, "Mrźké Kačiatko," *Statŏcný Cínový Vojačik*; trans. by Jaroslav Káňa; illus. by Albín Brunovský (Bratislava: Mladé letá, 1963).

15. *Andersenin Kauneimmat Sadut*; trans. by Sirkka Rapla; illus. by Maija Karma. (Helsinki: Oxava, 1972).

16. Hans Christian Andersen, *Das hässliche Entlein*; illus. by Toma Bogdanovic (Hanau: Peters, 1972).

17. Otto Wutzel, ed., *Dichtermärchen aus aller Welt*; illus. by Renate Schwarzer (Linz/Donau: Trauner, 1967).

18. Hans Christian Andersen, *Eventyr og Historier*; illus. by Herluf Jensenius (København: Nyt Nordisk Forlag Arnold Busck, 1963).

19. Hans Christian Andersen, *Roz právky*; trans. by Jaroslav Káňa; illus. by Vincent Hložník (Bratislava: Mlade leta, 1956).

20. Hans Christian Andersen, *The Ugly Duckling*; trans. by R. P. Keigwin; illus. by Adrienne Adams (New York: Scribner, 1965).

21. Barbaralee Diamondstein, "Inside New York's Art World: An Interview with Robert Motherwell," *Partisan Review* 3 (1979) 385–86.

22. Brian Alderson has given attention to this subject in "A View from The Island," *Illustrators*, pp. 20–43, and adduced a number of telling examples, especially in connection with style.

CHILDREN'S WORKS CITED

ANDERSEN, HANS CHRISTIAN. *Eventyr og Historier*. Illus. by Herluf Jensenius. København: Nyt Nordisk Forlag Arnold Busck, 1963.

———. *H. C. Andersen's Fairy Tales*. Trans. by L. W. Kingsland. New York: Walck, 1962.

———. *Das hässliche Entlein*. Illus. by Toma Bogdanovic. Hanau: Peters, 1972.

———. "Mrźké Kačiatko." In *Statočný Cínový Vojačik*. Trans. by Jaroslav Káňa. Illus. by Albín Brunovský. Bratislava: Mladé letá, 1963.

———. *O Patinho Feio e outros contos*. Trans. by Herberto Helder. Illus. by Jean-Léon Huens. Lisboa: Verbo, 1969.

———. *Roz pravóky*. Trans. by Jaroslav Káňa. Illus. by Vincent Hložník. Bratislava: Mladé letá, 1956.

———. *The Ugly Duckling*. Trans. by R. P. Keigwin. Illus. by Adrienne Adams. New York: Scribner, 1965.

Andersenin Kauneimmat Sadut. Trans. by Sirkka Rapla. Illus. by Maija Karma. Helsinki: Oxava, 1972.

CARROLL, LEWIS. *Alice in Wonderland and Through the Looking Glass*. Illus. by John Tenniel. New York: Heritage Press-Macy, 1941.

———. *Alice in Wunderland*. Illus. by Frans Haacken. Recklinghausen: Bitter, 1967.

———. *The Nursery Alice*. Illus. by John Tenniel. London: Macmillan, 1890.

———. *Priklyutcheniya Alicy v Strane Chudes*. Trans. by Borisov Zakhoderov. Illus. by H. Kalinovsky. Moskva: Detskaya Literatura, 1977.

CRAIG, M. JEAN. *The Dragon in the Clock Box*. Illus. by Kelly Oechsli. New York: Norton, 1962.

———. *Hadrakon bekufsat hasha'on*. Trans. by Rivkah Meshulah. Illus. by Ari Ron. Tel Aviv: Am Oved, 1975.

GOODE, DIANA. *Beauty and the Beast*. New York: Bradbury, 1978.

HAACKEN, FRANS. *Django*. Ravensburg: Otto Maier, 1979.

HÄRTLING, PETER. *Oma*. Illus. by Ingrid Mizsenko. Weinheim, Basel: Beltz & Gelberg, 1976.

———. *Oma*. Trans. by Althea Bell. Illus. by Jutta Ash. New York: Harper & Row, 1977.

MAYER, MARIANNA. *Beauty and the Beast*. Illus. by Mercer Mayer. New York: Four Winds Press, 1978.

MILNE, A. A. "Halfway Down." *The World of Christopher Robin*. Illus. by E. H. Shepard. New York: Dutton, 1958.

"Old King Cole," *Mother Goose*. Illus. by Bonnie and Bill Rutherford. Racine, Wis.: Western, Golden Press, 1978.

Poems and Rhymes. Childcraft—*The How and Why Library*, vol. 1. Chicago: World Book–Childcraft International, 1980.

PROKOFIEV, SERGEJ S. *Peter und der Wolf*. Illus. by Frans Haacken. München: Parabel, 1958.

WILDE, OSCAR. *El principe feliz*. Illus. by Marta Carrasco. Bellavista: Quimantu, 1972.

———. *El principe feliz*. (adaptation) Santiago de Chile: Ediciones Logos, 1973.

"Il vecchio Re Nicola." In *La scarpa in fondo al prato*. Illus. by Nicola Bayley. Milano: Emme Edizione, 1978.

WUTZEL, OTTO, ed. *Dichtermärchen aus aller Welt*. Illus. by Renate Schwarzer. Linz, Donau: Trauner, 1967.

10

Humiliation and Urgency in Two Key Scenes in Cinderella

In our generation the fairy tale is "in" again. In the thirties and forties education abhorred its lack of realism and the cruelty of its plots. Rational fiction was assumed to be child's faithful companion on his road to an autonomous adulthood. Today, however, the potential importance of fairy tales for the development of the human psyche is again recognized. They carry the child's mind far away from his everyday world, relating fantastic events whose heroes are rather abstract figures. They tell, in disguise, about basic human situations and relationships that the growing child may have to experience, about basic conflicts he will have to face, and about ways to resolve these conflicts. The child both enjoys the stories and at the same time unconsciously gets hold of some aspects of their symbolic meaning. This imaginary journey into the fanciful, archetypal world of the fairy story may give strength to the child in his efforts to master reality and aid him to understand more, again mainly unconsciously, about his own development into a mature personality.

Why this should be so is a question far beyond the scope of the subject at hand. So is the question of the processes taking place in the course of the twentieth century which brought the fairy tale back into the favor of the artist, the child psychologist, and the educator. These processes are modifications in the fabric of Western civilization. One very important element in this change is the development of in-depth psychology. Beginning with Freud, early in the century, and continuing with his disciples and then mainly with Jung and his school, the extended investigation of the fairy tale, in connection with that of the dream and the myth, offered insights which showed it to be a psychologically significant art form.

One of the most comprehensive studies in this area is Bruno Bettelheim's *The Uses of Enchantment*, a book that has been read widely by the public and has had notable influence on scholars in the fields of literature, psychology, and education.[1] In essence the book is a fervent plea, on behalf of psychology, for the fairy tale's role in education.

1. For a concise summary of in-depth psychological research on the fairy tale, see pp. 313–14, notes 10, 11, and 12.

One consequence of the rising interest in the fairy tale has been the proliferation of new editions, versions, and adaptations for children; increasingly these books include large numbers of illustrations.

Wishing to find out something about what illustrators do with (and to) this special art form, we single out for observation one tale, *Cinderella*.

VARIANTS OF *CINDERELLA*

Cinderella is an ancient story; over the centuries it has appeared in hundreds of variants in many countries and languages. Most versions known today are derived from the story as told either by Charles Perrault, at the end of the seventeenth century, or by the Brothers Grimm in the nineteenth century. Bettelheim, in his book, gives thorough attention to the story; his detailed analysis brings out rich patterns of meaning. He also stresses the psychological significance of the differences between Perrault and Grimm.[2]

While most modern versions of *Cinderella* are also derived from these versions, only relatively few of them include the classic text without any changes: more often it is rewritten, expanded, condensed; elements of the two versions are mixed for one purpose or the other; some cruel aspects will be toned down or expurgated; plot and language are simplified and certain scenes or motifs elaborated in accordance with the predilections and convictions of the adaptor: the sibling problem, the mother-daughter conflict or the passage from childhood to womanhood; Grimm's fairyland atmosphere or the subtle irony that colors Perrault's tale. On the other hand some motifs might be left out.

Yet there are certain motifs which will appear in any version or adaptation because they are essential to the fabric of the text. In order to learn what happens when illustrators approach a fairy tale and to compare their work and their attitudes, we have to choose from among such motifs.

The two motifs we selected are *Cinderella's degradation and humiliation* and *her sudden flight from the palace in the middle of the ball*. The contrast between the two motifs is great. The one refers to a prolonged state to which the herione has to adjust, the other one to a brief and decisive turning point in the plot. How do contemporary illustrators take up the challenge offered by these two scenes? What techniques do they employ in their representations and to what purpose?

In order to know more about this we searched for pictures of these two scenes in a large number of illustrated children's books falling into several categories: anthologies of classic stories for children; anthologies of fairy tales edited for children; collections of Grimm and Perrault; picture books on *Cinderella*. Over 200 books were examined. Not all the collections and anthologies included *Cinderella*. In some of those that did, the story or the particular scenes we were looking for were not illustrated. The final sample

2. *Ibid.*, pp. 236–77.

consists of 50 books published in 18 different countries after 1945.[3] Although there exist many more illustrated editions of *Cinderella*, the present sample can be considered representative.

CINDERELLA HUMILIATED

Cinderella, so the story tells us, has been rejected by her stepmother and her sisters. She has to do servants' work and has also been banished to the worst quarters of the house where she is to spend her days and nights quite alone. This is now her station in life; the situation does not, at first, offer any apparent hope for change. This is what all versions will tell us. Beyond this they tend to differ: the text speaks of hard or menial or dirty work; the mother and the sisters speak to Cinderella in varying tones of ill-will and abuse (the father rarely appears at all). But always—such is the *manifest* content of the story—the girl will have reason to be downcast and unhappy about the fate that has befallen her. Yet the *latent* meaning is at variance with the overt description of Cinderella's lowly state, as analysts of the story, both literary critics and psychologists, point out. Her humiliation is mainly external. The treatment she suffers from her siblings and her mother cannot break her spirit. While the sisters are lazy and self-centered, Cinderella is active and industrious; while they loll about she is busy with her work: the long period of relegation to lowliness and isolation is a time of preparation for the future. Max Lüthi, the well-known researcher into the world of the fairy tale, sees one of the attributes of the hero or herione in the presence of isolation. Because he or she is isolated he will later on be able to relate to the profane and the fantastic forces that may come his way.[4] For the heroine, development into a mature woman begins with being alone with herself: the Cinderella task is, in the opinion of Franz, to penetrate into the depths of her own secret affects and to bring consciousness and selective discrimination into that hidden nature of hers.[5] When she has, through her industriousness, realized the value of her own worth as an individual, she will be ready to liberate herself and ascend into the world of love and light and success. The humiliation is then, as was said, only external; behind the surface humility of Cinderella lies the conviction of her superiority to mother and sisters.[6] She accepts her role and goes about her work in a mood of expectancy, waiting until the time comes to break out of it and to attain maturity, recognition, and happiness. This is the deeper meaning of the story, and in it lies the reason why it is loved and appreciated so much.

How do illustrators cope with both the manifest and latent meanings of this motif—Cinderella humiliated? While they follow the outline of the text

---

3. See *"Cinderellas* Cited" at the end of this chapter for the list of books.
4. Max Lüthi, "Allverbundenheit," in K. Ranke, ed., *Enzyklopädie der Märchens*, vol. 1, p. 330 (Berlin: De Gruyter, 1975).
5. Marie Louise von Franz, *The Feminine in Fairy Tales* (New York: Spring, 1972), p. 153.
6. Bettelheim, *Uses*, p. 241.

before them they do not, in general, pay too much attention to the exact wording. Where the text tells about hard and dirty work the illustrator is apt to either paint a spotlessly clean kitchen where Cinderella does some sewing or else a gloomy cellar whose stairs she wipes. Another example: the text usually characterizes, very briefly, the sisters' attitude toward Cinderella; but the sneer or glare or contempt in their eyes as expressed in the picture might differ in mood from the text. In other words, when one examines a larger number of books one finds that the correlation between text and picture in respect to nuances and details is a rather slight one. Illustrators make their own choices creating the images that will, to their minds, fit the mood of the story, and not necessarily the exact wording of the text.

What impressions does one gather on meeting fifty visual reflections of Cinderella in her debased state? The first one is that the tale has been illustrated too often in a routine way. In the depiction of both her degradation and her isolation, pictures of similar structure recur: isolation is represented by an exaggerated physical distance between the sisters (with or without the mother) forming a group, and the lonely girl. Degradation is characterized mainly by four means: Cinderella works, broods, and sleeps on a *lower* level in the house; she does different kinds of housework from needlework to preparing a meal to cleaning the floor or the stairs leading downward; she is dressed in simple or poor clothes while her sisters are decked out in finery; the sisters look at her with scorn or derision or just plain satisfaction. In addition, with a few exceptions the story takes place in a historic period, somewhere in the eighteenth or nineteenth century; this period is presented with more or less authenticity. But whatever the period and the degree of debasement and neglect, Cinderella and everything near her is, in most illustrations, colorful and clean. Often this comes out too artificial: her blouse and skirt and apron are tidy and made of good material, except for a very neat token patch sewn on the skirt. Even when she kneels on the floor wiping it with bent back, her clothes do not get dirty and her hair is not disheveled; it is well-cut, well-combed, smooth, and shiny. What is worse is that the same smoothness is too often characteristic of Cinderella's face: while the sisters' laziness and nastiness are brought out strongly, her expression is stereotyped: her face is bland, her standard postures signalize "working hard" or "suffering" or "being beautiful." There is something cold and synthetic, almost phony, about this scene as it is presented in many of the fifty books we scrutinized; in only sixteen books does Cinderella express something of the liveliness of a young girl's spirit, not just a sweet doll going through her motions; in only eighteen editions are her gait and motions really indicative of industry and suffering and not merely disinspired clichés.

With this backdrop of recurring impeccable floor scrubbers and caricatured sisters a number of outstanding books prove that a scene that has been illustrated dozens of times and in fact easily attracts the artist to the sort of schematic solutions we have just described, can be represented ever again in new ways, in pictures that generate human interest and call for the viewer's compassion.

Cinderella and Her Sisters

Representing the relationship between them means many things to many artists. The illustration in book no. 6 on our list of fifty books is an example of the stereotype: a sweet girl; two sisters in fancy dress enjoying the view of her toiling away; the middle part of the picture left empty to heighten the impression of distance and difference between the two regions.

The picture in book no. 29 brings out the contrast between Cinderella and her family, mainly by means of composition (fig. 50). The conspicuous floor, folded up as in a child's drawing, emphasizes that the sisters are "looking down" on Cinderella. The persons differ from each other not mainly by dress. Their hands and arms are quite expressive, of Cinderella's anguish,

Fig. 50. Ádám Würtz, "Cinderella and Her Family"

From *Sneewittchen und andere Märchen der Brüder Grimm*, illustrated by Ádám Würtz, Spectrum, Stuttgart, 1970. Reprinted with permission.

her mother's severity, and her sisters' lazy satisfaction. But the faces are drawn with a caricaturist's pen and create a subtly ironic contrasting mood which makes it difficult to take the weeping servant girl seriously.

Book no. 33 represents a completely different conception. These are three modern girls of more or less the same age. They are characterized effectively by gait and facial expression. The sisters' haughtiness and their hate for their sister are quite believable. Everything in this realistic and balanced picture induces us to understand Cinderella's sibling problems.

Book no. 37, on the other hand, creates an outspoken fairy tale mood. The distance between the persons is there but not as a result of empty space; when our eyes move from Cinderella to the frolicking sisters, we pass over the attributes of her servitude—broom, pail, rags, pots. This is not a meek Cinderella. She looks at the silly sisters contemptuously. Her bony face is hungry not for bread but for recognition and change. Sitting there her body stretches, pushed up by her right arm. Look at her restless hands. This is a study in a grown girl's impatience with things as they are and her fervent belief that something will happen soon (fig. 51).

Fig. 51. Livia Rusz, ''Wrathful Cinderella''

From *Cenuşăreasa* by Fraţii Grimm, illustrated by Livia Rusz, Editura Ion Creangă, Bucureşti, 1976.

Industrious Cinderella

It is apparently not easy to depict her diligence in a significant way. Book no. 50 is an extreme example of the small chubby floor cleaner, superficial and silly.

Book no. 42 shows a poor and downcast Cinderella bravely going about her chores. The picture is drawn well in soft lines which bring out the gentleness in the simple girl (fig. 52).

No. 31, by contrast, comes out of fairy land (fig. 53). A noble Cinderella, her flaxen hair almost reaching down to the floor, concentrates upon her needlework. A sense of isolation is in the air. But that is not all. The calm in the center of the picture is only apparent. At its borders things begin to happen. At right stands the broom, the sign of Cinderella's degradation; opposite, at left, is the pumpkin, the vehicle of her future elevation. The diagonal lines which appear in her figure—her hair and her arm in one direction, her skirt, apron, and embroidery in the other—draw our eyes up to where magic images intrude: the mother and sisters on the left and the fairy godmother on the right. These visual lines leading from the evil family to the broom and from the good fairy to the pumpkin cross each other in Cinderella's figure. The illustrator achieves a remarkably beautiful and persuasive effect of tension by contrast: while the many static ornate elements (plates, pots, clock, spools) echo Cinderella's quiet concentration, the forces gathering about her create a quivering mood of things to come.

Cinderella's Expectancy

The illustration which we just discussed, successfully combines the representation of industry with that of expectancy. Few illustrators attempt to contend with this core element in Cinderella's personality. Many others and especially those who see her as a teenager interpret the expectancy as a meditative mood. In many books (see book no. 2) she momentarily stops working and gets lost in the strange thoughts that overcome her.

Book no. 4 shows one of the few truly destitute Cinderellas (fig. 54), bending slightly forward and gazing at the birds which flock in, while all around her odd fantastic faces crop out of the beams, the shelves, the cupboard: will the magic forces soon guide her on?

In book no. 14 a very young woman (whose well-groomed hair is at odds with the torn sleeves) wished to pierce the future with her eyes. The shape of an arrow recurs several times in the composition of her figure: right and left arm; arms and body; the two halves of her hair; her skirt's outline. The form of the arrow symbolically expresses her strong assertiveness and her readiness to soar up and away from her present state.

CINDERELLA'S FLIGHT FROM THE BALL

Cinderella's flight from the ball is an act of decision. The versions differ from each other about how often she is invited, once or twice or three times as the

Fig. 52. Svend Otto S., "Downcast Cinderella"
From *Askepot* by Grimm, illustrated by Svend Otto S. © Svend Otto S. 1978. Gyldendal, København, 1978.

Fig. 53. Errol Le Cain, "The intrusion of things to come"
Copyright © 1972 from the book *Cinderella or the Glass Slipper* by Perrault, illustrated by Errol Le Cain. Reprinted by permission of Faber and Faber Ltd. and of Bradbury Press, Inc., Scarsdale, NY 10583.

Fig. 54. Anton Pieck, "Destitute Cinderella"
From De Sprookjes van Grimm, illustrated by Anton Pieck, De Haan, Antwerp, 1959. By permission of Uniboek, Haarlem.

classic tale has it, and about whether she remembers to leave at midnight or has to be reminded by the fairy godmother. But it is always her own action springing from her urgent need not to spoil things, not to check the development that has begun. Consciously she leaves the palace because she wishes to preserve her newly won secret and adventurous freedom. Unconsciously "her running away from the ball is motivated by the wish to protect herself against being violated, or carried away by her own desires."[7]

The illustrator has to express the urgency of the moment. Other elements of the scene may be interpreted variously. Is this a girl proud of acting in a responsible manner or is she running away scared, furtively, afraid of being detected? Are we still in the palace? How does the prince figure in this? Is it the splendor of the palace or rather the dark night into which she runs that is emphasized? Does she still wear her dazzling party gown or is she already

7. *Ibid.*, p. 265.

dressed in her usual clothes? The illustrator has the double task of representing the urgency of the moment and of making clear what its connotations are, as he sees them: what does Cinderella's swift act mean to her and to the story? These elements have to be intertwined so as to be both credible and enjoyable.

Here again our sample includes a large number of pictures reflecting a very simple structure repeated again and again, and routine treatment of the aesthetic and the psychological aspects. A broad staircase leads down from the glittering ballroom. An excited and vacuously beautiful girl sweeps by in her delightful dress that is often more distinguished than the expression of its wearer. Somewhere in the background a nondescript prince appears; between them a more or less conspicuous slipper lies on the stairs. This typical solution, found in many variants, comes quite naturally. Are not all of us, storyteller, artist, and reader, easily fascinated by the magnificence of the king's mansions and the sparkle of the ballroom? Do we not rejoice in seeing the heroine still flustered with excitement, still wearing her shining gown as she runs out into the cool of the night? Do not most palaces have staircases which lead *down*? Is not showing Cinderella running *down* also a symbolic expression of the low state to which she temporarily returns? In two thirds of the books sampled the downward movement is very accentuated. In more than half of the illustrations she runs toward us, in a straight line or a sort of half-circle, passing by closely, involving us in her urgent desire to get away safely. In others she passes us sideways; we are just spectators. Still others, depicting her already outside the palace, show her moving away from us, into the unknown future.

Another element common to most illustrations is the accent on Cinderella's loneliness. In this important moment in her life she is isolated again (though in a manner that differs from her isolation at the beginning); nobody is to know what she is doing just now, nor why. This aspect of her flight is respected by most illustrators and brought out well by many. If so, then the prince really plays a secondary role; after all she runs away from him to avoid recognition and the danger of premature attachment. In sixteen editions the prince is not shown during the moment of flight; in most of the others he is depicted rather crudely; in eight books there is an expression of concern in his appearance. Usually he is at a distance from Cinderella; only in a few books does he almost catch up with her; only in one illustration does she look back at him.

Opinions are divided as to Cinderella's mood. In about two-thirds of the pictures she is frightened or worried; in one-third she is upright and somehow reflective. This is in part connected with the age that the illustrator attributes to our heroine: in four books she is a small child (for whom the story cannot really make sense); in twenty-five editions she is a girl somewhere between 7–12 years of age; in twenty-one, she is clearly shown to be in her teens. The illustrators who represent her as adolescent also tend to emphasize the more mature reflective mood.

Because this seems to be such a clear-cut scene it is probably difficult for the artist to be inventive about it, or it may not stir him to exert himself. The routine solution for representing the manifest content (sudden clandestine departure) by means of a rather self-evident structure (down and out), if it is executed well, may be quite charming and aesthetically satisfying, even if the illustrator avoids touching upon the more serious aspect of the moment and sticks to characterizing the external situation. We shall have a look at a few examples of this. But we will also show that illustrators dissatisfied with merely rearranging the same well-known components may, through their creative effort, contribute a new view of the scene and some fresh psychological insight into its meaning.

The picture in book no. 22 is typical of many inept renderings to be found. Bad draughtsmanship results in a tableau. Only the girl's right hand, raised to keep her balance or ward off the prince, has the slightest expressive quality.

No. 24 takes us further out into the night. Cinderella is already far from the palace, but only now does she lose the slipper; indecision seems to grip her as she stops for a moment. The dramatic moment does not come naturally.

Here are three examples to prove how the inventive illustrator may enhance the visual beauty and the meaning of the scene by illuminating it from a new angle.

No. 2 demonstrates how a different treatment can be applied to the all-too-familiar staircase structure (fig. 55). On the right the girl runs away and we are about to lose sight of her; our attention is drawn to the prince who gazes intently at the slipper he has just picked up. From now on the initiative lies with him; because of his persistence, the story will come to its happy end. (The allusion to their growing love, in the form of the statue of Cupid in the center, will be understood only by the adult reader.)

Fig. 55. Marcia Brown, ''The prince''
Illustration from *Cinderella* by Marcia Brown. Copyright 1954 by Marcia Brown. Reprinted by permission of Charles Scribner's Sons.

No. 30 depicts a Cinderella in rags, utterly alone in a gloomy night. As she trudges along she takes off her other slipper and carries it—she runs more easily this way; the servant girl is used to walking barefoot. Yet the rays emanating from the lantern enwrap her in an aura of warm yellow light, promising that all is not lost. The glow also enables us to see what a soft and lovable girl she really is.

The picture in no. 31 takes us back to the mood of enchantment. Cinderella hurries by. The magic spell is broken before our eyes as the princess turns into the housemaid under the watchful eye of the good fairy. In the brilliant sky the stars have become fantastic clocks all showing midnight—symbols of the conscience speeding her on.

THE HERO OR HEROINE AS EVERYMAN

The fifty books we discussed constitute only a part of many treating the Cinderella theme which have been published in the last decades. However, they are a fair sample representing different countries, styles, and conceptions. What conclusions can we draw from our examination?

In his book, Bettelheim states his opinion that the illustrated story book does not serve the child's best needs, that it robs the content of personal meaning which it would bring to the child who applied only his own visual associations instead of those of the illustrator.[8] One's first reaction is to protest against this severe statement; but the issue is not as simple as that. After going through dozens of pictures accompanying one fairy tale one cannot help wondering what effect the illustrations are apt to have on children.

The fairy tale is a literary genre whose importance derives to a great extent from the relative simplicity of its form and the generality of plot. The hero or heroine goes through dreadful and glorious experiences whose irrationality is significant on the unconscious level; these experiences represent or symbolize human situations and conflicts and developmental processes which apply to any child growing up. What happens to the hero or heroine concerns everyone of us. He or she is a kind of Everyman.

Now it is exactly this character of the fairy tale which is often misunderstood by the illustrator (and, by the way, by the adaptor of the text). Everyman is misinterpreted as an ordinary boy or girl, just like you and me. This is one reason why we get so many run-of-the-mill pictures, superficial glamour girls and clichéd compositions. Yet what the hero in the fairy tale is really intended to characterize lies not only in the processes and conflicts which are relevant to all children; *he also represents some aspects of that spiritual perfection all of us should strive to attain.* There is something distinguished and

8. *Ibid.,* pp. 59–60.

noble about the hero and his fate that is exemplary of the more humane side of human nature.

The artist who illustrates a fairy tale should have a measure of understanding of its underlying significance, either by way of conscious knowledge or intuitive grasp. He will then, if his talent permits, reveal elements of this significance to the child. If he is caught up in glamorizing the mediocre his pictures will not serve the child's best needs. To be sure, the impact of an illustration does not simply arise from its fidelity or proximity to the text. However, our sample suggests that a correlation exists between aesthetic creativeness and quality and the empathy the illustrator has for the deeper layers of the story.

The problem lies in the fact that hackneyed illustrations proliferate and flood the market. Not only the illustrator, but also the editor and the public are overwhelmed by this concentration on externals. Everyone falls for the sweet doll who moves in historic rags and party gowns through antique interiors and pseudo-historic palaces. Neither from an aesthetic nor psychological point of view is there any sense in the banal renderings of fairy tales accompanied by trite pictures.

If we realize that today, even more than in past times, the child needs the reassurance offered by the image of isolated man, capable nevertheless of achieving meaningful and rewarding relations with the world around him,[9] we will understand how powerful the superior illustration can be, how much joy the illustrator has to offer, and how he may call up profound humanistic values by his work.

*CINDERELLA*S CITED

The fifty editions of the story *Cinderella* sampled are listed in chronological order of publication. The last eight items bear no date, but are certain to have been published after 1945.

1. *Les Contes de Perrault*. Illus. by diverse artists. Paris: Laurens, 1948.
2. PERRAULT, CHARLES. *Cinderella, or The Glass Slipper*. Trans. and illus. by Marcia Brown. New York: Scribner's, 1954.
3. TETZNER, LISA. *Märchen*. Illus. by Regina Ackermann-Ophüls. Frankfurt a/M: Fischer, 1958.
4. *De Sprookjes van Grimm*. Illus. by Anton Pieck. Antwerpen: De Haan-Zeist, 1959.
5. *Perrault Masallari: Kül Kedisi*. Trans. by Tahsin Yücel. Illus. by Güngör Kabakciolo. Istanbul: Varlik Yayinevi, Ankara Caddesi, 1959.
6. PERRAULT, CHARLES. *Contes*. Illus. by Lucie Lagarde. Paris: Gedalge, 1960.
7. *Contes de Perrault*. Illus. by H. Romanini. Paris: Delagrave, 1961.
8. PERRAULT, CHARLES. *Cendrillon ou la Pantoufle de Vair*. Illus. by Claude Estang. Lausanne: Editions du Verdonnet, 1961.
9. *Contes de Perrault*. Illus. by Eliane Haroux-Métayer. Paris: Flammarion, 1962.
10. PERRAULT, CHARLES. *Contes de Fées—Die Märchen* (French and German). Illus. by Willy Widman. Ebenhausen bei München: Langewiesche-Brandt, 1962.
11. BRÜDER GRIMM. *Kinder- und Hausmärchen*. Illus. by Janusz Grabiański. Wien: Ueberreuter, 1962.
12. *Aschenputtel: Ein Märchen der Brüder Grimm*. Illus. by Erika Klein. Berlin: Kinderbuchverlag, 1963.
13. *Die Kinder- und Hausmärchen der Brüder Grimm*. Illus. by Werner Klemke. Berlin: Kinderbuchverlag, 1962.

9. *Ibid.*, p. 11.

14. APARICIO, TERESA. *Cenicienta: Cuento de Perrault.* Illus. by Pablo Ramirez. Barcelona: Ed. Cervantes, 1963.
15. BARRON, NOEL, and SCANTIER, LIONEL. *Gibborey Hasepharim Hanifla'im.* Trans. by Benjamin Tamous. Illus. by Jean Steen and Lisa Marin. Tel Aviv: Misrahi, 1965.
16. *Die schönsten Märchen der Brüder Grimm.* Illus. by Horst Lemke. Düsseldorf: Hochverlag, 1965.
17. *Likhlukhit.* Trans. by Uriel Ofek. Illus. by Borellini. Tel Aviv: Misrahi, 1966.
18. PERRAULT, CHARLES. *Populuška.* Trans. by Hana Ferhova. Illus. by Ivica Kroslakova. Bratislava: Mláde letá, 1966.
19. ARIEL, S. *Be'eretz Hahalomot.* Ramat Gan: Massadah, 1967.
20. G.E. G. GRIMM. *Le fiabe piu belle.* Illus. by Ivan Gongalow. Milano: editrice a-m-z, 1967.
21. PERRAULT, CHARLES. *Contes.* Illus. by Janusz Grabiański. Paris: Flammarion, 1967; Wien: Ueberreuter.
22. FRAȚII GRIMM. *Povești.* Trans. by Dan Faur. Illus. by Done Stan. București: Ed. Tineretului, 1968.
23. *Cinderella.* Illus. by Dick Bruna. London: Methuen, 1968.
24. PERRAULT, CHARLES. *A Gata Borralheira.* Trans. by Marie Teresa Mega. Illus. by Jean-Léon Huens. Lisboa: Edd. Verbo, 1969.
25. PERRAULT, CHARLES. *Cinderella or The Little Glass Slipper.* Illus. by Shirley Hughes. London: Bodley Head, 1970.
26. BRÜDER GRIMM. *Kinder- und Hausmärchen.* Illus. by Otto Ubbelohde. Marburg: Ewert Verlag, M. Sändig, 1970.
27. PERRAULT, CHARLES. *Aschenbrödel (Kopiuszek).* Retold by Hanna Januszewska. Illus. by Božena Truchanowska. Warszawa: Nasza Ksiegarnia, 1970.
28. *Al bas likli çocuk ve Kül Kedisi.* Trans. by Gani Yener. Istanbul: Inkilap ve Aka, 1970.
29. GEHRTS, BARBARA, ed. *Sneewittchen und andere Märchen der Brüder Grimm.* Illus. by Ádám Würtz. Stuttgart: Spectrum, 1970.
30. PERRAULT, CHARLES. *Bajki.* Retold by Hanna Januszewska. Illus. by Janusz Grabiański. Warszawa: Nasza Ksiegarnia, 1971.
31. PERRAULT, CHARLES. *Cinderella or The Little Glass Slipper.* Illus. by Errol le Cain. London: Faber, 1972.
32. PERRAULT, CHARLES. *Sprookjes van Moeder de Gans.* Retold by Christine Doorman. Illus. by Rie Cramer. Den Haag: Van gor zonen, 1972.
33. *Märchen der Brüder Grimm.* Illus. by Bernhard Nast. Berlin: Kinderbuchverlag, 1973.
34. DISNEY, WALT. *Cinderella.* Trans. by Sh. Lapid. Pictures and illustrations by Walt Disney Studio from the motion picture. Tel Aviv: Yavneh, 1974.
35. *La Cenicienta.* Bilbao: Ed. Vasca Americana, 1974.
36. *Grimm Märchen.* Illus. by Marlene Reidel. München: Betz, 1975.
37. FRAȚII GRIMM. *Cenușăreasa.* Illus. by Livia Rusz. București: Ion Creangă, 1976.
38. ŠH. PERRO. *Skazki matushki gusuyni.* Illus. by G. A. V. Traugot. Leningrad: Hudožestvennaya literatura, 1976.
39. PERRAULT, CHARLES. *Contes II.* Illus. by Alice Huertas. Paris: Bias, 1977.
40. *Aschenputtel: Ein Märchen der Brüder Grimm.* Illus. by Bernadette Watts. Mönchaltorf: Nord-Süd Verlag, 1977.
41. *Biblia Dora Gia Mikra Khaidia.* Illus. by St. Bazileioy. Athens: Angyra, 1977.
42. GRIMM. *Askepot.* Illus. by Svend Otto S. Kóbenhavn: Gyldendal, 1978.
43. *Likhlukhit.* Retold by J. Nun. Illus. by Isa. Tel Aviv: Amihai, n.d.
44. *Likhlukhit.* Trans. by A. Kadimah. Illus. by Roberto Sgrilli. Tel Aviv: Massadah, n.d.
45. *Cinderella Ve'ahayoteiha.* Illus. by R. Bresillon. Tel Aviv: Arieh, n.d.
46. *Cinderella.* Illus. by Rose Art Studio, Tokyo. Tel Aviv: Yavneh, n.d.
47. *Likhlukhit.* Trans. by Lea Goldberg. Dolls by Amalia Serkin. Tel Aviv: Sifriat Poalim, n.d.
48. BRÜDER GRIMM. *Schönste Märchen.* Illus. by Hans und Marie Mannhart. Reutlingen: Ensslin & Leiblin, n.d.
49. PERRAULT, CHARLES. *Contes de ma mère l'Oye.* Paris: SFIL, n.d.
50. *La Cenicienta.* Illus. by C. Busquets. Editorial Roma & Barcelona, n.d.

11

Between Dream and
Social Utopia

Janusz Korczak (1878–1942) was a Polish-Jewish educator. Originally trained as a pediatrician, he decided to dedicate his life to the welfare of children. For many years he headed an orphanage for Jewish children in Warsaw. When in 1942 the orphans were transported by the S.S. from the Warsaw ghetto to the extermination camp, Korczak, though offered freedom, chose to accompany the children to their death.

Korczak was a progressive educator who fought all his life for the child's right to be loved, to be recognized as a complex human being and allowed to grow up according to his individual needs and abilities. He was a prolific writer who recorded his beliefs and ideas on education in his diaries, articles he wrote for parents and teachers, and in other works written for the children themselves. He also wrote a large number of stories of varying length for children.

He was well-known in Poland in his own time. In the fifties and sixties, a Korczak renaissance set in that brought international recognition to him as a person, his writings, and his beliefs.

Among Korczak's fictional writings for children the story *King Mathew I*, first published in 1923, has stood up rather well to time. It is probably Korczak's best children's book.

It is the story of Mathew who, while still a young boy, ascends the throne when his father the king dies. At the beginning of his reign Mathew, who plays at being king, is met with derision by his ministers and servants. Yet as time goes by, the boy learns to understand and accept his responsibilities. When war breaks out he joins his army anonymously and fights with his soldiers as one of them. The senseless suffering and cruelty of war appall him, but victory is achieved because of his heroic feats. He affirms his belief in peace and the unity of mankind by showing leniency to his enemies, the foreign kings. When he returns to the capital he embarks upon comprehensive reforms that change the face of society and create more justice and equality for the people, especially for the children. Time and again Mathew finds out how naive and inexperienced he is, and how stupid, wily, and unreliable the people are for whom he labors, children and adults alike. But he does not give up; he learns quickly and studiously. Finally he overcomes opposition and ill will, and the new society rises, built on his ideas. In his kingdom and far beyond its frontiers Mathew is hailed as the great young reformer. Next he improves his country's economy by setting out on a daring and hazardous journey to Africa where he succeeds in engaging the assistance of the rich black tribal king for his plans. Then Klu-Klu, the king's clever and gracious daughter becomes his friend. When Mathew invites them to his country he has an opportunity to demonstrate his belief in the equality of races.

But then Mathew, urged on by one of his counselors—who really is a spy disguised as journalist, and who has been planted by enemies to misguide the young king—grants an inordinate measure of power and authority to the children of his realm. The adults are sent to school and are treated as inferiors. The economic and social fabric dissolves. The foreign kings attack again and defeat the weakened kingdom. Mathew is abandoned by his people and condemned to death. At the last moment the sentence is converted to banishment. Mathew, discredited and disenchanted, is sent to a barren island.[1]

The strength of the story lies in the characterization of the boy-king and in the plot, with its swift succession of adventures. Except for a few episodes which now have an antiquated ring, the book still impresses the reader by the naturalness and logic with which things happen. Korczak also succeeded rather well in weaving in his views on society and education without bearing down too much on the narrative. The book is full of the daring enterprises and unexpected incidents that children love so much, yet this does not prevent the author from relating how the boy, who at first understands his kingship in terms of a game, grows up to face his responsibilities: in an early scene Mathew stamps his foot, insisting that his government buy the biggest doll in the world for a girl he has met in the public gardens. Yet in a later scene, when his best boy friend asks for a merry-go-round, he replies:

Just look, you are not a king, you don't understand that. Well, I'm not against the merry-go-round, but I don't want only one. At the next meeting, I'll tell them to put swings and merry-go-rounds with music in all schools.[2]

—and toward the end, when he burns the letter he received from the Sad King and hurts his hand, he muses:

my soul suffers more than my fingers.

The boy develops an ardent desire to act, initiate action and change, and also to reflect on his own actions and those of others—children, soldiers, ministers, kings. He is willing to appreciate his opponents' point of view, but he is not deceived by superficial argument. Even when his frustration becomes obvious, his belief in humanity is not entirely lost. At the same time he is and

1. A sequel to the story relates Mathew's adventures there, ending with his death.
2. My translation.

remains a real boy, not yet in his teens, and that is why some of the tricks applied by adults, journalists, counselors, and kings are beyond his grasp and trip him.

A certain tenseness prevails in the story: there is the tension between the lively and at times prankish playfulness of the typical boy, and the demanding decisions Mathew has to face;[3] between his dynamic optimism, which in Korczak's eyes epitomizes the inherent qualities of childhood, and the inertia, hypocrisy, and egotism rampant in the society he strives to change; between the haunting loneliness of the young hero (at the best of times he has one or two friends in whom he can confide and scarcely anyone who understands what goes on in his mind), and his fierce commitment to moral and social decency.

A different kind of tension exists on the formal plane. While the story is told in a very realistic and matter-of-fact vein, it is in fact a fantastic utopia. The author persuades the reader to accept as quite logical events of high improbability and to consent to Mathew's visionary mood—though he writes in an utterly rationalistic style. The fact that he succeeds in this is a proof of his craftsmanship. Yet the strain is there.

These stresses come to a head with Mathew's downfall. When the story ends in an anticlimax, a dilemma, even a conflict, arises in the child's mind; an ending like this negates the habitual sense of success to which the child's mind is geared by his psychological needs and by uncounted stories and tales and myths. But in this ending lie two important messages: the best intentions are not sufficient; one needs experience and wariness and patience. A hero's spirit may be unbroken though his mission has failed. These messages reflect Korczak's ideas on education: let us strengthen children's belief in themselves, but at the same time prepare them for life in an unreliable adult society where you have to fight for your ideas.

These antagonisms in content and structure reverberate throughout the story. Yet it is precisely through them that the story is saved from succumbing to stereotyped patterns; they aid in turning the book into an expression of humanistic ideas. Thus Hentig, the well-known educator, was able to say more than fifty years after the book first appeared, that it was a story full of adventures, instructive accounts, and parallels to our own time, and very much a children's book.[4]

In the period after 1945 *King Mathew I* became a popular book; it was published and translated into several languages. Illustrators were called upon to create sets of pictures for the different editions.

What are we to expect of the artist who illustrates this book? He should perceive the dynamics of the story and be able to feel and communicate empathy for its hero; his pictures should illuminate facets of the story in a

---

3. This has been well emphasized by Adir Cohen, "King Matya I," *Janusz Korczak the Educator* (Tel Aviv: Czerikover, 1973), pp. 160–65.

4. Hardtmut von Hentig, quoted on the back cover of Janusz Korczak, *König Hänschen I*, trans. by Katja Weintraub (München: Deutscher Taschenbuchverlag, 1974).

way that will assist the child reader to get nearer to its social significance. More specifically, the illustrator might focus on the energetic and yet lonely figure of the child king; on the widening geographic and social horizons that open up before Mathew, and on a few of the key scenes, both intimate and public, that give a new turn to events. Beyond that, one would expect the illustrator to express some of the stresses and tensions that characterize the book and to communicate to the reader the spirit of skeptical humanism that pervades it.

We were able to examine the published work of five artists. They are, in chronological order, Irene Lorentowicz in the English adaptation; S. Cohen in the first Israeli edition; Jerzy Srokowski in the Polish edition (whose illustrations also appear in translations, such as the German editions, the Russian edition and the second Israeli edition); Veronica Leo in the Swedish edition; Waldemar Andrzejewski in a new Polish edition. In addition, the sample includes two as yet unpublished sets of illustrations by Brakha Alhassid and Esther Katz.[5]

The seven artists represented here demonstrate widely different techniques, styles, and views. Besides, the editions vary as to the number of illustrations they include. The English edition has dozens of pictures and vignettes, the Swedish one over thirty; the others much fewer. In order to convey an impression of the illustrators' individual approaches to the story, six illustrations from every set were selected for examination, either because they are good examples of the artist's style and intentions or because they illustrate important events or phases in the story, and often for both these reasons.

LORENTOWICZ AND COHEN

Lorentowicz's volume is profusely illustrated with simple drawings that remind one of children acting on a stage, quite young children incidentally, who are able to feign following the course of the story, without actually comprehending its meaning. There is something artificial about the pictures, as if the illustrator were winking at the reader, suggesting that the whole affair should not really be taken seriously. Mathew is a small expressionless boy. The mood is artless and glib. Cohen scatters a number of black and white drawings here and there, most of which look as if they were unfinished. But on the whole the illustrator prefers to draw stereotyped figures and masses of people. Neither of these illustrators creates an impact.

SROKOWSKI

This excellent illustrator painted a colorful series of pictures with rich yellow and golden tones predominating. These pictures interpret the story in a very

---

5. Brakhah Alhassid and Ester Katz, Two Sets of Illustrations for *King Mathew I*, created for and exhibited at the Korczak Centennial Symposium, Haifa University, April 1978.

special and personal way. Mathew spins his own fairy tale. The young king is a sensitive child caught in a daydream. His look turns inward to contemplate this bittersweet dream. There is a sadness in his beautiful almond eyes that will not easily be forgotten. Everything in the story, so the illustrations seem to tell, happens in the fanciful realms of Mathew's imagination, and not in a fictional reality. It is an illusion, odd and playful at first and increasingly tragic; but there is no real drama: in the first illustration in the book, the hour of his father's death, Mathew's face bears a nostalgic expression that is similar to the one in the last when he is led away to prison. Is there no difference between losing a father and losing a kingdom?

The other side of this essentially romantic conception is found in the sarcasm with which the ministers and the foreign ambassadors are drawn.

Mathew's loneliness and his distance from reality is made conspicuous by the pointed use of perspective (for instance, when he is acclaimed by the people and in the zoo). Only when he meets Klu-Klu is he shown slightly more "here and now."

If Mathew is seen as being spellbound by the images that rise within him, then it is not surprising that he is rather tranquil and inactive, a sensitive boy, alert to his reverie, whom the illustrator portrays with intimate intensity. This view also determines how other themes in the book are treated: in these illustrations silence reigns; only faint echoes of the turbulent outer world come through. Mathew's flight to Africa is the only picture that shows him in action. No picture refers to the war.

LEO

Here, too, as in Srokowski's illustrations, we come face to face with Mathew's sad eyes first when his father dies and then again near the end when all is lost. But the troubled child who sat on the knees of the wise old doctor who guided his first steps (fig. 56), has grown into an upright boy (fig. 57): Mathew changes as the story unfolds. Between these two pictures there are others that represent, again and again, the boy-king who has a dream, but also the world in which he acts. The artist is very much conscious of this double task and uses the elements of her style with versatility. Rich textures, reminiscent of art nouveau, mark the palace and the jungle where the king finds Klu-Klu. But the picture of Mathew the soldier, exposed to the atrocity and terror of war, has fewer, strongly contrasting shapes. The children's parliament in session is drawn realistically.

This illustrator sees Mathew as a lone dreamer who fights for a better future, but the fight draws its meaningfulness from the social background: it happens out there. That is why people in these pictures are shown as real human beings. When they first meet the new king the ministers are haughty courtiers, not caricatures.

By various combinations of realistic and romantic style elements the artist creates a range of moods. They are expressive of the warm human interest she takes in the story and which she wishes to arouse in the reader.

Fig. 56. Veronica Leo, ''Mathew's father dies''
From *Lille Kung Mattias* by Janusz Korczak, illustrated by Veronica Leo, Raben & Sjögren Bokförlag, Stockholm, 1974.

Fig. 57. Veronica Leo, ''A kingdom lost''
From *Lille Kung Mattias* by Janusz Korczak, illustrated by Veronica Leo, Raben & Sjögren Bokförlag, Stockholm, 1974.

ANDRZEJEWSKI

The first illustration is a powerful introduction to the story. A child, unsure of himself, steps into a hostile world of giants. The arrogantly indifferent attendants and the palace buildings merge into one frightening construct (does the main tower have an apprehensive stare?). A fairy-tale mood of great immediacy is intimated. But the pictures that follow do not develop the mood. They vary too much in style and in composition, and no sense of continuity is created. The way Mathew is represented makes it hard for us to feel close to him—somehow we are kept at a distance.

The illustrations also deviate from the text. Any illustrator will do that; straightforward documentation is the last thing called for in illustrations of fiction. But in the present series emphasis is too often put on subjects or arbitrary details that are not really relevant to the story; the garden scene with the child in the diving suit and a lobster in each hand, does not appear in the story, and is not particularly interesting; when Mathew, on one of his great and happy days entertains the foreign kings, he and his royal guests are scarcely visible, and we are treated to an exhibition of catch-as-catch-can; in one of the last illustrations a submissive Mathew is led away, while the last chapter expressly tells of his dignified behavior up to the last minute. These deviations create fragmentation instead of continuity.

If there is a continuous motif to be found in these illustrations, it is a mood of anxiety. With the possible exception of that of the colorful festive city, all the pictures are dominated by a kind of hidden threat. While this is justified in the first picture, Mathew's first insecure steps into kingship, and in the African scenes, it is not the pervading mood of the story. But as the artist's skill and power of expression—and his involvement in the anxiety-arousing elements of the story—are considerable, he conveys this feeling too strongly.

ALHASSID

These are simple pictures, rather typical of children's books illustrations— neat, picturesque, focused on action. Mathew is a little boy acting out his daydreams in his habitual small world, walking in the palace garden, longing to play in the snow as he was allowed to before he became king, discovering disruption in the city and playing the game of politics. Here and there caricaturistic features appear, in the portrayal of ministers and in the trip to Africa. This is a child king who, after he has overcome a moment of embarrassment, plays his role with zest, untroubled by apprehension. This is a humorous, slightly funny version with some affinity to the very first chapters of the book when, as yet, no depths are suspected beneath the shallows.

KATZ

Rich and sensitive colors characterize these illustrations. It is a real and quite serious world to which we are introduced, from the first picture where workers tidy up the palace garden for the king's pleasure. This is neither dream nor fairy tale. It is the story of a boy who works hard and fights courageously against heavy odds. This is the message imparted by the picture where Mathew learns about the war with the faint red glow beyond the twisted iron bars (fig. 58), or when he returns from the war, throws

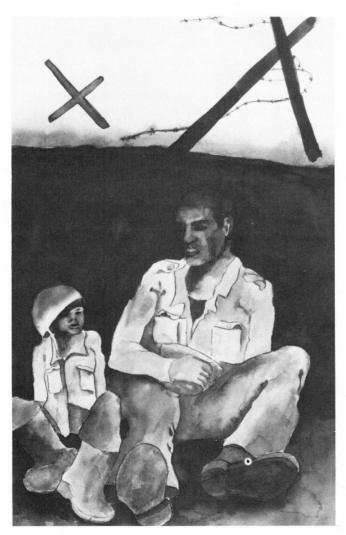

Fig. 58. Esther Katz, ''Mathew in the war''

From the exhibition, Two Sets of Illustrations to the Story, created for the Korczak Centennial Symposium, Haifa University, April 1978. By permission of Esther Katz.

down his bundles, and sits down at a late hour of night to catch up on state correspondence: his feet dangle above the floor and an abandoned teddy bear tries in vain to catch his attention. This is also the meaning implied in the last two pictures: Mathew confronting his judges with an infinitely sad but composed expression on his face; then Mathew in his last hours, meeting the apprehensive stares of his fellow children and citizens (fig. 59). These are studies of dignity in failure.

The pictures are small works of art; every one has a composition, a color scheme, an aesthetic quality of its own. They are expressive of the illustrator's earnest involvement in the book and representative of her conception of its meaning. But we have to note that this concentration on every scene somewhat interferes with continuity. The pictures are very dissimilar to each other, and not sufficient visual transfer is created (through similarity of motifs, faces, colors or compositions) to carry the viewer from one illustration to the next.

This illustrator interprets the tragic side of the story in terms of poetic realism. The readers she has in mind are somewhat older than those the

Fig. 59. Esther Katz, "A kingdom lost"
From the exhibition, Two Sets of Illustrations to the Story, created for the Korczak Centennial Symposium, Haifa University, April 1978. By permission of Esther Katz.

other illustrators aim at. The beautiful picture of an adolescent Klu-Klu looking out from amongst flowers, a completely poised girl, is proof of this.

How do the illustrations compare with the expectations we expressed above? What common features and what personal accents can we observe in the illustrators' approach to the story of *King Mathew I*?

A number of the key moods and concepts of the book are brought out by most illustrators:

Mathew's awkwardness when he first confronts the ministers is depicted with acuity.

The young king's solitariness is brought out impressively.

The grotesque features which characterize many of the adults in the illustrations visually render the sarcasm with which the author describes the establishment: the ridiculous court ceremonial, the supercilious routine under which the government and the army are run, and the stiff hypocrisy that hides behind the routine.

The frequent use of very marked perspective in many pictures is an effective visual symbol of Mathew's uphill fight in a society of adults.

But when we want to find out about the measure of empathy for the hero and attention to the dynamics of the story, the differences between the artists and their series of illustrations become marked. Andrzejewski and Alhassid view the strange boy and his games from a distance, as it were. Srokowski and Katz, on the other hand, let us come very near him; yet each of them calls attention to only partial aspects of his personality and his fortune. Srokowski shows us the sweetness of Mathew's dream, but he cuts him off from social interaction. Katz omits the lighter, boyish side of his adventures. Only Leo's pictures reflect Mathew's person as he grows in the real world he lives in; they urge the reader to follow his development. Leo also comprehends the dynamics of the story and shows in her pictures how a child's playfulness and anxiety become a fantastic dream that leads to action and failure. And still, the romantic elements in Leo's style gracefully uphold the spell of Mathew's dream. Even she, though, does not relate significantly to the social upheaval and its profounder issues.

It comes as a surprise that practically all the illustrators see their contact with the contents, dynamics, and meanings of the story on so narrow a plane. They attach themselves to a few aspects of the story, and draw or paint pictures that present their associations to these aspects. But when, as in this story, a child's mind grows, the range of his experience widens and his activities expand, the illustrator should be aware, and aid us to become aware, of these processes. He should enrich the reader's experience, not lead him astray. This mandate does not imply a restriction of the illustrator's creative inspiration; it implies an application of his consideration for the child's aesthetic impressionability and for the nature of the story.

This is a tale reminiscent of a dream, for it relates events that could happen only in the imagination of a child. Yet it is also the account of a social experiment whose protagonist is a creative boy: society is criticized, social beliefs and ideals are probed; human nature is put to a test. In his dream Mathew is very industrious, very much involved in his task, continually alternating between action and interaction with others and solitary reflection.

The story has the power both to arouse the reader to flights of fantasy and to awaken his mind to themes of social significance. The illustrators, on their part, are caught more than the author and his hero in the playful and, in the end, cruel dream and pay too little attention to the construction of a quasi-realistic utopia, and to Mathew's effort, doomed to failure, to improve society by the rational means of education, law reform, and enlightened government. That is the reason why some of their work is too facetious and some of it too despondent, and why many of the pictures and the series of pictures do not have a true ring or communicate a sense of "rightness."

Beautiful pageantry is fine for the dream. But the utopia, too, is in need of visual support for its claim to relevancy in the child's mind: so the book still waits for the illustrator who will do justice to its spirit.

CHILDREN'S WORKS CITED

These works are listed in chronological order of publication.

SULKIN, E., and SULKIN, S. *Mathew the Young King.* Illus. by Irena Lorentowicz. London: Dobson, 1946.

KORCZAK, JANUSZ. *Hamelekh Matya Harishon.* Trans. by J. Lichtenboim. Illus. by S. Cohen. Tel Aviv: Twersky, 1950.

———. *Król Macius Pierwszy.* Illus. by Jerzy Srokowski. Warszawa: Nasza Księgarnia, 1953.

———. *König Hänschen I.* Trans. by Katya Weintraub. Illus. by Jerzy Srokowski. Göttingen: Vandenhoeck & Ruprecht, 1970.

———. *König Hänschen I.* Trans. by Katya Weintraub. Illus. by Jerzy Srokowski. München: Deutscher Taschenbuchverlag, 1974.

———. *Lille Kung Mattias.* Trans. by Mira Teeman. Illus. by Veronica Leo. Uddevalla: Rabén & Sjögren, 1974.

———. *Król Macius Pierwszy.* Illus. by Waldemar Andrzejewski. Warszawa: Nasza Księgarnia, 1978.

———. *Korol Matius Pervei.* Trans. by N. Podolsk. Illus. by Jerzy Srokowski. Moskva: Detskaya Literatura, 1978.

———. *Hamelekh Matya Harishon.* Trans. by U. Orlev. Illus. by Jerzy Srokowski. Jerusalem: Keter, 1979.

12

Jonah: Seven Images of a Prophet

The Book of Jonah in the Old Testament tells, in four concise chapters, an episode in the life of one of the minor Hebrew prophets. One day God called upon Jonah and commanded him to go to Nineveh, the great capital of Assyria and to warn its people that He would destroy their city unless they repented their many sins. Jonah demurred and fled to Joppa, where he embarked on a ship bound west for Tarshish to remove himself even farther from God's reach. God sent a high wind, which endangered the ship; when the sailors began to pray to their various deities, Jonah went down into the ship and fell asleep until the captain woke him and asked him to pray to his god, too. Meanwhile, the sailors threw lots to find out who had brought the storm upon them. Thus Jonah's guilt came to light; he asked them to throw him into the sea to save the ship and themselves. He knew that God had found him. When the sailors reluctantly threw Jonah overboard, the wind and the waters calmed down. God sent a big fish to swallow Jonah; he stayed inside the fish for three days and three nights, praying to God to deliver him from the deep and promising that he would listen to His voice. God told the fish to spew Jonah onto the land; He spoke to him again, repeating the command that he should journey to Nineveh. The prophet did so and preached to the people, telling them that they had another forty days to repent. The king and his people listened to Jonah and repented their sins. God spared Nineveh. At that, Jonah became angry because his prophecy had been proved void; he asked God to let him die. Then he left and sat down in the shade of a hut he had built for himself outside the city, to wait and see what would really happen. God made a plant grow quickly beside the hut; it offered shade over Jonah's head which pleased him very much. But on the next day God sent a worm to gnaw the plant and destroy it. Once more Jonah was angry at the Lord and asked for his own death. Then God spoke to Jonah for the third time: if you feel pity for a short-lived plant shall I not feel pity for the many thousands of people and beasts of Nineveh?

This ostensibly simple biblical tale can be, and has been, understood on different levels. It is a religious tale in which God appears as the one and only god of all mankind, a universal deity. There is no escaping from His will and command. His wisdom and foresight are to be trusted above all. Yet man is able to forge his own destiny: both the recalcitrant prophet and the sinful people of Nineveh may repent and be saved. Jonah is described as a very sensitive human being; he has his self-respect, his anxieties, and his own independent ideas. But he undergoes a development, exemplary for all believers, and at the end he is a better man because he now knows about God's grace, which is above justice. In Jewish exegesis the story is one more example of God's love for man; in Christian exegesis it is one of the prefigurations of Christ's death and resurrection.

From the psychological point of view the story has been interpreted in various ways; but mostly the accent is on Jonah's adventures as symbolizing a learning process, during which he rises to face the responsibilities of a mature and fully developed adult. The plot is understood to hold a sequence of symbols which stand for an inner experience, at first a search for increased isolation and protection, a withdrawal from communication with others. When the steps (the ship, the ship's belly, the belly of the fish) of the escape into security result in imprisonment, Jonah returns, somewhat more mature, to the point in life where the escape had begun.[1] A man sinks into his childhood memories; not wishing to accept a difficult assignment, he retreats psychologically from the world existing around him and finds himself in deepest spiritual darkness. But during this unconscious retreat into a state of regression he links back with his instincts; he reactivates, reorganizes his spiritual contents, and reappears in the world, strengthened by the mysterious experience. Thus, too, the story may be helpful to whoever comes across it because its symbols represent a way of preventing psychic energy from being immobilized.[2] The story is seen as one, though not fully structured, variation of the symbol of the night-sea journey, the dangerous plunge into the unconscious; the successful return expresses recuperation, the overcoming of one's spiritual standstill or death.[3] It is also interpreted as the magical passage through the female womb, as a symbol of rebirth and regeneration, and as the emergence of a heightened consciousness. This is why (and here psychological aspects intertwine with theological ones) in the medieval Biblia Pauperum, for instance, Throwing Joseph into the Well, the Entombment of Christ, and Jonah Being Swallowed by the Whale are represented side by side in one picture; and again, another picture portrays a threefold example of the Reappearance of the Hero: Samson with the Temple Doors, Christ Arisen, and Jonah Emerging from the Whale.[4]

In literature Jonah and his vicissitudes have turned up, for instance, in

---

1. Erich Fromm, *The Forgotten Language: An Introduction to the Understanding of Dreams, Fairytales and Myths* (New York: Rinehart, 1951), pp. 20–23.

2. Carl Gustav Jung, *Symbols of Transformation*, trans. by R. F. C. Hull (New York: Pantheon, 1956), p. 409.

3. C. E. Cirlot, *A Dictionary of Symbols*, 2nd ed., trans. by Jack Sage (London: Routledge & Kegan Paul, 1973), pp. 228–29.

4. Erich Neumann, *Die grosse Mutter: Der Archetyp des grossen Weiblichen* (Zurich: Rhein-Verlag, 1956), pp. 159–60. Joseph Campbell, *The Hero with a Thousand Faces* (New York: Meridian, 1956), pp. 94, 218.

Melville's *Moby Dick*,[5] where Father Mapple cites Jonah before his congregation as a model of repentance for the sin of disobedience, as one who progresses from hardheartedness, through fears and punishment, to the joy of preaching the Truth to the face of Falsehood.

We have assembled evidence on the many facets of the story mainly to support our surprise that it should also be considered as a tale especially suited for children. It has long had its place in chrestomathies and anthologies of religious texts, in the original version or else adapted according to prevailing needs, and usually accompanied by one or two (melo)dramatic illustrations—swishing beards, swaying ships, swooping gales, soaring towers—with notable exceptions of truly expressive pictures contributed by great illustrators like Albín Brunovský[6] or Janusz Grabiański.[7]

But lately the story has turned into a preferred subject of picture books, which by their nature are very different from the customary religious books for children and youth, and usually are intended to reach a somewhat younger audience.

Now there is no doubt that the story contains several elements which easily attract the attention of the child at different ages. There is much adventure, there is magic with picturesque scenes and surprise turnings; there is the child's intimate understanding of the wish to escape a tiresome duty, and his experience, just as familiar, with moral authority, which will lead him toward responsible action. There is the unconscious fascination with the symbols of being swallowed, the bliss of regression into uterine security, and of rebirth and spiritual growth. Still, the story harbors some difficulties for children. The moral message is quite intricate and has almost scholarly nuances. The stages of the hero's moral progress demand attention, more than children appreciate. The last part, after the repentance of Nineveh, is quite abstract and even anticlimactic in the eyes of children. And does the story really make it clear how far Jonah is a human being whose destiny is operated for the benefit of other men and women, and to what extent he is a self-reliant hero of the kind children love to identify with?

Be this as it may, within a short period a number of picture books have taken up the subject and treated it, by way of textual alteration and elaboration and with lavish illustrations. How do the various combinations of retold texts and sets of illustrations work out?

Jona und der grosse Fisch is a picture book for young children. The story is retold briefly in very simple terms; wisely, it ends with the salvation of Nineveh. The pages of the small-format book are dominated by vivid illustrations; the text is scattered here and there. The pictures play with the story and elaborate upon it in a purposely naive style, spiced with nice touches: We see the ship leave the harbor from a gull's eyes' view; as the storm

---

5. Herman Melville, *Moby Dick* (New York: New American Library, 1961), p. 59ff.
6. Ivan Olbracht, *Biblické Príbehi*; illus. by Albín Brunovský (Bratislava: Mládé letá, 1968).
7. G. Fussenegger, "Giona il disobbediente," in *La Bibbia*; trans. by E. Martinez; illus. by Janusz Grabiański (Milano: Mursia, 1975).

grows, the sailors throw bags, barrels, and jugs overboard; in the next scene the whale appears before the text refers to it; Jonah sinks into the whale's mouth in an underwater seascape with fish, a coral reef, and the remnants of old wrecks (fig. 60); the road to Nineveh, an oriental city, leads through lush vegetation. Throughout, the sea is pictured in endless stylized blue-green waves. Jonah himself is a chubby child with an outsize beard who goes peacefully through the motions required by the plot. His repentance in the whale's belly is a series of callisthenic gestures. The moral is there in the text, but the pictures externalize it by clothing it in joyful agitation. The book is a pleasingly innocent attempt at early religious education; it is one in a series of biblical tales. The idea seems to be to have the child meet sacred texts the easy way, without aiming as yet at much more than that.

Jona, illustrated by Kees de Kort, is also part of an extended series of picture books on themes from the Old and New Testaments, published by Dutch and German Bible societies. The text is abbreviated, concise, and straightforward. But with the exception of the growing bush nothing essential is omitted. The story ends with God explaining to Jonah why the people of Nineveh will be saved, with the added sentence, "All human beings are

Da wurde das Meer still.
Der Sturm hatte sich gelegt.
Gott ließ einen großen Fisch kommen.
Der verschlang den Jona.

Fig. 60. Stefan Lemke and Marie-Luise Lemke-Pricken, "Jona in the seascape"
From *Jona und der grosse Fisch*, illustrated by Stefan Lemke and Marie-Luise Lemke-Pricken, Gerd Mohn, Gütersloh, 1976. By permission of Gerd Mohn.

my children." There is great force in de Kort's expressionist illustrations. Background and garments are historical, Mideastern, painted in saturated colors. But the figures in the story are the stocky, earthy, common people of any era (fig. 61). The main emphasis lies with human expression. Surprise, tension, anxiety, and anger are reflected by the illustrator in the faces of the sailors and the inhabitants of Nineveh with credible straightforwardness in a manner matching the text but imbuing it with a glow which turns the simple words into drama. In none of the other editions considered in this chapter is Jonah's face so humanly expressive of what goes on within him. The fact that Jonah, a heavy and somewhat slow man, is depicted so vividly creates continuity of impression and unity of composition characterizing the book.

The down-to-earth-approach is strongly felt in the sea episode. There are no delicate sailors in this book: they shout at the yawning Jonah; they are taken aback by his avowal that he has caused the storm and throw him into the water with brutal satisfaction. Then, when Jonah prays inside the fish, the illustrator paints only the unbounded wavy sea: the miraculous is best left to the imagination. Next, Jonah, lost in thoughts, kneels on the shore as

Fig. 61. Kees de Kort, "Jona and the sailors"

From *Jona*, illustrated by Kees de Kort, Dutch Bible Society, Haarlem, 1976. Illustration Kees de Kort © Docete Foundation Hilversum Holland–Netherlands Bible Society.

the savage fish turns away from him. (This is the center picture halfway through the book. It is repeated on the cover.)

De Kort uses colors convincingly. The first picture, when God calls Jonah, is a pastoral corner dominated by yellow fields. When the prophet castigates the sinners in Nineveh, a pale green coats everything. Composition and color are powerfully combined in the last two pictures. In the first Jonah sits in the shade amid lush vegetation, pointing and looking expectantly at the blue-white clay houses bound to be destroyed at any moment. In the next picture, the last one in the book, the flowering bushes have wilted, Jonah has turned away from the city; he holds his head in both hands, his face red with anger—a portrait of incomprehension. The illustrator has the courage to underline the unsolved conflict in Jonah's mind, immanent in the biblical ending. Jonah has not yet learned from his experience.

While the book seems to be intended for younger children, to judge from the adaptation of the text, the illustrations endow it with depth. This is also true of many of the other books in this series, with pictures by the same illustrator.

Yonah Hanavee is a far more problematic version. It is a large-format picture book for older children and young adults. The story is retold rather faithfully; it upholds the serious mood of the original, with simplifications and elaborations here and there. The text is accommodated below and between the many pictures, close to seventy, that make up the book.

From the visual point-of-view this is quite a feast for the eyes: at least at first one is struck by the hieratic mood which pervades the pictures. There are glowing oriental sceneries: the tawny and light green semiarid slopes; city gates made of hewn stone; priestly figures in biblical attire and exhibiting dramatic gestures. All these combine to offer to the viewer a sense of solemnity.

The illustrator draws both on the techniques of film art and comics to create the style of his pages. Long shots, medium shots, and close-ups swiftly move us through space; some pictures occupy a whole page; others are cut up into vertical or horizontal panels with abrupt changes from one page to the next. Dramatic, well-chosen colors express the rectangular pictorial spaces and shapes of various sizes: the terrible moment when Jonah is thrown overboard in the storm is shown full-page. The facing page has three small, glass-like vertical panels picturing his rapid descent into the turbulent waters. As he slows down, wide horizontal strips show him, head downward, ever closer, sinking into the seaweeds toward the fish's mouth. The color of this whole sequence is blue-green. Now all of a sudden we are in the belly of the fish, four close takes show a repenting Jonah on a deep crimson background, and then the clear blue sea with the fish spouting a stream of water. Next, Jonah being cast ashore, is a study in lines with horizontals dominating: the sky and the horizon, gales rolling ashore, Jonah's legs and the white stripes of his gown, and a few diagonal waves matching his upper body and shoulders; in the foreground, the strongly contradictory verticals of his propped-up arms, his wet black hair hanging down, and the folds in his gown. Now comes the epic journey to Nineveh: three horizontal pictures, one below the other. The upper one is small, with Jonah kneeling and thanking God for his rescue; the larger one in the middle shows an upright prophet, ready to set out on his mission, in vertical lines (body, arms alongside body, striped gown), leaving a strongly accentuated diagonal shoreline behind him; in a slender strip, Jonah espies the great city from afar. We feel the momentum as the prophet enters the city. Vertical pictures show him collecting his first impressions of evil-doers, from medium shot to close-up; and so it goes on. The last sequence, the prophet and his bush, springing up and withering, is presented with stately visual deliberation. At this point in the story most pictures occupy a whole page: the book represents a successful effort to employ visual dynamics—shape, size, color, composition—to maximum effect.

Where aesthetic authenticity is concerned, things are different. The pictures are mainly beautiful photographs of seemingly Mideastern sceneries and sites; some are painted. The human beings appearing in them are usually painted cut-outs pasted on the photographs, a fact which is not very well disguised. Those superimposed figures are cleverly designed and arranged. Their relative sizes indicate perspective. But they are static; they exhibit monotonously exaggerated postures and gestures of awe, repentance, sudden illumination. The illustrator's interpretation, too, tends to be stereotyped. Thus, when the text tells us that Jonah walked the streets of Nineveh and saw evil-doers, the illustrations specify sexual temptation and carousing. Does sin always have to be sex and drink? Must sex so often be presented to young people in its negative aspects? Was there no brutality in Nineveh, no bribery, no theft?

The technically impressive work of the illustrator results in a number of stirring pictures. Yet the overall effect is of a collection of stills from a movie picture, or of actors on a stage. The beauty is marred by superficial histrionics and cardboard tricks. In spite of visual dramatization the tone of the pictures is impersonal and informative—"illustrative" of the text. This sleek, showy style, found everywhere, is very much in favor with children and adults because it complements the surface meaning of the story; but being an aesthetically cheap montage, it is devoid of individual artistic expression.

Jonah: An Old Testament Story, by Beverly Brodsky, is textually a lucid first-person account of the prophet's own adventures. Changes from the original are few, except for the fine ending coming after God's admonition, "I was ashamed, but I wept for joy." The illustrations are glowing and evocative. They are done with an expressionist, emotional brush often embracing the text, and very pliantly: towering gales alternate abruptly with the city's heavy stone structures, heavy Assyrian faces, and the quiet concentration of man and beast fasting. Several times these modes clash persuasively: when God calls Jonah for the first time, the prophet is about to be encompassed in a yellow and blue ark emanating from a personified deity; but instead of yielding to it, he resists by thrusting his right arm toward God, his elbow forming a sharp right angle. In another example the sailors who throw Jonah into the raging sea are pictured motionless to express their unwillingness (fig. 62).

There are more visual allegories and metaphorical touches in the book. The ship Jonah finds in Joppa has a large eye (of conscience?) painted on its bow. Near the end, when God reminds his prophet of the many people and animals in Nineveh, whom he, Jonah, had been willing to abandon, the illustration is a large revolving sphere showing the different domains of creation—sun and moon in the sky, trees and beasts, man, fish, the deep sea—a powerful reminder.

Leviathan is represented with special visual force; no sinking into the sea here. The harsh personal experience is depicted in three pictures of the huge fish: Jonah entering his mouth from the left; Jonah inside his belly, an expressionist turmoil of lines and colors; and the fish spitting Jonah out toward the right. These three pictures create one continuous momentum.

This is a vivid, beautiful book. If one is not completely satisfied with its visual message, this results from two elements found in the artist's style. One is the lack of a continuous rhythm throughout the book. So much imagination and energy is invested in the creation of each page that they tend to be too dissimilar and isolated from each other. The Leviathan sequence is an exception. The other element lies in the low expressiveness of the human figures. They wear artificial expressions, to the point of appear-

Though they knew I spoke the truth, the men tried desperately to bring the ship to dry land. But it was no use. The storm only grew worse, and they threw me into the raging sea.

Fig. 62. Beverly Brodsky, ''Jonah thrown into the sea''

An illustration from *Jonah: An Old Testament Story*, written and illustrated by Beverly Brodsky. Copyright © 1977 by Beverly Brodsky. By permission of J. B. Lippincott, Publishers.

ing stolid. This is true even for Jonah with one fine exception when, being angry at God, he is portrayed seething with barely controlled emotion. In the rest of the pictures, including the last one where he weeps with joy, there is more external pageantry than internalized, and visualized, emotion. It is, after all, the man Jonah who tells his story in the first person, with whom we should communicate.[8]

Jonah and the Great Fish is an elaborate and intricate book. The text relates that Jonah farmed his own land; he had a house and a garden and a donkey to pull his plow, explaining why he was reluctant to leave and go and save the Assyrian enemies. So when God had called him, he waited until nightfall before he rode away on his donkey. In the morning he fell in with a band of traders who took him to Joppa by the sea. There he had to sell his donkey to pay his fare. And so elaboration continues. While biblical conciseness is abandoned, the spirit of the tale is preserved. Only the child's imagination and intellect are left with fewer questions.

The illustrations appear on full pages opposite a white text page. Sometimes, as in the episode on the ship, three pages of text follow each other, alternating with five pages of illustrations; but only rarely do text and picture mix in this book. The illustrator fully accepts the author's elaborateness. She lets herself be guided by him, but not disciplined. While the author attempts to make the magic more real, self-evident, and understandable, the illustrator creates, in her complex style, wondrous pictures of symbolic force to show how strange the man was and how mysterious the events that befell him.

Graphically, the pictures are rather simple, but their structures and colors wish to convey unmistakably mystic overtones. It all starts innocently, as it were, on the dust cover. There is a palm grove in the blazing sun; the air is hot, red and orange, and the donkey is tied to a peg. Again, on the credits page, the tied donkey on a green meadow. Then the story proper begins and we see Jonah in a picture made up of dark brown colors; he is a simple pensive man, and he is plowing his field with his donkey. Next we see him lying in the dust, frightened and envisioning Nineveh's orange-colored walls and turquoise flames burning the city (fig. 63). Then a picture of the farmer's house, shut and shuttered against the Lord's will, with a bleak sun in a dark heaven; as our eyes move downward, the ground becomes burnished orange. As night falls, Jonah furtively rides away on his donkey: we can see him in the upper right-hand corner of a satiny brown-black picture; the furrows of his field converge in that corner; a dark moon threatens in the sky. Then Jonah leaves Joppa on a small vessel; the donkey he sold is tied to the pier. In the next picture a tiny light blue ship is swept in and out of brown-black vortices. Then a last vision of the ship, staid and tall, in the

8. It is worthwhile to compare Brodsky's *Jonah* with a previous important book by the same writer-illustrator. There she achieved pictorial continuity; the lack of facial expressiveness is less felt there, because the protagonist is an artificial being. See Beverly Brodsky McDermott, *The Golem, A Jewish Legend* (Philadelphia: Lippincott, 1976).

Fig. 63. Helga Aichinger, "Jonah's vision of Nineveh"
An illustration by Helga Aichinger from *Jonah and the Great Fish* by Clyde Robert Bulla. Illustrations copyright © 1970 by Helga Aichinger. By permission of Thomas Y. Crowell, Publishers.

center of the water, now calm and glowingly blue. A picture of the lucent blue fish with its whitish mouth, shut tightly. Then we follow Jonah again. First he is shown standing quietly within a circular spout of water, being propelled onto the sand-colored shore. Now he is standing at the red-hot gate of Nineveh, seeing again the vision of the bluish flames rising above the city. A bleak picture of the city-dwellers rejoicing at their salvation. In the olive-green night Jonah is sitting on a crimson hill, wearing a crimson gown. The plant which grows near—and which he has begun to love as he would love a friend, so the text says—is a palm tree, whitish under the full white moon. On the next page, a small sketch of the worm which has come to kill the plant. The final double-page picture: To the left rises a dark green mountain; to the right is the brilliant sun, concentric rings of white, yellow, and orange. Underneath, the donkey stands in the meadow, but free, untethered.

This description offers only a hint of the power of the colors (almost every picture is dominated by one saturated color) and to the originality of structure and composition displayed in the book. It cannot but allude to the mystic mood pervading it. The artist, as we said, was guided but not ruled by the author's intentions and style. In some respects she contradicts them. While Bulla describes Jonah as a simple man who acts and reacts rationally according to circumstances—albeit extraordinary ones—as he understands them, Aichinger's Jonah is more of a passive, meditative figure to whom things happen as if he were caught in a dream. There is another moving picture to emphasize this, the frontispiece; it shows Jonah walking along the shore. The wind shapes the waves, the sand, and Jonah's yellow gown into one rhythmic pattern: Jonah is united with the forces of nature.

The landscapes of the dream change beyond recognition from one picture to the next. The detailed continuity of the rambling adventure tale, the text, is broken up into disparate visions whose imperious beauty, here and there slightly mannered, demands the viewer's full concentration and draws him into contrasting contemplative moods: the disquiet of Jonah's vision of burning Nineveh; the oppressive anxiety gripping the house into which he retreats; the majesty of the mandaloid blue fish; the riddle of the last picture.

But Aichinger takes visual symbolism much further. At first, Jonah wears a dark brown frock, a farmer's one. But dark brown and black are, throughout the book, the colors of lowliness, seclusion, and resistance to the force of God, whose color is bright orange. When Jonah emerges from the fish, to set out on his mission, he wears a festive red gown. And why is the hill on which he is sitting during the night flaming red? Because when he begins to love the plant as he would have loved a friend marks the first time that Jonah is gripped by a true emotion, and he begins to understand what love might mean. Here the illustrator is inspired by the author who, going beyond Jonah's anger in the biblical text, speaks of the love which stirs in him and fulfills his spiritual education.

Another visual motif, even more important, is found in the figure of the donkey. Again, the idea comes from the author. By way of elucidation he mentions the donkey which pulls the farmer's plow. Then again he tells us that Jonah sold it as he needed money for the ship's fare. Aichinger turns the donkey into a major symbolic motif. Several times the innocent animal appears tied to a peg. Then Jonah leaves it at the pier. Yet when the story ends, we find the donkey standing in the sun, by itself, near a palm tree: the donkey appears to be the visual image of the instinctual, the intuitive aspects of Jonah's personality, fettered and abandoned through his rational and seemingly clever actions, and miraculously liberated and regained as

Jonah learns to love. The artist introduces into the tale the ancient fairy tale symbol of the dumb beast, despised and betrayed, whose deliverance and whose assistance are essential to the success of the hero. This interpretation also offers the clue to the riddle of the last picture in the book. The text ends on the previous page, stating that Jonah thanked the Lord for his mercy. The final illustration goes beyond this. It shows, we said, on the left a dark green, bulging, threatening mountain; to the right, the donkey in a light green meadow, made warm by the glowing sun. As Jonah returns home, to himself, having learned about justice and grace and love, this is his ultimate vision. Evil is banished to the left and is clearly separated from the brilliant light of day. The donkey is free and awaiting his master: now Jonah's spiritual world is whole and sane. In this symbolic landscape of his inner world, Jonah is not portrayed bodily.

This is a book of great artistic distinction. The issues it raises have surely become obvious during this analysis. Most important, author and illustrator combine to pull us in different directions. Their intentions and moods touch only associatively, tangentially. Though this is a not infrequent occurrence in art, when media meet, it becomes more questionable in a children's book. Children will benefit from Bulla's tale and from Aichinger's paintings; the combination of the two make it hard for the child, both intuitively and cognitively, to determine what kind of experience, a lucid, coherent one or a mystical one, he is urged to cull from the book.

The intricacy of the illustrator's style also poses difficulties in visual communication even for older children. Not too many will easily comprehend even unconsciously, the symbol of the donkey, because of its intentionally naive and clandestine appearance. Then, too, it is not easy to get used to the utter silence which reigns in these paintings. We do not hear anything visually, so to speak; the flames do not crackle; the joy of Nineveh is mute; even the roaring sea does not ring with sounds. It is all visions in a dream.

An outstanding book. Is its message open to children?

If Brodsky's illustrations are deeply felt religious history and Aichinger's a solitary mystical experience, Miyoshi's *Jona* is an iridescent myth.

The text is adapted for young children. Jonah is said to be a young man. He has a house and a donkey. When, in the end, he returns home he marries and lives happily with his wife and their children. They know that God's grace is with them, too. Elaboration refers mainly to Jonah's feelings and states of mind. When he is tossed onto the shore, he enjoys the warm sunshine. After he has spoken to the people of Nineveh he quickly runs away because he is afraid they will come after him. Extensions like these are set off by the omission of other episodes in the original, so that the text is short and easily understood by the child.

Yet there is one significant alteration in the role of the fish. The story begins with the fish, which shone, so the text says, in all the colors of the rainbow. One day the fish emerged from the sea and saw a young man sleeping on the high cliff. Then a voice spoke to the young man in his sleep, and Jonah understood that it was the voice of God (fig. 64). When he sailed away in the ship, the fish followed him all the time. The story also ends with the fish—it had many children and grandchildren, all bearing the colors of the rainbow. To this day, so the story says, they remember how Jonah came to understand that God's grace is greater than His wrath.

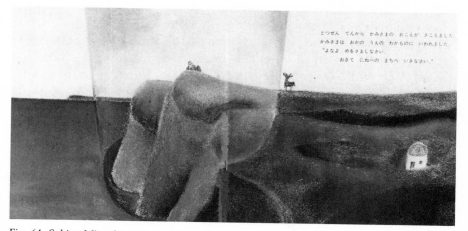

Fig. 64. Sekiya Miyoshi, ''God speaks to Jona''
From *Jona* illustrated by Sekiya Miyoshi, Shiko-Sha Ltd., Tokyo, 1977.

The special role of the fish is also emphasized in the illustrations. In the beginning, though, it is invisible. There is the blue sea; then the sea reaches the cliff on which Jonah is sleeping. Then comes his flight from home. Only when he falls asleep on the ship, does the fish appear in the waters below, watching him closely. It continues its watch during the storm. Then, when it has swallowed Jonah, there is a double-page portrait of the fish, with an attentive look turned inward, and no background at all. Three days later we see the fish spewing Jonah ashore in a rainbow of water. Later, when the prophet is sitting in the shade of several bushes which grow up around him, the fish watches from afar; it raises its head apprehensively from the water as Jonah lifts an angry finger toward God. Finally, in the last picture the big fish benignly crosses the sea, its descendants following behind.

This variation of a motif found in the original story somewhat changes the nature of the tale. Instead of being the dumb instrument of God's will at a certain point in the plot, the fish turns into a creature having a mission of its own all through the story. In a way this becomes the fish's tale and accomplishment. Jonah, being a young man, is certainly to be excused if he makes but slow progress in grasping God's wisdom. Only afterwards is he mature enough to marry and have a family. Has the fish been sent by God to intercede and to watch? Or is it a symbol (similar to what we found in

Aichinger's donkey) of Jonah's unconscious, submerged animal sagacity? The big fish ranges through the book through a delicate combination of the verbal and the pictorial, its meaning as iridescent as its colors.

This might also explain why Jonah himself is portrayed in a quite ordinary fashion. He wears a red gown and his behavior is always appropriate to the situation he finds himself in. But his face lacks expressiveness except for one picture. Certainly no child would recognize it as a *young* man's face. Jonah's distinction is, as we shall see, brought out by different means.

The fact that one person created both text and illustrations (so we may assume, though this is not stated specifically in the book) enhances its unity. The mythical mood of the former is brightened and enlivened by the latter. The pictures are painted with gay crayon colors, in a decorative style, with some abstract and a few cubistic elements introduced here and there, and with large, glowing spaces in one color. While the pictures differ much in content, point of view, and structure, each is quite obviously an intensification of the accompanying text, and the composition is transparent and attractive to the imagination.

But this is not simply a picturesque book. The colors clearly have emotional and symbolic values: the vast stretches of blue sea and the green and brown hues of the land are peaceful enough. But when Jonah furtively leaves his home, fearing God's wrath, the illustration shows him doing so as night falls and a red sun hangs low in the sky; he moves away into the violet night, quizzical disbelief in his eyes, his face violet, too, and even the text page opposite turns a light mauve. When Jonah is angry with God, he, the withered bushes, and the earth below all turn red, while on the facing page the sea is unnaturally white: above, a large yellow space represents God's grace and Jonah's perception of it. For yellow is the color of the numinous, the divine: in the beginning, when Jonah first hears God's voice in his sleep, a yellow emanation enwraps him (fig. 64).[9] In the last picture in the book Jonah is pictured near his home and family, again surrounded by a yellow halo; he is also standing inside a pink mandala, a circle symbolic of fulfillment and wholeness. So, too, the rainbow hues of the big fish are an allusion to the great Flood: Jonah's story, like Noah's, is one more proof that God will forgive suffering humanity when it finds its way back to Him.

There is more symbolism in the composition of some of the pictures. When Jonah first hears God's voice, the donkey is shown standing outside the yellow numinous halo. But, when, in the end, the prophet is standing inside the pink mandala, the donkey is there with him too. Is this pure chance, or does the donkey, now part of Jonah's wholeness, fulfill a symbolic function similar to what we found in Aichinger? Then we remember, of course, that the redeeming Messiah is said to come riding on a donkey. And suddenly we notice on Jonah's outstretched hand, in a halo of its own, a small bird—another reminder of Noah who sent the dove to find out if God

9. See also chapter 4.

had yet forgiven the sinners? Or is the bird symbolic of the Holy Ghost? Jonah as a prefiguration of Christ?

Miyoshi also plays with the design of the book. When the story opens we enter into it from the left through the blue sea. As the story ends, we are led out of it, continuing in the same direction into the sea. When we open the book in the middle, the central picture is the large likeness of the fish. When we turn the book round, there is the fish on the cover.

A sophisticatedly innocent religious spirit pervades the book. It treats a serious subject in a lucid fashion with a concise text and intense pictures. Its beauty springs from the motif of the big fish's mission; from the well-sustained contact and balance between the verbal and the visual; and from the acumen with which the two levels—the manifest fantastic and the latent symbolic—are combined in such a way that younger children may be attracted by the tale, and older ones may gradually detect or be led to understand, some of the hidden meanings. This is a good approach to presenting myths to children.

Finally, Cocagnac's *L'Opéra de Jonas* is a modernized version, where the substance of the ancient tale and of contemporary life and rational and fantastic elements are blended ingeniously in a seemingly matter-of-fact way.

Monsieur Jonas is an insurance agent, a quiet man living a simple life. His files reflect many kinds of catastrophes, large fires, railway accidents, etc. But to him these are no more than heaps of papers, claims to be settled, and checks to be written out. Jonas is a tranquil, modest man. One day, though, a postman in unusual attire brings him a letter sent by a mysterious person, demanding of him to announce to the inhabitants of a city called Nineveh that the nuclear bomb which they have built will explode in the very near future. Monsieur Jonas does not care for trouble. To get away from this demand he books a cruise in the Mediterranean. Just when he is embarking, he sees behind him the strange postman once more, following him, with outstretched wings. Jonas is certain that this is an illusion. But his peace of mind is upset. What is more, when the ship leaves the pier, Jonas smiles, and his smile is met by a smiling fisherman on the shore who unfolds his angelic wings. Jonas is disquiet, but as is his habit, he goes to bed early and sleeps it off. On the next day, just as he begins to enjoy the trip, he suddenly finds the letter in his pocket; he reads it once more and throws it away, but a bird catches it in mid-air and flings it into one of the ship's air vents. The letter lodges in a valve and the ship stops. Jonas confesses that he is the one to blame. When the engineers deal with the trouble, all of a sudden the letter flies into Jonas's mouth, he swallows it, feels sick, loses his balance and falls into the water, now certain that he will not escape his destiny. As he drifts down, past staring fish, the letter in his stomach inflates and carries him up again. Jonas prays; he is ready to go to Nineveh. As he regains the surface, a submarine comes to his rescue. It is operated by a hippie family who long ago left the mainland in order to survive the explosion of the nuclear bomb which they are sure has already taken place. Jonas, smiling, tells them of his mission. They are grateful to know a prophet (who is defined by Mother Hippie, for the benefit of her son, as a gentleman who always says yes and goes wherever he is sent). Jonas tells the child all kinds of wonderful catastrophe stories, including (and we already perceive why) the adventure of one Noah who was clever enough to take out an insurance policy before the great Flood swept the earth.

Jonas sets out on his mission. He is not afraid anymore, but full of doubt. He crosses the desert and, seeing the city from afar, he is very irate at the stupidity of its people who invent instruments of death. He happens to arrive in Nineveh right in the middle of two violent demonstrations organized by the supporters and the opponents of the nuclear bomb project, who are locked in dangerous combat. Jonas succeeds in giving his message to the already worried and irresolute king. Then he hurriedly leaves the city and waits for his words to come true. He falls asleep and in his dream the angelic postman hovers around him and mocks his misfortune. In the meantime the king of Nineveh has discarded his sumptuous clothes and is practicing yoga and meditation. Jonas, on his part, dreams of destruction. When he wakes up, the leaves have fallen from his tree, no doubt because of the blast from the bomb. But the city stands intact. Jonas grows furious. At this moment who should appear before him but a winged shepherd, his angel again (fig. 65). He explains to Jonas that God had mercy on Nineveh; that a miracle has happened, the black box of death has been rent by a large flower growing from it. Jonas comprehends that God is patient with the men and women of Nineveh.

Monsieur Jonas returns home to his insurance business. He now has larger eyeglasses to better understand what happens to the right and left of him. The flower he keeps on his desk (resembling the one of Nineveh) sometimes reminds him that behind all the forms and accounts there are

Fig. 65. A. Maurice Cocagnac, "Monsieur Jonas and the angel"
From *L'Opéra de Jonas,* written and illustrated by A. Maurice Cocagnac, Editions du Cerf, 1970. By permission of A. Maurice Cocagnac.

people. He assures the flower he will never forget what he has learnt by his adventure.

This is but a short summary of a long, astonishing, and well-wrought story. It gives an idea of how old and new motifs are brought together, and how the natural and the supernatural are mixed. The summary cannot do justice to the instances of humor and mild irony which characterize this version. Humor and irony both ease and accentuate the moral, educational intention. For Cocagnac has a clear view of what he wishes to achieve. The God of Jonas, so he intimates in the foreword, has a sense of humor which offers a chance for some smiling instruction that does not preclude serious teaching.

The point is that in modern civilization, both in Monsieur Jonas's office and in Nineveh, Good and Evil struggle for humanity's future. Man can win this fight only through the intervention and guidance of divine providence. But God also needs, so the story spells it out, man's good will and cooperation even if he has to be coerced. During the story God and his angel overcome three manifestations of evil: the smugness and indifference of Jonas, the petty bourgeois in his complacent alienation from his fellow human beings and their misfortunes; the carefree withdrawal, the abandon of the hippies who, by their own free will, lose touch with ordinary people; and the political powers, vying for ascendancy through destruction. Slowly, step by step, with funny situations and scarcely believable phenomena hiding the seriousness of the issue, the numinous, intruding upon bureaucratic and technological reality, has its way—using the good services of an insurance agent whose conscience has to be prodded by the recurrent mediation of the angel.

The facts and the symbols are all there in the written story. What role does the author assign to himself as illustrator?

The illustrations are large, clear pictures that convey outspoken impressions both of the narrow world of the bureaucrat, his office, his indifference, his rising involvement, and the far-flung areas where his story takes place. Structures vary; there is much alternation between spacious landscapes and seascapes, and close-ups without a background. This is a common-sense style drawing upon traditional fashions of illustrating and cartoon drawing, but with vigorous and tasteful color schemes. The pictures support very well the main intentions of the text: the concrete mingles successfully with the fantastic; the recurrent appearances of the angel in disguise come out as natural pictorially as they do verbally. Jonas's alienation is brought out by his stocky self-satisfied gait, until the bird snatches the letter. Now Jonas renounces his indifference. When he swallows the letter and drops into the sea, he appears four times in the same picture (in continuous narrative), his body color changing from brown to yellow to green. From now on emotions grip him, concentration, wrath, worry; in the end he sits at his desk again, smiling at the flower, wearing larger eyeglasses and a T-shirt with *love* imprinted on it.

The illustrations do justice to the first two parts of the book, Jonas's recalcitrance, and the agitated episodes taking place in seascapes relating to his change of heart. Then comes a breathtaking double page, in terra cotta hues, of Jonas crossing the desert on his way to Nineveh. From then on, though some of the pictures are quite good, they are less convincing. Just when the text becomes more serious, the illustrations become too funny. This is especially true of the portrayal of the king of Nineveh. He is an old-fashioned feudal ruler, with a headgear reminiscent of a Viking or else of Asterix, the famous cartoon character. He looks plain silly when he practices yoga. It is difficult to associate him with the doom of humanity—irony becomes farce.

This does not happen haphazardly. These pictures were done by an expressive and experienced illustrator. And by its appearance this is a picture book; some two-thirds of the book are occupied by pictures. But it is a picture book for older children and youth. It is quite clear that Cocagnac the writer intended the text to dominate and assigned to Cocagnac the illustrator the task to accompany it, to accentuate the fun, to underline the ironic distance, but to leave the role of presenting and interpreting the symbolic, moral fabric of the story to the written word.[10] He states, in the foreword, that the neglect of inward health is still the great temptation of our age, yet God's patience offers us the time to remove it. This message comes through in this updated version of Jonah's adventure, but not in the pictures. One result of this discrepancy between the text and the illustrations is that the age level, and power of sophistication, of children and youth who will be drawn to the text is much higher than of those who will be attracted mainly by the illustrations. In this version the word deals, in its own intriguing style, with the transcendental. Not so the picture. Still, this is an uncommon picture book, treating its grave subject in a light vein, in a way which makes it accessible for children of different ages.

Looking at these images of the prophet one may say that on the whole Jonah fares well. His story is treated with dignity and thoughtfulness. All retellings embody the religious concept that the human being is moral only because of the intervention of superior powers. They convey this idea by different means because they wish to appeal to children in different age groups, and because they represent various religious beliefs. They pronounce and emphasize their message by displacing some of the ancient motifs and introducing new ones. Yet in all these versions Jonah remains himself. His is not a strong personality. He is no hero, though he is compelled to carry out feats of heroism and compelled to comprehend that his mission was unavoidable. There is something of the anti-hero in him, and this may possibly account for his popularity with children's book publishers today. After all, the anti-hero is one of the major preoccupations of contem-

10. This is a prose story. There is nothing operatic about the book, except for a song, words and melody, added at the end, quite unnecessarily.

porary literature and film. It seems that there is a need, felt by writers and artists, to communicate to the child the major existentialist concept that the non-heroic human being, too, is capable of moral conduct. This is certainly an important trend in picture books. Children will be able to show interest in Jonah's adventures and feel empathy with his fate. They will not easily identify with him.

As to the measure of aesthetic quality and meaningfulness which these books achieve in their attempts to represent the dynamics of the plot and Jonah's spirit, the versions bear witness to the wide range of iconic and symbolic functions to which the illustration may be put.

CHILDREN'S WORKS CITED

BRODSKY, BEVERLY. *Jonah: An Old Testament Story*. Philadelphia: Lippincott, 1977.

BULLA, CLYDE ROBERT. *Jonah and the Great Fish*. Illus. by Helga Aichinger. New York: Crowell, 1970.

COCAGNAC, A. M. *L'Opéra de Jonas*. Paris: Le Périscope, Les Editions du Cerf, 1970.

FUSSENEGGER, G. *La Bibbia*. Trans. by E. Martinez. Illus. by Janusz Gabriański. Milano: Mursia, 1975.

Jona. Illus. by Kees de Kort. Utrecht: Docete–International, 1976.

Jona und der grosse Fisch. Illus. by Stefan Lemke and Marie-Luise Lemke-Pricken. Gütersloh: Mohn, 1976.

MIYOSHI, SEKIYA. *Jona*. Tokyo: Shiko-Sha, 1977.

OLBRACHT, IVAN. *Biblické Príbehi*. Illus. by Albín Brunovský. Bratislava: Mláde letá, 1968.

Yonah Hanavee. My Bible in Pictures, edited by Uriel Ofek. Tel Aviv: Revivim, n.d.

13

The Benign Image of Dehumanization

INANIMATE OBJECTS AS PROTAGONISTS

Literature of all times and peoples has always told of man-made objects that took on a magic quality and served their owners in miraculous ways. But inanimate objects as protagonists of tales can be found only rarely before the latter half of the nineteenth century. In order to be the hero of a tale, the object has to undergo a process of animation; it is transformed by technological processes to be useful to man, perceived as an entity, and endowed with life: the leap that fantasy has to take is much greater than in the anthropomorphization of talking beasts.

A few examples can be adduced. From the Caucasus comes the old motif of the kitchen utensils' rebellion against man; excited pots and pans will not stand their servitude any more, but the good housewife finds a way to pacify them. In one version of "The Pot," a Danish folk tale, the story's hero is a pot that wanders from one home to another in the village and endeavors to bring food to the poor.[1] The pot speaks and replies when spoken to; it shows understanding. Yet its owner received it from the hands of a good witch, and it is at her command that he has taken up the task of going from door to door looking for the deserving poor. In another version of the same tale, the pot is in a poor man's possession and "skips" to more fortunate homes and farms and steals food, grain, and money for its owner; it talks and acts independently and responds to questions.[2] It was given to its owner by "a fine-faced stranger." The tale bears social significance: it is a kind of Robin Hood pot, but of definitely magical origin.

In Goethe's "Wandering Bell," the church bell leaves its steeple and harasses the child who refuses to come to church for Sunday prayers.[3] The

---

Parts of this chapter are reprinted from Sara I. Fenwick, ed., *A Critical Approach to Children's Literature* (Chicago: Univ. of Chicago Pr., 1967), pp. 78–95, by permission of the publisher. Copyright 1967 by the University of Chicago. All rights reserved.

1. "Der Topf," in Max Lüthi, ed., *Europäische Volksmärchen* (Zurich: Manesse, 1951), pp. 51–57.
2. Mary C. Hatch, "The Talking Pot," in *Thirteen Danish Tales* (New York: Harcourt, Brace, 1947), pp. 16–24.
3. Johann W. Goethe, "Die Wandelnde Glocke," in *Goethe's Gedichte* (Berlin: Minerva, n.d.), p. 83.

child has been forewarned by his mother that this might finally happen; the bell therefore appears to have been sent by some higher power.

The common characteristics of the objects in the tales cited seem to be that, though personified, they appear in stories that are actually parables and that man's superiority is not questioned. And, as has been mentioned, the examples are relatively rare.

All this was changed by the appearance of the first writer of modern fantasy, Hans Christian Andersen.[4] His unusually sensitive mind discovered life in everyone and everything; whatever his fantasy touched upon became for him the bearer of a destiny, the symbol of the pervading sadness and happiness he saw all around him, and the vehicle for his intensely human message.

Andersen's animation of man-made objects manifests itself in various ways. Some of the stories are frankly allegorical. In "The Shirt Collar," a would-be Don Juan conducts unhappy love affairs with several objects associated with females: a garter, the hot iron, a pair of scissors, and a comb.[5] When he gets old, he, like Casanova before him, retells his adventures in a form embellished by his memory. But other tales create a more emotional atmosphere, calling upon the reader's feelings just as if their heroes were human or animal. "The Old Street Lamp" becomes more and more human as the story develops, and in the end he feels that the old couple whose rooms he brightens are fond of him for his own sake: "I'm really like a child to them."[6] In "The Old House," one of Andersen's most tranquil tales, the old house, the new houses, the little boy, the flowers, the old man, the birds, the brass knobs on the railings, the carved trumpeter, and the tin soldier curiously live side by side in "one world" and even a scrap of pigskin covering "has something to say."[7] Only with difficulty could one determine who really is the hero of this story: no one really stands out, and the general mood, of life passing away from all of us, serves as the great equalizer in this story.

Andersen's animated man-made objects inhabit a strange land. They are alive, so it seems; they are personified and equipped with human attributes; they are conscious of their existence; they contemplate their experiences and become wiser for doing so; they are very sensitive creatures. But these objects are wrong in assuming that they are important to man; they are alive, but they are so much wrapped up in their narcissistic memories that they never realize that they are not free to act; they strive for independence but fail to attain it. Their existence is, from man's point of view, a tragic and ridiculous illusion—yet again, they are alive enough to lead their illusory existence. Behind it we can discern Andersen's existentialist view of human

4. Hans Christian Andersen, *H. C. Andersen's Fairy Tales,* trans. by L. W. Kingsland (New York: Walck, 1962).

5. *Ibid.,* pp. 309–11.

6. *Ibid.,* pp. 290–98.

7. *Ibid.,* pp. 299–308.

life. Man uses his tools and prides himself on them as long as they are new and fit his purpose. As they become dented and cracked they become worthless, and we throw them away. Some of the wiser among the objects are aware that this is so.

The "Tea-Pot" gains more insight into the conditions of existence in this world than any other object.[8] She knows, in spite of her pride in herself, that she is in fact much less important than she would have us believe. As this deeply symbolic tale develops, the suffering teapot slowly perceives something of elementary importance—*the superiority of organic substance over the inorganic*. "Even as I stood there, my better life began: you are one thing, and then you become something quite different . . . Earth was put inside me and for a tea-pot that's as much as being buried . . . in the earth a bulb was planted . . . the bulb lay in the earth, the bulb lay inside me." And the teapot begins to believe in her own transformation: ". . . it became my heart, my living heart . . . there was life in me, there was strength and force."[9] This ecstatic hymn to life is rudely interrupted when people point out that the beautiful flower deserves a better pot. The teapot is thrown out into the yard; even there she is forever ennobled by her illusory experience of organic wholeness and pregnancy. In "The Nightingale," Andersen states even more unequivocally that the living animal is superior to the artifact.[10]

In an uncanny way, Andersen moved creative fantasy ahead toward the animation, in fantasy, of inanimate man-made objects, exactly at the time when the influence of the Industrial Revolution was about to alter man's life beyond recognition. It is as if he had intuitively, seismographically, understood that mankind, in his own time, stood on the threshold of a new age and would soon recast his material environment and, beyond that, would become involved in technological and psychological attempts to adjust to the inanimate works of his own creation.

Andersen called forth the "industrial revolution" in children's literature, the animism in modern fantasy. In the generations following him, man-made objects have managed to improve their lot and their relative importance, both in reality and in the realm of fantasy.

MAGIC OBJECTS AND AUTONOMOUS OBJECTS

From Andersen's stories about animated objects two types of children's literature have grown: stories about animated dolls and toy animals; and stories about useful and serviceable objects (tools, gadgets, and machines).

Although dolls and toy animals that come to life in children's daydreams and fantasies, and in the fantasy stories written for them, are man-made objects, they have been specifically created for the purpose of serving as objects to which the child is supposed to become attached; their function is

8. *Ibid.*, pp. 325–27.
9. *Ibid.*, pp. 326–27.
10. *Ibid.*, pp. 172–84.

to represent biological beings toward whom real emotional attachment—love, hate, confidence, admiration, etc.—is possible or even necessary. They are significant symbols of projection and identification processes. They are, moreover, the descendants of what Garland has called the great tradition of anthropomorphism—the descendants of sacred effigies and statues and images that symbolically represented gods and goddesses in countless cults and, of course, of the toys that children cherish in almost every culture and every generation.[11] And they are, after all, anthropomorphic or theriomorphic—they resemble real creatures, human or animal, who have faces and limbs and personalities. Learning to relate to these real beings, even when they are represented by proxy, is a decisive aspect of growing up.

Another no less important point becomes manifest when we look at the development of the doll and toy animal stories in the nineteenth and twentieth centuries: animation more often than not takes place in an exceptional, often magical, situation or because the child loves his toy so much that his wish comes true. Coming to life is an exceptionally rare experience, as it were, not an ordinary, everyday occurrence. Some examples are Collodi's *Pinocchio*, Margery W. Bianco's *Velveteen Rabbit*, A. A. Milne's *Winnie-the-Pooh*, Elizabeth O. Jones's *Big Susan*, Enys Tregarthen's *The Doll Who Came Alive*.

The fantasy situation adopted by stories of this type is one in which the child relates in a psychologically meaningful way to the fantastic creatures of the writers' minds; they, the animated toys, usually depend on the child and are not his equals. The human child's superiority is—exactly as in animal stories and in the child's relation to his pets—one of the educative values of those relationships because it partly balances and partly compensates for his inferiority feelings toward the adults in his life.

However, the other type, stories about functional, useful artifacts, does not possess these educationally valuable attributes. Here and there one can find objects that belong to a magic world: "And the soup ladle was walking up the table towards Alice's chair, and beckoning to her impatiently to get out of its way."[12] Yet the twentieth century has evolved *stories about man-made objects that are represented as "naturally" active, autonomous in their actions, co-existing with the child on a basis of equality and even, on occasion, being superior to him.* They share the child's world in a matter-of-fact manner, relate to him, and care for him out of their own free will, as it were.

ANTHROPOMORPHIC VEHICLES AND MACHINES

The personified, anthropomorphic machine as the hero of stories, has become a trend, especially in picture books; it has also been carried over to other types of children's literature for various age groups.

11. Madge Garland, *The Changing Face of Childhood* (London: Hutchinson, 1963), p. 76.
12. Lewis Carroll, *Through the Looking Glass* (New York: Macmillan, 1943), p. 211.

Children's literature is one of the means by which children are socialized and are acquainted with important aspects and features of their civilizations. It is, therefore, only natural that gadgets and machines should loom prominently in children's books in an era and a society that is, in fact, based on technological development. Some of the essential attributes of machinery— its colorfulness, its acoustic quality, and its usually locomotive character— make it especially attractive to children. The many stories and poems in which inanimate machinery plays an important role have the additional task of catering to the child's daydreams and serve the goal of wish fulfilment in fantasy: while the child who dreams of operating machines cannot yet do so in reality, he can do so in fantasy. At the same time, machinery in stories, as in play, aids the child in overcoming fears of the powerful contraption that he harbors in his mind. A good example is the story about "Johnny's Machines," where the little boy tells his grandfather that he likes to push buttons; so grandfather brings in more and more machines, and the farm becomes mechanized while Johnny and grandfather are continually proud of and fascinated by the mysterious things.[13] "It was all because Johnny likes to push buttons." Another example is "Smoky and the Red Fire Engine."[14] A stray dog who is fascinated by the red fire engine one day succeeds in riding on it to be present at a fire where he saves a girl's doll. By this act he gains a home for himself. The machine's important role is brought out well, but people and dogs are even more important.

In these stories, machines are presented to the child as interesting and intriguing; yet they are mechanical creations of man's ingenuity and nothing else. Adults or children are the actors and heroes in the stories. With the appearance of stories and pictures of anthropomorphic machines in children's literature, however, this is changed decisively. They, the machines, are animated; they usually have names and the ability to think and, even more, to relate emotionally to others like themselves and to animals and human beings.[15] They become co-protagonists or sole protagonists of the story. The child is expected—this is what the story proposes to him—to enter into a meaningful emotional fantasy relation to it-him-her, exactly as he would be expected to do in a story about a human being or an animal. In other words, he is asked to identify with the machine-hero's exploits and personality. It is assumed that he will learn from them and that these stories will advantageously influence the development of his personality. The fact that, unlike humans and animals, and (in fantasy at least) effigies, dolls, and toys, machines have actually only a strictly functional raison d'être is neglected.

Within the confines of the story that humanizes machines, several more

---

13. Helen Palmer, "Johnny's Machines," in Ellen L. Buell, ed., *A Treasury of Little Golden Books* (New York: Golden Press, 1960).

14. Joseph DeMers, "Smoky and the Red Fire Engine," in Arthur L. Gates, Miriam B. Huber, and Frank S. Salisbury, eds., *Friends and Fun* (New York: Macmillan, 1931).

15. This corresponds with the child's inclination to animate the inorganic. But we are concerned here not with the working of the child's mind, but with what adults offer to it, and with what trends these adult fantasies represent.

or less distinct types can be recognized. The distinction appears to be created mainly by the criterion of *the degree of autonomy granted to the machine as a meaningful protagonist who is able to decide upon his own course of action.* In general, the more important the machine is in the story, the more will it-he-she be endowed with biological and psychological attributes.

This point is also borne out by the illustrations appearing in the machine books. Machines can be presented visually in a number of ways, matching the degree of their autonomy. Altogether, the emotional appeal to the child, to understand and love the machines, seems to spring more forcefully from their high-powered, conspicuous images than from the repetitious texts. The illustrators have an important share in the development of the genre.

Type 1. The machine can make no choice. There are stories in which machines are portrayed in a mild form of personification as having only slight emotional attributes. The emphasis is on the work done together, but mutual cooperation and respect pervade the story: men care for machines just as machines care for men. In Virginia Burton's *Mike Mulligan and His Steam Shovel*, both work better when admiring people watch their common effort. In the end, they bask together in the town's esteem. The driver of "The Taxi That Hurried" is proud of his smart little car: *"We're* a speedy pair" (our italics).[16] Jean Berg's *Tuggy the Tugboat* and Captain Larson grow old together and do not easily adjust to technological change. "We like steam boilers, don't we?"; in the end they are happier than they ever were before.

Ivor the Engine, by Oliver Postgate, lived in a shed and did its work conscientiously, in harmony with its human operators. One day, however, Ivor hears the choral society practicing. From that moment he is not his old self anymore. That night he went to bed very, very sad. Soon the humans notice; he is examined, and the examiner states, ". . . mechanically speaking, I've never seen a better one. It's my belief he's upset. You haven't spoken to him harshly, have you?" In the end, the human operators find out what is wrong because a tear drops from Ivor's window. Organ pipes are fitted to him, the choral society looks forward to his participation, and the railway company agrees to it. Before the rehearsal starts, Ivor suddenly felt funny in his boiler. Nervous he was. But then he was so pleased that he quite forgot to feel nervous. The story ends with the choral society standing and singing with Ivor on the railway tracks—*ad maiorem machini gloriam*—as in olden times people gathered close to the organ, only the organ did not weep, and people did not sing to help it. But now, similar to what happened in *Tootle*, Ivor's psychomechano-therapy is carried out, as it says on the dust jacket, with the help of nearly everybody else in that part of Wales.

The "Washing Machine Golden Arrow" by Liukko-Sundström is another example. After being thrown onto the rubbish heap, then found by a young couple with a baby who cleaned it, Golden Arrow was so happy that it started working at once.

---

16. Lucy S. Mitchell, Irma S. Black, and Jessie Stanton, "The Taxi That Hurried," in Buell, *Treasury*.

These machines are not quite autonomous, but man's superiority over them is only slight; the machines cannot operate without aid, and, most important, they are alive.

Type 2. The machine can make choices but chooses to cooperate only with a human. While the accent is as yet on the machine's performance, the emotional attachment becomes more outspoken and the machine more central as protagonist. *Maybelle the Cable Car* by Virginia Burton tells the story from the cable car's point-of-view of how San Francisco's cable cars were saved by the enthusiasm of the city's inhabitants. While at the beginning the story relates that she (the car) has a conductor and a gripman, in the end she, in an autonomous decision, gratefully invites the people to a free ride. The reader is told what she and her sisters think, remember, and feel; the difference between machines and human beings is felt less. *Henriette Bimmelbahn* by Krüss and Stich is actually a grandmother figure; together with her engineer she chugs on, readily leaves the rails to bring the children to the woods, waits patiently until the last of them has picked all the flowers he wants; together with the engineer she is very upset when the train collides with a cow, and returns home tired but still good-natured (this is one story in a series).

Type 3. The machine makes a heroic, hence autonomous, choice on behalf of humanity. This type is the newest version of the "tale of the young hero," the hero being the machine. In the face of grim odds and after dangerous adventurous exploits, the hero is victorious, and the spice of the story is provided by the contrast; whoever was strong and powerful suddenly finds himself dependent on the achievements of one who was until now held to be small, helpless, bashful, and inferior.

In fact, this type is a transmutation, a continuation, of the age-old myth of the young hero, one of the oldest and most persistent motifs in mythology, legend, and literature, whose profound psychological significance has been analyzed, in our time, by many writers.[17] It is intimately connected with the motif of rebirth through suffering and has been told from time immemorial as the story of young gods and of mortals, bearing, for the weak and oppressed in every culture and for the small and subdued in any generation, the message of eternal hope—that one day the despised will stand out as saviors, restrain the mighty, and administer justice. Moses and Pharaoh, Joseph and his brothers, David and Goliath, Hercules and his tasks, Siegfried and the dragon, Cinderella and her stepmother and stepsisters are variants of this paradigm. During the last decades, with the development of children's literature, this motif has been reworked countless times in stories

---

17. Among the important authors who have treated the subject one might mention:
Otto Rank, *The Myth of the Birth of the Hero*, trans. by F. Robbins and S. E. Geliffe (New York: Journal of Mental and Nervous Disease, 1914).
Joseph Campbell, *The Hero*.
Erich Neumann, *The Origin and History of Consciousness*, vol. 1, trans. by F. C. Hull (New York: Harper/Bollingen, 1954).
Vladimir J. Propp, *Morphology of the Folklore*, trans. by Laurence Scott (Austin: Univ. of Texas Pr., 1970).

of adventurous young children who are held in scorn, doggies, kittens, young bears, etc., who defy the authority of their elders and return triumphant, having learned something about themselves and the world, and so forth. On the way, the motif has often acquired a trivial or picayune mode; yet its unflagging universal popularity testifies to its psychological significance. It has also become the nucleus of accounts of adventurous and misjudged young machines.

The *Little Red Engine* by Rahel Caspi is held in contempt by the big overland streamlined locomotives. All he does is slowly trudge his way over small distances. Yet the day comes when the super engine bearing the king and his entourage jumps the rails in a snowstorm. The stationmaster is in despair, but Little Red Engine saves the day. After an excited dialogue between the two, the stationmaster entrusts the undersized engine with the king's train. During his long journey, the engine good-naturedly talks with engines, frogs, and people. After triumphantly entering the capital, he returns home and, acclaimed by all the big, important engines, returns to his former modest life, full of inner happiness.

Young Homer is a shiny red caboose. In Hardie Gramatky's story he is gay, "lively as a newborn colt . . . railroad steam is in his blood, and there's adventure in his eye." He becomes separated from his train and makes friends with animals, human beings, and an old engine of a circus. When they all are in danger of being derailed and thrown into the deep gorge, Homer, putting his right wheel forward, in concert with the animals and against incredible odds, saves them and himself from certain death. No human intervention is needed. Human beings appear only at the end of the story, when the whole town turns out to acclaim Homer the hero and to cheer the brave animals.

The main characteristics of this type of story are these: The hero is inferior and weak, and he is an outsider; a catastrophic situation of some kind— storm, fire, breakdown, and so forth—reveals the machine as the one and only rescuer; the task he fulfills is socially significant and connected more or less with his work or function as a machine; and in the end the former social stigma is replaced by grateful recognition of his feats.

Up to this point, the type follows the general outline of the young hero story. It differs from it in two ways: (1) While the traditional young hero becomes, after his return, the leader of his kind, this is not true here: socially he becomes equal to them but subsides into his old position. The achievement of a leadership position is not as important as gaining full social status by proving oneself and shedding one's role as an outsider. (This is also true of the modern young child-hero and the animal-hero.) (2) The other dissimilarity results from the peculiar nature of the new hero. He usually maintains cordial relations, based on mutual understanding, with humans and occasionally with animals. They all live in "one world."

Actually, this is a mixed type, considering the extent of autonomy. Some of the machines depend upon the close cooperation of men in their work;

others operate in full autonomy, driven by their own discernment and conscience.

Type 4. The machine is taught, by experience and human guidance, that attempts at autonomy are not successful. Stories of this type state unequivocally that a machine should act in a responsible way. It is one form of the modern moralizing and cautionary tale.

Some of these machines become involved in adventures because they feel an urge to be free of the restrictions placed upon them by man: they are essentially inferior to and dependent on human beings, and while they are allowed to enjoy the adventure, they learn that work and responsibility are preferable.

In "The Story of a Holiday" by Berestov, the truck for once wanted to have a good rest on his day off. He felt hot under his roof and left. The green traffic light winked, saying, "Where is your driver?" The automobile understands the problem: "I cannot run alone, and still I do run alone; so what? It's my day off today, and it would be a sin not to go for a trip." Reflecting further on his own strange situation, he finds that they probably decided to direct him by radio. So what, after all this is the twentieth century, the century of miracles, he concludes: Let's go on! The truck pulls off the road and into the woods. The drops of resin smell, so he thinks, not worse than gasoline. After a good rest, his responsibility asserts itself again, and wandering lonely between oaks and birches, he collects a full load of mushrooms which he carries back to his garage. Now he is happier and carries his loads better.

Choo Choo, again, is the story of a little engine who ran away. Normally the little engine had an engineer, a fireman, and a conductor; she pulled passenger cars and a baggage car and did her job well. One day, however, she was tired and told herself that she could go farther and easier by herself. She escapes, goes wild, jumps over an open drawbridge, rushes through the big railway yard, and loses her way. When she is rescued by the combined efforts of many people, she is very glad to be found and tells Jim, the engineer, that she will not run away again.

Choo Choo's adventures are described as delightful, precisely because the machine is normally operated by human beings, yet the cautionary accent is there. In other stories the moralizing intention is stronger and more outspoken. The human operator disappears and the engine acts on his or her own.

"The Little Freighter" by Lambart is socially a lower-class boat; other boats deride her: she is so squat, so deep in the water. When she is unloaded, she dances lightly on the water and feels better, more like the others. Then she becomes frightened in a storm—"Oh dear, what is happening to me?"—is again derided by her fellow boats, and wishes to be loaded again and deep and safe in the water; then the other boats will not be jealous. Adventure teaches that it is best to keep one's social station and acquiesce in it.

Tootle by Gertrude Crampton is an outstanding example of close mutual relations and understanding among humans, machines, and animals. Tootle is a young locomotive who goes to engine school. His fellow students are engines, his teachers men. The two main lessons taught in the school are "Stop at the red light" and "Stay on the rails no matter what." The reward for being a good student is to become a big streamliner. Tootle is one of the best students the school has had in a long time. Yet one day he finds out how delightful it is to leave the tracks and to look for flowers, so "the dreadful thing" happens, and Tootle becomes quite giddy with all the sunshine, flowers, and frogs. He is seduced by a black horse and races it across the fields. Tootle's human teachers are consternated. Tootle's fellow (engine) students look down upon him. The school principal informs the mayor, who in turn alerts the citizens, and all combine to return Tootle to the track. By holding up red flags wherever he turns in his escapades among the flowers, they bewilder him; then he discovers his teacher, who stands on the track signaling him with the green flag. The young engine who was so enthusiastic about flowers and fell in love with a horse is chastised by men's care and solicitude. By foregoing his individualistic leanings and conforming to the signals, he will earn an A + .

The notable characteristics of this type of story are, then, rather narrowly moralistic. The spirit of adventure leads to errors of judgment and to disaster. One's elders know better, so one should listen to them and prove oneself by hard work and keeping to one's station in life.[18]

These books constitute a small sample of the existing literature in many countries. They made their appearance a long time ago: Merkelbach mentions the story of a personified machine, "The Dear Train" by Wilhelm Schulz, published in 1926.[19] Piper's *The Little Engine That Could* came out in 1930. A list of machine literature for children and adults by H. Künnemann, contains some two hundred items in six languages, many of them stories about personified machines.[20] Numerous machine stories have been published in Great Britain.[21]

The anthropomorphic machine has gained importance mainly in picture books for children aged three to seven. But it has not stopped there. It has also appeared—influenced by contemporary scientific developments—in literature written for older children, especially in the form of stories about androidal robots.

This type of literature has an interesting early forerunner, *The Wizard of Oz*. Two man-made creatures, very different from each other, appear in the

18. This last aspect of *Tootle* has been exhaustively analyzed by David Riesman, Nathan Glazer, and Reuel Denney, *The Lonely Crowd* (New York: Doubleday, n.d.), pp. 129–31, 144. (Originally published: Yale Univ. Pr., 1950)

19. Valentin Markelbach, "Tendenzen im Bilderbuch der Zwanziger Jahre," in K. Doderer, and H. Müller, eds., *Das Bilderbuch* (Basel, Weinheim: Beltz, 1975), pp. 279–80.

20. Horst Künnemann, *Bibliographie Muse und Maschine* (Munich: International Youth Library, 1965).

21. Hamish Fotheringham, *List of English Books on Anthropomorphic Machines* (Munich: International Youth Library, 1966).

story. One is the Scarecrow. He knows that " 'I don't know anything. You see, I am stuffed, so I have no brain at all,' he answered sadly." The last word proves that at least he has emotions. As the story develops he demonstrates no little helpfulness, and he has the great advantage of never being tired. The other man-made figure is the Tin Woodman. He is made of tin yet he once was a perfect human being who lost his biological body, part by part, because of his stubborn love for a girl that was opposed by some wicked woman. Limb after limb was replaced with a tin one made by a tinsmith. Now he has no heart and so does not care. Yet he *feels* that something is missing. This modern fantasy is halfway between Hans Christian Andersen and the latter half of the twentieth century: the animation of the inanimate is possible because the setting is a magic country, and a magically endowed girl performs it in harmony with the age-old tradition. On the other hand, the problems of how superior man is to his creations and of humanization-dehumanization definitely have a modern ring. The Scarecrow and the Tin Woodman are man-made contraptions able to emotionally appeal to humans.

Children's books about robots, inspired by adult science fiction, treat robots as equal to humans. The two following examples are representative. *Andy Buckram's Tin Men* by Carol Brink is an adventure story for boys. Its hero is a boy who builds robots out of tin cans. In the beginning they are ordinary robots fit for just one very simple job and operated by an ordinary current. At a certain moment in the story, however, lightning that strikes them causes a transformation: while they still have no minds, in their new state of electrification they are able to understand human language. From then on—actually even before this point—human beings relate to the robots, have feelings for them, attempt to make them feel joyful. The three children, a boy and two girls, one a baby, intermingle with the four robots, one "girl" and three "boys," one a baby, and rely on them for their safe return from danger; yet the role of the mastermind remains securely with Andy.

The most curious element is the development of Campbell, the youngest of the robots. As the story evolves it becomes clear that he is a mutation of the traditionally despised and later victorious young hero. Campbell arouses emotions from the first. For about two-thirds of the story he is liked by all the female figures in the book and held in scorn by his creator; he, too, develops the power of emotion. Later, he saves the human baby from the big bear, and Andy recants and recognizes the real hero in him. At the same time, Campbell has somehow matured.

The story ends in a strange way. Because of a wrong command given by Andy, the robots row away, and they and the boat are lost. Andy and his girl friend very speedily console themselves for the loss by prying out of the sand a new tin can, the start of a new batch of robots. This throws a strange light on the emotional attachments that evolved through the almost two hundred pages of the story: there is a certain inconclusiveness concerning the relations between men and their machines.

The Runaway Robot by Lester Del Rey is the story of a robot's indelible friendship with the son of his owners, as told by Rex the robot himself. His personality is very rich in its emotional possibilities: Rex learns to worry, to care, and to act independently. He is motivated by love and can even be happy. He becomes involved in moral questions when a police sergeant informs him that he will have to learn that humans say a lot of irresponsible things. Humans aren't as reliable as robots.

While the question of superiority of human over robot is not solved, it is clear that the hero is the robot, not the boy.

PSYCHOLOGICAL ROOTS

These, then, are some of the animated artifacts and machines that serve as protagonists. The child reader is supposed to identify with them, their adventures, and their visual images; he is asked to learn from them and to emulate them; he is induced to relate to them; it is assumed that in his fantasy he will look upon them as communicating with him. The machines are his and her benign and benevolent partners. They constitute a new and questionable type of hero. By extending the limits of animism, modern fantasy has originated *the story in which animated and personified objects and machines are equal to and often superior to the human beings* with whom they live together in one world.

Children's literature is not, and never has been, an isolated phenomenon. Very early in the evolution of modern technology, the overt attitude of admiration and pride, and the usually covert one of uneasiness, ambivalence, and fear, created an unconscious conflict about machines in the mind of Western man. As so often in the individual and collective history of man, when he is confronted with an ambivalent mental attitude toward forces that seem to be beyond his control, he turns, in his attempt to solve the conflict, to the device of projecting onto these forces the human attributes of emotion, reason, and volition by way of animation and personification. In this manner the modern anthropomorphic myth of the machine for adults is born. Its imagery is symptomatic of man's concern with his role in society and with his human essence. The animated machine in children's literature is just one branch of a growing myth.

Animation and personification of the inanimate are not rational processes—not the recognition of something that exists objectively, but symptoms of irrational, and largely unconscious, processes, a projection of human characteristics onto objects that in fact cannot actually possess them. This is natural in children. When it is done by adults, even for children, and consistently over a long period, it reveals the problematic importance of this category of objects: the personification of the machine as human is, then, the result of a repressive tendency, a transformation, a masking, in the face of mounting anxiety.[22]

Specifically, animation and personification that portray the inanimate object as benevolent and intimately responsive, as existing on the same level as man, symbolize the intensification of anxiety to an unbearable degree. The conflict is ousted from consciousness by the projection of humane, attractive, and pleasing attributes onto the objects. Thus the conflict is hidden or at least disguised. The machine that has a soul or mind is not dangerous anymore; it is reasonable. This is, of course, a double delusion because it assumes that human beings, having soul and mind, are reasonable by that token.

DEHUMANIZATION

The process of projection has a reverse side, an almost natural correlate: the sense of inferiority engendered by the machine seeks relief through one more defense mechanism, the process of identification.

The functioning of this unconscious mechanism, together with the ubiquitousness of machines in modern life, makes it understandable why, supplementing the attribution of human characteristics to machines, modern fantasy for children and for adults alike offers so many instances of conferring machine-like traits upon human beings. This feature is typical for a technological civilization that struggles for its maturity. It can be documented by examples on all levels of the creative arts. In much of the creative expression of our time, in art and in science, there can be found a strange, growing awareness of man and machine living in one world and drawing nearer to the point of becoming, in a sense, mutually interchangeable.

Even this began in the nineteenth century. McLuhan made the point that, as early as 1872, Samuel Butler's *Erewhon* explored the curious ways in which machines were coming to resemble organisms not only in the way they obtained power by digestion of fuel but in their capacity to evolve into new types of themselves with the help of the machine tenders. Butler saw, says McLuhan, that this organic character of the machine, was more than matched by the speed with which people who minded them were taking on the rigidity and thoughtless behaviorism of the machine.[23]

One day, probably, Walt Disney's animated cartoons will be recognized as a major symbol of this process of mutual interchangeability: are those jerky creatures not both mechanical men and hominoid mechanisms?

How serious is all this? Serious enough to attract the attention of the

---

22. The psychoanalyst Reik once stated that the conscious knowledge of the nature of a mechanical device could sometimes coexist with a nonrational magic conception of an instrument. The two views were on different psychical levels and could contradict each other only if both were conscious: Theodor Reik, *Listening with the Third Ear* (New York: Farrar, 1949), p. 114.

23. Herbert M. McLuhan, *The Mechanical Bride: Folklore of Industrial Man* (New York: Vanguard, 1951), p. 99.

scientist, the psychologist, and the philosopher. Norbert Wiener, who created cybernetics, once said that it would be wrong to assume that machines
could not possess any degree of originality, or to assert that machines made
by man must remain continually subject to man. *The Sorcerer's Apprentice* and
the story of the genie and the fisherman in the *Arabian Nights* are, to his
mind, just two of the tales which are based on the assumption that agencies
created or liberated by man might be both effective and dangerous.[24]
Fromm,[25] Bettelheim,[26] Tillich,[27] and Grotjahn[28] are only a few among the
scholars who have grown apprehensive about the confusing relationship
modern man develops towards the objects and machines he makes.

In children's literature all this finds expression in the machine hero who is
proffered to child readers and viewers as an object of admiration: He-She the
artifact will not fail them, will not stop thinking of and feeling for them.
He-She may be emulated and identified with.

THE POWER OF THE ILLUSTRATOR

The convincing impact of the machine stories really originates with their
illustrations. In few kinds of stories is the visual image so decisive in
influencing the child's willingness to be impressed.

A number of these books, classics by now, are illustrated extremely well.
Choo Choo is a book of exemplary beauty to this day. The author-artist,
working with charcoals, creates a mood of continuous motion, of rising
excitement gripping humans and engines. Together with them we are
thrown, by her swift lines and forceful shapes, into centripetal and centri-
fugal gyrations, with some moments of rest in between. The contrast of the
black and white technique heightens the tension as the plot develops. The
pictures vary considerably in size and structure, and in point-of-view. Each
one is composed with an unfailing sense for the distribution of the visual
forces applied in it.

Tootle is different. No doubt it is one of the most original machine tales. Its
illustrations are truly funny and telling. The plain, plastic style of the
illustrator makes it easy for the child to look at the pictures in the book
almost without noticing that full-color pages alternate with black-and-white
drawings in the text; we never lose contact with Tootle, the student engine
who learns his profession in school. Characterization is vivid; it is difficult
not to be stirred—in a way that is beyond the power of the text—by the
picture of young and unexperienced Tootle who has jumped off the rails,
moodily lying in the grass, while five groups of railway workers, railway
engines and ordinary, well-disposed citizens, all of them wearing a worried

24. Norbert Wiener, "Some Moral and Technical Consequences of Automation," *Science*, 6 May 1960, pp. 1355–58.
25. Erich Fromm, *Man For Himself: An Inquiry into the Psychology of Ethics* (New York: Rinehart, 1947).
26. Bruno Bettelheim, *The Informed Heart: Autonomy in a Mass Age* (Glencoe: Free Press, 1960).
27. Paul Tillich, "Modern Man and Freedom," interview in *The Listener*, December 14, 1961, p. 1025–26.
28. M. Grotjahn, *The Voice of the Symbol* (New York: Dell, 1973).

expression on their faces, debate how they might best help the transgressor to mend his ways; or by the other picture, where Old Bill, the principal of the school, confronts Tootle with the portrait of his ideal, the New York-Chicago Flyer. They make us laugh; yet the moral is unmistakable.

The trend that is recognizable in the illustrations in *Tootle*, exaggeration, especially in the portrayal of the machine heroes, becomes very outspoken in many machine books, probably also because of the influence of comics and Disney's animated cartoons. Over the years, hosts of machine heroes have appeared, distinguished by their ever-appealing demeanor and by human features that are overstated in coyness, naiveté, vulnerability, or smugness.

In the earlier books such as *Choo Choo* or *Tuggy*, there is no personification, or only slight personification as in *The Little Engine That Could*, where the funnel becomes a face whose expression changes perceptibly with changing circumstances. The face is more bizarre in *Mike Mulligan and His Steam Shovel*. Or, as in Gramatky's *Hercules*, where a human head is simply added and protrudes from the fire engine without becoming part of its structure, so that it looks like a baby in his carriage. In *The Magic Bus* by Dolbier, Jenny twists her front fenders and wheels and headlights when she feels the children's affection, for that is what Jenny always needed.

The more autonomous the machines become, the more personification tends to take over the whole body (robots are usually drawn as pseudo-humans). In *The Little Red Caboose That Ran Away*, by Polly Curren, the whole caboose turns into a face. Rafa's *Mr. Frelon*, a helicopter who rises to heroism in wartime, is represented as a perfect blending of a soldier in battle dress having the outlines of a helicopter, featuring one hand and some landing wheels, a propeller on top of his beret and eyes that also serve as searchlights. The truck in "Holiday Story" actually undergoes a metamorphosis while he roams the forest. In the first of four pictures that illustrate the poem he looks like a truck, with just a hint of an animal face. Successively his body and wheels change until in the fourth picture, on the cover, he is somewhere between a truck and a dog. Transformation may also work in the opposite, dehumanizing direction. In *Queen Esther and the Bulldozer*, by Avi-Yonah, a boy's body and limbs change, by stages, into a bulldozer.

As the years go by, redundancy sets in. Decades after Tootle jumped off the rails to escape to the countryside in 1946, Bertrand Solet's *Little Train (Who) Goes Away* does so again, because nobody loves him, to the surprise of the musing cows.

Throughout, the idea of people, animals, plants, objects, and machines living together in one animated world is reinforced by having them mingle freely, care for each other and communicate most naturally, in the illustrations. Their easy mutuality is exhibited chiefly by the way they look at each other, with admiration, tense compassion, or glowing happiness. The illustrator of Krasikov's *Tales* personifies a piano and an accordion at its side, a tree with eyeglasses and a tractor conversing with a tank, not to mention a few animals performing human tasks; he also includes a number of human people. Snunith's poem "What am I going to be when I grow up?" offers to the child some unusual personal goals for self-fulfilment: the boy in the poem wishes to become, in this order, a tower, a motorcycle, a clock, a whistle, a captain and, after his return from the sea, a car. Three machines, two objects and one human being. The illustrator introduces his own strong accents, with the illustrations being about ten times as large as the text. He excludes the captain and the car; the captain is represented by a ship on the high seas, one more machine. In the center is the daydreaming boy's head; behind him roll the huge gales of the sea and the daydream, while on his head stands a large, heavy alarm clock. This is a symbolic expression exactly analogous to the motif Riesman, Glazer and Denny detected in *Tootle*: the contest between the wish for freedom and the forces demanding responsible functioning.

A grotesque strain pervades many of the stories and exerts its spell on the illustrators. There are Chuggy the little engine and Lucy the Caboose, created by Lydia and Don Freeman, in love with each other, bashful, happy living beings, communicating with the railway workers. Yet when the switchmen celebrate Chuggy's heroic deed they do so *inside Lucy*, the warm living-loving object. Then there is Lornsen's Tobbi, the boy who, together with Robbi the computer, constructs a flying machine; they are shown sitting *inside it*, smiling; the flying machine, too, exhibits a broad smile. Another story of love fulfilled is *Ra ta ta tam* by Peter Nickl, where a small locomotive springs to life to join her beloved creator, little strange Matthaeus, after harrowing adventures. Delicate illustrations, done in a fantastic style with surrealist elements, create the rich, satisfying lyrical mood of a dream, and beautifully and impressively stress the ecological idea that the small locomotive who continually issues clouds of steam and chooses to forsake the sooty city and live with Matthaeus in a village high up in the mountains is an agent of environmental renewal. Mahood's *Clanky*, the junior robot who has been adopted by a human couple and sent to school, is depicted as failing at the blackboard, when he reckons that $2 \times 2 = 7$. But we know—do we really need the text to assure us?—that within a few weeks he will be top of the form, towering above his teacher and his human fellow students intellectually as he already does now physically. And there are all those machines ogling at flowers and butterflies and elks and children and adults, with their smiling headlights, which *perceive* light, like animals, at the same time that they *emit* beams of light.

Even though there is admittedly much clever humor in these pictures; even though they are beloved of children and adults alike (*The Little Engine That Could* has sold millions of copies; *Robbi, Tobbi* etc., has been mentioned for a German award in juvenile literature, and so on); even though we know that those pictures may easily be justified on psychological grounds by the child's animistic mode of thinking; even though it is no doubt true that, according to psychological theory many of the machines are phallic symbols and mother symbols and other dream symbols, an aspect which we did not touch upon in spite of its importance, because we did not want to overload the argument; even if it is certainly necessary that the illustrator should be responsive to the child's fascination with machines, engines, and apparatuses and appliances and everything that moves and has a rhythm of its own—we suggest that adult illustrators catering to the child's fantasy should be made aware that the representation of man-made mechanical or electronic shapes as organic does not contribute to the child's sound aesthetic and spiritual maturing.

THE ANTHROPOMORPHIC MACHINE
AS AN EDUCATIONAL EXPERIENCE

If the hypothesis offered is correct, and benevolent animation is the result of anxiety repressed and forced into the unconscious, to reappear in the form of human characteristics projected onto the machine, then stories about animated objects, written and illustrated by adult writers and artists for children, are a medium through which adults unconsciously communicate to children their own repressed anxieties. If this is so, then this type of literature and art unwittingly prepares the child for acquiescence to a "one-world" situation,[29] for life in a society whose members experience an unconscious inferiority vis-à-vis machines and make an effort to adapt to them. Then engines can teach the rules of life; that is, they assume superego functions. Machines are looking at us—let us cherish their conformist righteousness. It may allay unconscious anxiety.

As repressed anxiety is clearly a psychological hindrance to the development of a healthy personality and to mature (as against dehumanized) adjustment to life, children's literature of this kind cannot be viewed favorably from the educational point of view.

Another issue is the danger of functionalization of human relations in a machine age. The machine hero and its story can be easily recognized as a particularly apt medium through which to reinforce these tendencies: the machine's pride lies first and foremost in its functional perfection, in its flawless performance; it is satisfied with a relative paucity of relationships. The machine actually has no individuality; it has the typically trivial personality that is representative of, and unwittingly aids to prepare children for, the functional cooperative anonymity required by industrial society. In addition, machines almost never are allowed to play; they usually work and work and are quite happy with it. They are represented as children, but they do not live a child's life. They are happier and more adjusted when they do some useful work. They are reliable because they have learned that the spirit of adventure and of playfulness leads to disappointment. They are repre-

---

29. In the sense in which this term has been used in the present context: humans, animals, and machines living together.

sentatives of a very narrow functionalistic technical ethos: when you conform to the expectations others have of you, you will be satisfied and fulfilled. This is a misrepresentation of the child's reality.

Should so much weight be attached to a type of literature that is, after all, only one among many? Again and again one is tempted to put these stories aside and shrug them off.

But then, these stories are read by millions of children. Psychological, sociological, educational, and scientific writing makes it clear that they are but one facet of that modern myth which has sprung up in our era, and not a myth alone: the struggle between the dehumanization of man and its alternative, the humanization of industrial society, takes place both in man's fantasy and his reality on the psychological as well as on the technological level. Erikson once warned psychologists and educators that our child-training customs had begun to standardize modern man, so that he might become a reliable mechanism prepared to adjust to the competitive exploitation of the machine world.[30] Certain modern trends in child training seem, to him, to represent a magic identification with the machine, analogous to identification of primitive tribes with their principal prey.

To some extent man has become trained to conform to standardization. To another extent man struggles to assert his humanity over the machine.

What the child needs are books and images that are conducive to the maturing of his own humanness, by offering him sound objects for identification that guide him to enjoy and respect life and the living; in the present context, by emphasizing the superiority of the person to the machine.

CHILDREN'S WORK CITED

ANDERSEN, HANS CHRISTIAN. *H. C. Andersen's Fairy Tales.* Trans. by L. W. Kingsland. New York: Walck, 1962.

AVI-YONAH, HAVA. *Esther Hamalkah Vehadahpor.* Tel Aviv: Am Hasserfer, n.d.

BAUM, FRANK L. *The Wonderful Wizard of Oz.* Illus. by W. W. Denslow. Chicago: Hill, 1900.

BERG, JEAN H. *Tuggy the Tugboat.* New York: Wonder Books, 1958.

BERESTOV, VALENTIN. "Skazka pro vykhodnoi den." In *Kartinki v Luzhakh.* Illus. by M. Miturich. Moskva: Izdatelstvo Detskii Mir, 1962.

BRINK, CAROL R. *Andy Buckram's Tin Men.* Illus. by W. T. Mars. New York: Viking, 1966.

BURTON, VIRGINIA L. *Choo Choo: The Story of a Little Engine Who Ran Away.* Boston: Houghton Mifflin, 1937.

——. *Maybelle the Cable Car.* Boston: Houghton Mifflin, 1952.

——. *Mike Mulligan and His Steam Shovel.* Boston: Houghton Mifflin, 1939.

CARROLL, LEWIS. *Through the Looking Glass.* New York: Macmillan, 1943.

CASPI, RAHEL. *Ma'assah bekattar kattan adamdam.* Illus. by Zvi Malewanczik. Tel Aviv: El Hama'ayan, n.d.

CRAMPTON, GERTRUDE. *Tootle.* Illus. by Tibor Gergely. New York: Simon & Schuster, 1946.

CURREN, POLLY. *The Little Caboose That Ran Away.* Illus. by Peter Burchard. New York: Wonder Books, 1952.

DEL REY, LESTER. *The Runaway Robot.* Philadelphia: Westminster, 1965.

DEMERS, JOSEPH. "Smoky and the Red Fire Engine." In *Friends and Fun,* edited by Arthur L. Gates, Miriam B. Huber, and Frank S. Salisbury. New York: Macmillan, 1931.

30. Erik H. Erikson, "Ego Development and Historical Change," *Identity and the Life Cycle. Psychological Issues,* vol. 1 (New York: International Univ. Pr., 1959), p. 46.

DOLBIER, MAURICE. *The Magic Bus.* Illus. by Tibor Gergely. New York: Wonder Books, 1948.

FREEMAN, DON, and LYDIA FREEMAN. *Chuggy and the Blue Caboose.* New York: Viking, 1951.

GOETHE, JOHANN W. "Die Wandelnde Glocke." In *Goethe's Gedichte.* Berlin: Minerva, n.d.

GRAMATKY, HARDIE. *Hercules.* New York: Putnam, 1940.

————. *Homer and the Circus Train.* New York: Putnam, 1957.

HATCH, MARY C. "The Talking Pot." In *Thirteen Danish Tales.* New York: Harcourt, Brace, 1947.

KRASIKOV, SERGEI P. *Basni.* Illus by A. Eliseyev. Moskva: Izdatelstvo Malysh, 1973.

KRÜSS, JAMES, and LISL STICH. *Henriette Bimmelbahn.* Berlin: Kinderbuchverlag, 1956.

LAMBART, CLARA. "Little Freighter." In *Believe and Make Believe*, edited by L. S. Mitchell and I. S. Black. New York: Dutton, 1956.

LIUKKO-SUNDSTRÖM, HELJÄ. "Satu Pesakone Kultanualesta." In *Heljän lempeitä satuja.* Helsinki: Otava, 1977.

LORNSEN, BOY. *Robbi, Tobbi und das Fliewatüüt.* Illus. by F. J. Tripp. Stuttgart: Thienemann, 1967.

MAHOOD, K. *Clanky The Mechanical Boy.* London: Collins, 1971.

MITCHELL, LUCY S.; IRMA S. BLACK; and JESSIE STANTON. "The Taxi That Hurried." In *A Treasury of Little Golden Books*, edited by Ellen L. Buell. New York: Golden Press, 1960.

NICKL, PETER, and BINETTE SCHROEDER. *Ra ta ta tam: Die seltsame Geschichte einer kleinen Lok.* Hamburg, Mönchaltorf: Nord-Süd Verlag, 1974.

PALMER, HELEN. "Johnny's Machines." In *A Treasury of Little Golden Books*, edited by Ellen L. Buell. New York: Golden Press, 1960.

PIPER, WATTY. *The Little Engine That Could.* Illus. by Ruth Sanderson. New York: Platt and Munk, 1976.

POSTGATE, OLIVER. *Ivor the Engine.* Illus. by Peter Firmin. London: Abelard-Schuman, 1962.

RAFA. *Adon Frelon* (recording). Ramat Gan: Hed Arzi, 1968.

SCHULZ, WILHEIM. *Die liebe Eisenbahn.* Oldenburg: n.p., 1926.

SNUNITH, MIHAL. *May yesh li la' assoth?* Illus. by Avi Margalith. Ramat Gan: Massadeh, 1969.

SOLET, BERTRAND. *Le petit train s'en va. . . .* Illus. by Sylvie Buisson. Paris: Éditions la farandole, 1974.

"Der Topf." In *Europäische Volksmärchen*, edited by Max Lüthi. Zurich: Manesse, 1951.

14

The Role of the Illustration in the Child's Aesthetic Experience

CHILDREN'S BOOK ILLUSTRATION AS AN ART FORM

The illustrated children's book is a special case of visual communication. Its fictional forms and types, which have concerned us in this book, also make it a branch of art. It might be a strange one in the eyes of some of its observers. Certainly its mixed ancestry and lineage are apt to make some people raise their eyebrows: So many kinds of literature, so many visual media—plastic art, film, comics, advertising—so many didactic assumptions and educational philosophies have had a share in the development of this genre, that one may well be skeptical about its claim to be called an art. But here it is, alive and kicking, kicking very vigorously, growing in quantity and, we believe, in quality and exhibiting manifest proofs of its existence and identity.

It is an art form because it bears the characteristics by which we recognize art. It communicates in symbolic language; it expresses its intentions by creating, from verbal and visual elements, an aesthetic order carrying content and meaning; it creates illusions of realities which are partly similar and partly dissimilar to the one that men and women operate in practically; it uses figurative, metaphorical, and symbolic means to call forth a deceptive, imaginary world—richer, fuller of surprises, more astonishing, more innovative, more serious or humorous, more beautiful or else uglier, and also much tenser, dynamic and complex than our daily lives. It is supposed to take us away, for a period of time, from this narrow existence, and make us react to a deeper level and wider scope of life, beyond what we ordinarily accept as reality. It also strives to induce us to meet, consciously or unconsciously, ourselves. Does not the illustrated poem and story for children attempt to achieve all these?

The illustrator of children's books is not, of course, the only one who presents aesthetic objects to the child. On the contrary, the child's relatively small world is full of such objects vying with each other for attention. But he is the first one to present the child with aesthetic messages, symbolic deceptions which are specifically created for the child. He presents to him and her the first and almost only art form existing on a broad basis, which has the child in mind. The illustrator's potential importance for the aesthetic experience of the child is, then, considerable: the contents and structures he offers communicate to the child that there exist these illusory ways of breaking away, temporarily, from habitual settings; that there are dreams which may make one a little wiser or satisfied or curious or sad or just arouse a smile, and make it easier to return to the routine, which is slightly less important now. Art in children's books, as Doderer has put it, should have the effect of liberating the child from the excessive coercion of reality.[1] It does so by playing with expressive, significant, non-real structures.

The importance of illustrated books also stems from the fact that they exert their influence non-systematically. They are not, as textbooks are, taught in a consecutive order nor do they belong to a fixed hour of day. Their potential lies in their being around, to be taken up, loved, and preferred, or never to be looked at again, in an incidental fashion. This is their chance to leave a mark on the child's mind. It is irrelevant, in this respect, to what extent the child becomes aware of what is in a book, what a book does to him; some of the most significant things in life, and in man's encounter with art, happen on an unconscious level. It is relevant and of utmost importance that apart from the meanings the illustrator puts in his pictures, the child should be able to detect personal meanings, whether intended by the illustrator or not. This is one aspect of liberation through art. It requires that illustrations should be of different kinds—pictures offering clearly confined and outlined information (defined as "closed form" by Halbey), and another kind, whose composition should allow the individual perceiver to bring in personal associations ("the open form").[2] For perception is, lest we forget, a motivated, selective activity. The development of the child's aesthetic sense is an extended process in the course of which he and she also learns that every art specializes in the communication of knowledge and emotions that cannot be expressed in exactly the same manner in any other form, through artistic symbols which, though they are not translatable, may be supported and interpreted by the symbols of other arts.

Authors writing on aesthetic development and education offer a great many definitions of their objective: how to cultivate the growing child's ability to create, experience and appreciate art. However, it is possible to discern, among other things, two, though by no means neatly separated, attitudes. There are those for whom the principal objective lies in leading the child toward being capable and motivated to take part in the art life of his place and time, to take in beauty, harmony, drama, joy, laughter, as they are presented and represented by the arts, and to make the child a willing future customer of the aesthetic phenomena found in his society. To others, developing the child's aesthetic sense means more. In their eyes the importance of the aesthetic originates at existential, even evolutionary levels: man and woman have developed the ability to communicate and to be moved by

1. Klaus Doderer, "Illustrationen im Kinderbuch als Kunstprodukt," in Eva Šefčákova, ed., *Bienále Ilustracii Bratislava '67–'69* (Bratislava: Obzor, 1972), pp. 141–43.
2. Halbey, "Die offene und geschlossene Form im Bilderbuch," *Festschrift*, pp. 533–38.

symbolic forms, as part of their prolonged struggle to become spiritual beings. Symbolic forms have the power to reflect issues of individual and collective existence. Leading the child toward greater competence in aesthetic perception means aiding him and her to become more humane, to partake more in his unique human heritage. This process of humanization is partly congruent with, and partly very much distinct from, the process of socialization.

The ubiquitous illustrated book and its artist, or rather the good book and the superior illustrator, can play a role in the realization of these processes.

AFFECTIVE, ASSOCIATIONAL, AND AESTHETIC
RESPONSES TO ILLUSTRATIONS

The elements, structures, and strategies by which the illustrator offers to the child the possibilities of aesthetic experience have engaged us in the previous chapters of this book. Now we wish to recall a few aspects of the discussion and call more attention to others which were passed over too quickly. We shall attempt to do this aided by remarkable illustrators whose work is eminently conducive to the enhancement of the aesthetic experience.

Before we do so, we should stress two points concerning the nature of aesthetic perception. One is that the aesthetic stimulus arouses attention mainly by its emotional appeal. A picture attracts affectively first, followed by an attempt to understand what it contains and means. Attention may be triggered by a figure, by a combination of shapes and/or colors, by a corner of the picture whose details are utterly clear, or else misty and lacking distinct form. One picture may lead back to the text and on to the next picture. The first response is an affective one; it may arouse interest or terminate in indifference.

The other point concerns the difference, not to be neglected even with children, between contemplating a picture or a natural view, etc., and looking at an illustration. In the first case the highest degree that can be attained is what Weismann called "pure" seeing: attending to an object because it is valuable in itself, as distinct from operational (utilitarian) and associational seeing.[3] In the case of the illustration it is clear that it inspires associational seeing: it is connected to a text and reminds us of textual passages. Though surely all of us have seen children who get lost looking at an illustration for a long time, just as they are apt to repeat parts of the text over and over, the usual and natural course is to shift back and forth between the two media. For such is the nature of our art form. However, as the combined product, the illustrated story, evokes interest for its own sake, we may speak of "pure response" to an aesthetic object. Besides, it seems that associational responding is for many people and probably for most, if

3. Weismann, *Visual Arts*, pp. 18–21.

not all, children, a necessary developmental step toward "pure" responding, toward enjoying and appreciating art.

Let us recapitulate a few of the concepts we have introduced on how text and illustration may stimulate associational and "pure" responding by examining one excellent illustration and its text. It is the first page of *Tiny One*, a story we briefly referred to in chapter 2, about the first grade boy who had to suffer because of his small stature. The lower part of the page contains the text, relating how on the first day in school mother brings her son Peter to school, how she is a little ashamed because the other children are taller, how the teacher calls Peter Tiny One and the nickname sticks. Above the text nearly half of the page is left empty. Above that, a rather small strip, comes the illustration. We see Peter from behind, with a heavy schoolbag on his back; his head is partly cut off by the upper edge of the page. To his left stands his mother, to his right the teacher turns toward them, receiving them; of both adults we see only the lower part of their legs; the rest is above the margin; Peter, then, scarcely reaches up to their knees.

This is no imitation of reality. It is the figurative elucidation of a moment in the life of little Peter. The visual motif is dramatization. We see the boy high up on the page, entering a new, reputedly loftier world, the next stage in life. He is made to feel so small and inadequate that the grownups seem to be remote giants of whose countenance he is unsure. The spatial distribution of text, picture, and empty space in between also reinforces the sense of instability and of anxious anticipation. By his choice of elements and their arrangement on the page, the illustrator achieves a vibrant interpretation of the anguish gripping Tiny One, while the text describes the situation in plainly factual terms. The intention is to stimulate associations to what goes on in Peter's mind and to arouse empathy for him. At the same time the page, with its large empty space and the three faceless persons, opens possibilities for "pure" reflection on loneliness and frustration. The dramatic effect of this page, its emotional and cognitive significance, is the result of what its composition does to our perception. Very few children will be able to conceptualize why the picture may impress them as it does, and by what means. But the important point is this: the potential persuasiveness of the picture and the text together lies in the metaphorical reality created by the distribution of visual forces, and the opportunity this offers for associational and "pure" responding.

ABSTRACTION

Good books intending to develop the child's aesthetic sense can take many forms. *A Necklace of Jewels* by Eftimiu is a volume containing an adapted historical play for children. It is illustrated by dozens of colored sketches bordering on the text with changing accents on dress or suggestions for stage direction, and interspersed with a number of full-page pictures. It is a beautiful romantic introduction to the theatre. A book may bring to children the beauty of architecture by celebrating, in the guise of a child's dream, the radiant charm of a city, all sugar and spice, warm colors, and slightly funny figures as in Zavřel's *A Dream of Venice*. Or an illustrator may apply, in a children's book, the color symbolism propounded by the great abstract painter Kandinsky,[4] and create, in forty-one illustrations, an enchanting, stylized, almost mysterious version of Andersen's *The Nightingale*, where colors represent the flow of moods (fig. 66).

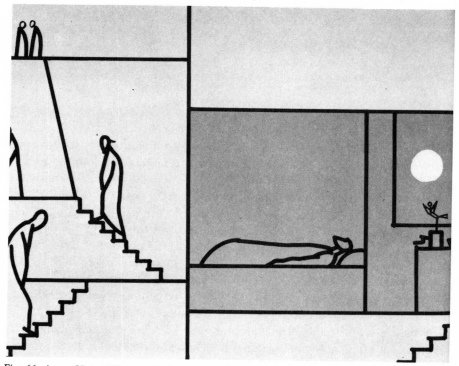

Fig. 66. Amos Hetz, "The search for the nightingale"
H. C. Andersen: *Hazamir*, The Dvir Co. Ltd., Tel-Aviv, n.d.

This last volume brings up abstraction. In a broad sense any pictorial representation of people and objects and backgrounds is an abstraction from reality. Even so there is a difference between the illustrator who wants to imitate reality faithfully and the one who does not care so much about this or rejects it (whatever the reason for this may be in art history). The effects will be different. Here, *The Nightingale*, with forty-one illustrations, page after page dominated by one or two colors only, and with firm black lines stylizing palaces, gardens, and figures, becomes a tense, introverted,

4. Wassily Kandinsky, *Concerning the Spiritual in Art and Painting in Particular 1912* (New York: Wittenborn, 1970).

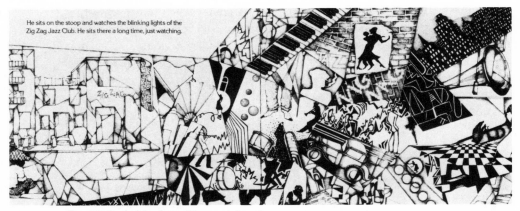

He sits on the stoop and watches the blinking lights of the Zig Zag Jazz Club. He sits there a long time, just watching.

Fig. 67. Rachel Isadora, "Ben watching"
From *Ben's Trumpet*, by Rachel Isadora, Greenwillow Books (A Division of William Morrow & Company), New York, and Angus and Robertson Publishers, Cremorne Junction, N.S.W. Copyright © 1979 by Rachel Isadora Maiorano.

ideational fantasy; in another book, pictures captivatingly characterizing Chinese seasons, landscapes, architecture, and fashions illuminate a yarn spun about strange and moving events that happened a long time ago in a faraway country, and thus widen the child's narrow horizon. If the story by Ursula Rellstab about the professor who travels around the world to catch the big red fish were illustrated by realistic pictures this would have underlined an intention of lightheartedly adding to the child's knowledge of what foreign countries, the sea, and all kinds of vehicles look like. As it is, the stylized ornamental patterns through which the realistically depicted professor moves suggest an experience that is more personal, internalized, basic: the motif of searching—for what? Happiness? Achievement?

Stylistic mode confines to an extent the associations that may give rise to aesthetic experience. We believe that the child should meet both the representational and the abstract mode in books, and also that the representation of reality in illustrations should not be a mere imitation.[5] That is why much significance is attached to books that succeed in combining representational and abstract means of expression, as happens in Isadora's *Ben's Trumpet*. It is the story (mentioned briefly in chapter 2) of a boy who dreams of playing the trumpet, until one day the trumpeter of the jazz club finds out about him and agrees to teach him. The first pictures show Ben, his neighborhood, and the club in an agitated, expressionistically enhanced reality with an abundance of visual rhythms in the lines of houses and streets (fig. 67). But then Ben manages to see the trumpeter in action and is struck by the sight—so the trumpeter is repeated six times in one picture. Suddenly white lines crowd in and zigzag across the page, creating the illusion of visible sound. From now on Ben is enraptured. So he recedes even more into his dream world; he

5. This is being stressed by many writers, for instance: Lucia Binder, "Die Illustration im Kinderbuch," Waltraut Hartmann et al., eds., *Buch—Partner des Kindes* (Ravensburg: Otto Maier, 1979), pp. 131–34.

cares only about playing his imaginary trumpet. This state of mind is illustrated by formal rhythms, encroaching on the pictures. Though we continue to see Ben, his family, his skeptical boyfriends, the visual sound patterns occupy part of every picture, changing from one page to the next. Only when the trumpeter takes on Ben as his student do things calm down, the rhythms disappear, the houses stand straight. This visualization of the boy's preoccupation with his dream, his withdrawal into himself, and his reawakening interest in the outside world which now offers wish fulfillment, is achieved by a blending of representational and abstract symbols of a quality that makes it aesthetically satisfying and psychologically meaningful.

This mutual intrusion in our mind of outer and inner reality is a basic theme in aesthetic creation, as it is in human existence. Let us take one significant instance of it. When we fall asleep and begin to dream, events, objects, sights, voices which aroused our interest during the day, residues of the outer world, experiences with which we have not done yet, trespass and trigger our fantasies, often fashioning our dreams. This is a universal dream mechanism that has survival value. The illustrator in children's literature touches upon this more often than we are usually aware of.

Thus, in *Where the Wild Things Are* (can one ever get far away from that book?) some main elements of Max's fabulous voyage and kingship are prefigured on the first two pages—by the puppet dangling from the clothes hanger, by the tent, the stool, and the blithe monster drawn by Max. Similarly, in Mayer's *There's a Nightmare in My Closet* the pachydermous benign Nightmare bears some resemblance to the billowing window curtain that might have inspired it. So, too, on the wall above the sofa on which Alan goes to sleep, in Van Allsburg's *The Garden of Abdul Gasazi*, hangs an etching of a landscape (fig. 68), much like the one through which the boy will wander a little later (fig. 69). And is it not Fritz the dog who is transformed into the magician of the dream? The dog's nose, protruding from under the sofa, suspiciously resembles Abdul Gasazi's chin; both are vicious, too, and in the end the dog has Alan's cap which he had lost to the magician. In each of these books an external object becomes a catalyzer of the motifs that are worked through and overcome in the dream sequence.

In this context let us return to Burningham's Shirley books (chapter 2). Here, again, we find the mutual infringement of outer and inner reality, albeit as contrast, the fantasy plot compensating for the frustrations of reality, dynamic independence versus static overprotectiveness, creating a common message. It teaches us that the human mind and human behavior are more complex than meets the (in this case, mother's) eye (fig. 70). It says something about the polyphonic ability of the human being.

The fact that illustrators can put their symbols and configurations to serious use and still create pictures so naturally humorous or dramatic, or both, on levels enjoyable for children and suitable to their perception and experience, is an important achievement.

Fig. 68. Chris Van Allsburg, "Alan asleep"

From *The Garden of Abdul Gasazi* by Chris Van Allsburg. Copyright © 1979 by Chris Van Allsburg. Reprinted by permission of Houghton Mifflin Company and Hamish Hamilton, Ltd., publishers in the United Kingdom.

Fig. 69. Chris Van Allsburg, "Alan's dream"

From *The Garden of Abdul Gasazi* by Chris Van Allsburg. Copyright © 1979 by Chris Van Allsburg. Reprinted by permission of Houghton Mifflin Company and Hamish Hamilton, Ltd., publishers in the United Kingdom.

That's the third and last time I'm asking you whether you want a drink, Shirley

Fig. 70. John Burningham, *Come Away from the Water, Shirley!*
Illustrations from *Come Away from the Water, Shirley!* written and illustrated by John Burningham. Copyright © by John Burningham. By permission of Thomas Y. Crowell, Publishers, and Jonathan Cape Ltd., Publishers.

INTERMEZZO: THE UNDESIRABLE

Before we continue the exploration of the ways by which the illustrated book can contribute to the development of the child's aesthetic sense, we cannot obviate the task of examining the undesirable. If we do so briefly, it is mainly because we chose to concentrate on superior illustrators and valuable pictures, and to treat the categories of the poor and the inadequate rather summarily, though somewhere in a hidden corner of our heart we believe that an anthology of such pictures might work wonders as an eye-opener for many persons who are responsible for the creation and distribution of illustrated books.[6]

What we consider to be aesthetically harmful is not, primarily, bad craftsmanship, though untalented artists, careless printing, cheap paper, and negligent binding are regrettable occurrences. But there is much more damage inherent in several categories of illustrations although or because they exhibit a high level of artistic talent, and the printing, paper, etc., are satisfactory. The books we are thinking of at this moment are created by gifted illustrators whose work attracts attention and exerts influence. To offer a simple example of what we mean: in chapter 2 we discussed the multipurpose illustration, the case of the one picture accompanying several poems. Some of these illustrations are meaningful, but the device easily deteriorates into the manufacture of sleek alluring pictures, made to order and lacking real expression. Talent does not assure quality, just as quality does not demarcate intention.

What we have in mind are illustrations which, in a remarkably effective way, cheat and deceive the child whose interest they arouse. The common denominator of a number of very diverse categories we refer to is lack of integrity.

6. We have, on other occasions, treated more elaborately two specific aspects of the undesirable: the lack of consistency (Joseph H. Schwarcz, "Meheymanutoh shel ha'iyyur besifrey yeladim," *Hahinukh*, Tel Aviv 5 [1969], pp. 427–42) and the aesthetic and pedagogic definition of Kitsch (Joseph H. Schwarcz, "Al hakitsch ba'iyyur," Problems in Children's Literature: A Symposium, *Eyyunim behinukh*, University of Haifa 3 [1974], pp. 79–98). Both articles are supported by illustrations.

Factual Inconsistency

There are more illustrators than we might assume who cheat the child's perception by presenting to him and her inconsistent imitations of reality. There are all those small and, frequently not so small, things: the girl's green necklace that is described as red in the text; the headphones worn according to the text but absent in the picture; the house of The Three Bears, whose elaborately designed chairs, blankets, beds, doors, and so on, vary in details considerably from one picture to the next; conspicuous changes in the countenance of prominent persons in a story, such as color of eyes, hair, and relative height. Examples like these can be found easily. They seem to result as much from slipshod work as from an inclination of illustrators to entertain themselves by playing with shapes and colors. In either case this shows that they do not care too much about the customer. But the child has the right to get books which are representationally consistent. This does not mean that the illustrator should abstain from introducing lively changes of sizes, proportions, angles, etc., according to his style. It means that figures, animals, objects, and backgrounds have to have a recognizable identity beyond these variations.

Lack of Authenticity

The desperate search by authors for a new, unheard-of-plot gives rise to contrived stories. It happens quite frequently that the illustrator tops the writer by using visual tricks. There exists a book about a tree who wandered through the countryside, homeless until the children saved him from being cut down, a story with ecological pretensions. Throughout the story the tree is pictured red; only when he is weak and in danger of falling down does he turn green. Then there is the book that relates how a girl, together with her cats, dogs, and bears, conquered the moon. This time the text and the pictures simulate scientific exactitude. For instance, there is no air on the moon, so the girl and her companions wear heavy headgear. But at the same time they plant a tree, which supposedly needs air and water. Or, in a story that is a variation of Andersen's *Ugly Duckling*, about a hen who hatches a little crocodile, the illustrator has no choice (except not accepting the job) but to faithfully portray them. These are a few examples of books whose illustrations are drawn or painted quite skillfully. They are artful rather than artless.

The unauthentic has many facets. The simplistic, affected representation of persons and animals and their artificial ways of communication are two particularly harmful ones. Putting pretentious accents on decorativeness is another one.

The Stereotypes and Their Exaggerations

The stereotype in art for children has been often described and deplored, and rightly so, because there is no greater enemy of the child's aesthetic and human development.[7] It is the very incarnation of the unauthentic.

---

7. An excellent concise treatment of the stereotype is Donnarae McCann and Olga Richard, "Stereotypes

There are the artificially sweetened landscapes, neighborhoods, and houses, ready for sale.

There are the perfectly beautiful, spotlessly clean, and naively infantile figures and animals with their famous large heads, ready to be loved.

There are the grimaces, the affected caricatures, and the outright grotesque physiognomies, ready-made to be laughed at.

The first category results in a persiflage of beauty; the second, in a parody of tenderness; the last one, in a suspension of humor and fun.

The multitude of books dedicated to the skillful celebration of these abominations fill the shelves, and the eyes of children and adults alike. Why? Because in any art form the stereotype, with its seemingly decent, innocent, and easily recognizable exaggerations, with its preference for the typical over the individual, has ever been, and will probably always be quantitatively dominant and qualitatively reputable. Books of this kind are also produced quickly and therefore usually with less expense. They also make extensive use of popular schemata advanced by the less fortunate creations in the domain of the animated cartoon, comics, and advertising. But there also exist more profound reasons for the widespread acceptance of stereotypes. The sweetly naive and the unblemished surely reflect an unconscious nostalgia, in adults, for a paradisical, gorgeous world that never was; the grimace reveals deep-seated adult hostility which can be comfortably alleviated by doing some artwork. But this explanation does not constitute a justification for abusing the child.

Excessive Beauty

Quite apart from the facile attractiveness of the stereotypes, there exist books whose rich, careful illustrations are of incontestable quality and usually accessible to the child's imagination. But their beauty spoils the text; we never get near it. As Alderson puts it, they swamp, crush, and overwhelm the text.[8]

Adult Level

An increasing number of illustrated books are being published which are over the heads of children. Their subject matter and its pictorial accompaniment are far beyond the child's perceptual, affective, and experiential horizons. This is a statement which we would ask the reader to accept judiciously, and to check against the books which we will discuss in the last part of this chapter. One can easily be wrong about the limits of a child's abilities. The more so, as here we are speaking of illustrators whose style and execution are full of interest and captivating. Yet not a few of them work with adults in mind, or just themselves, and not for children. This seems to be true, for instance, for some books created in a surrealist vein. We mention this with some reluctance, for there is much fascination and beauty in

in Illustration," *The Child's First Books—A Critical Study of Pictures and Texts* (New York: Wilson, 1973), pp. 19–21.

   8. Alderson, *Illustrators*, pp. 39–44.

surrealism, and no little affinity between its imagery and the child's imagination. But such books have to be conceived and executed carefully, with an eye on the child, and this is rarely done.

We should not let books of this kind, which themselves are an engaging product of the genre's rapid development, draw children prematurely into an adult world.

The Morbid

How else are we to define books like a picture book relating the fortune of a nose that got detached from its face (inspired by Gogol?). Or another quite gay one, whose text is adapted from Edgar Allen Poe, about the man who killed his wife and buried her behind the wall, until the cat's meow aided the police in discovering the crime. The list could be continued.

Lack of Understanding

Throughout these categories in children's illustrated literature are found the illustrators who do not understand the text and its possible meaning for the child. This happens either because they do not care to take the time to try to understand and so they pursue their own ideas; or, because the complexity or integrity of a story is beyond their grasp. This is not the same as what we called "deviation from the text" in chapter 2. Here we mean disregard; there we spoke of an illustrator's confrontation with the text.

Lack of Style

This refers not so much to illustrators who have not developed a novel and distinct style of their own as to a lack of unified style. We know a volume of poems, for instance, full of pleasing pictures; but it is a veritable collection of associations to known artists such as Rousseau, Magritte, Dufy, Kreidolf, and others. Adjusting the illustration to the mood of the poem is a good thing; but this is going too far. Similarly, there exists an edition of tales by Andersen, where the style and technique applied to many pictures change with almost every one of them. Pen drawings, photography, watercolors, montage, speech balloons and more, create partly romantic, partly "cool" moods within one and the same story, without any recognizable relation to the text. Such style mixtures may result in attractive pictures, but they leave one with the feeling of being played with, and removed from contact with the text. A lack of unified expression is detrimental to experience. If this happened in a writer's style, it would be noticed, and no one would justify it or be willing to accept it. It is a measure of our visual illiteracy that this is not true to the same degree with pictorial messages.

UNITY OF EXPRESSION

If a lack of unified expression detracts from the communicative power of an aesthetic message then, turning the statement around, unity of expression in a book is an essential element in stimulating an aesthetic experience. For it is this unity, as aesthetic theory has stated many times, which gives satisfaction because we are in the presence of a whole story, whose parts, pages, passages, and pictures gain their essential meaningfulness from being combined in a certain order and with certain intentions.

When we apply this principle to the consecutive sequence of illustrations in a book, an immediate corollary arises from the fact that the pictures come one after the other: time goes by while we turn the pages. Unity involves a time factor. Unified expression is created step by step, as some of the elements and configurations of expression reappear, unchanged or modified, according to the necessities of the evolving story. In serial messages aesthetic unity naturally implies continuity.

The artist illustrating a children's book has at his disposal the infinite possibilities of his art. He can balance and contrast materials, space, and colors; he can select patterns and play with them. Unity is achieved in various ways. But we frequently discern elements and motifs which are especially charged with the creation of that continuous sequential flow of impressions, the patterns of visual continuity in time.

It may be tone and texture. In *Circus Spaghetti* by Van Tuinen, a picture book made of torn paper, a yellow-red-brown motif appears on every page, attaching itself to different objects and moving along with us (excepting one page depicting a situation of great danger). In *Staying Home Alone on a Rainy Day* Iwasaki shows us misty textures, rain, and damp windows, suddenly clearing up in the last picture when mother returns home. In *The Snowman* by Briggs, the glowingly ice-cold charm of wintry textures leads us through exciting adventures toward the melancholic end.

It may be design. We have commented earlier on a number of books which are outstanding in this respect: The dynamic interplay of visual forces in *Choo Choo*; the waxing and waning of visual space in *Where the Wild Things Are*; the intricacies of *Thirteen* by Charlip-Joiner. Or take what we have just said about *Ben's Trumpet*: though each page is composed and structured differently from any other and the illustrations' functional change and point-of-view is manipulated extensively, a progressing rhythm arises from the way representational and abstract configurations are combined and imposes a pattern on the flow of events and moods.

In many books the effect is enhanced by the writer and the illustrator sharing a common approach and working in similar styles. We have already discussed important examples of this affinity of pictorial and textual expression, such as in the editions of *Beauty and the Beast* mentioned in chapter 10—one being stylized and elegant, the other emotional and dramatic; or several of the versions of Jonah. In some of these cases adaptor and illustrator are one and the same person. Garfield and Blishen's *The God Beneath the Sea* is an exceptional attempt at rendering Greek mythology as one successive tragic development, carried along by unmitigable passions. Charles Keeping's black and white illustrations heighten the excitement and deepen the despair. The stark expression in the faces and bodies of these gods and goddesses dramatically reflects their lust for power and lonesome bit-terness; long, drawn-out skeins and meshes of black lines dominate the pictures, symbolizing the misery that entangles them. Another example of close contact between author and illustrator is *A Dancer Had the Knack to Hope, He'd Dance a Little on the Rope* by Hans Halbey. It is a volume of sparkling inventive rhymes in the tradition of the nonsense verse, but definitely oriented toward the contemporary child living in the big city. The illustrator peoples his pages with four clowns who perpetrate, together with a few goblin companions, circus tricks and feints paralleling the author's play with words and situations found in the text. The illustrator supports the author's effervescence, pushing it a bit further toward the absurd.

Commensurability of styles is, as we know from "Variations on a Theme," only one of the means that may create unity. Contrast may be another one. More than that, as we shall see presently when we discuss the books of Ezra Jack Keats, personal creative expression can be based on a discrepancy of the verbal and visual styles of one person.

Probably the most important factor, or even condition, by which the significance of a sequence of illustrations that is a pattern of unity in time can be brought about, is the representation of the protagonist, the hero of the story, whether child, adult or animal. He appears again and again; it is on him that the child concentrates; he or she is supposed to arouse admiration, empathy, or even identification. In a good book the other means serving unity link up, tie in with the central figure, and aid him in becoming the focus of interest. From the rich store of intuition and style arise untold possibilities of inventing convincing images. Two elements seem to be essential in accomplishing this:

One is the representation of the hero as an individual person, recogniz-able throughout the book by unchanging features identifying and character-izing him and, as well, by changes in his facial expression, posture, gait— how he or she speaks, listens, reads, runs, jumps, fights, sleeps—present-ing him or her as an acting, communicating being, exhibiting behavior characteristic in the circumstances called forth by the story: the protagonist as a credible (illusory) living being.

The other element is what might well be called stage direction. It refers to the ways in which the illustrator marshals his visual forces in successive pictures so that, on changing backgrounds, in varying conditions of figures and objects coming together, through modulations of angles of vision, the hero will more or less consistently remain in the center of our attention.

Examples of how experienced artists guide their heroes through a story? Take any of Sendak's adventurous boys and follow him, turning the pages slowly, analyzing how he fares and how he acts and reacts. Or accompany Kalinovsky's attractive Alice through the absurdities of Wonderland. Look again at Haacken's Peter who, though he appears in less than half of the pictures in the book, exhibits a forceful presence and calls for sympathy and a smile every time he crops up again. Or McKee's humorous *Magician and the*

Scorcerer, of whose vivacity we spoke in chapter 2. In the medley of incessantly changing pictorial arrangements Melric, the benevolent magician, chased around and about in the rapidly developing plot, manages to keep his good-natured but wary countenance—and our interest. He creates an individual impression precisely because other figures in the story also have their own funny expressions.

Look again at Mayer's *Beauty and the Beast* and try to absorb how the artist carries the heroine through changes of style, Flemish Renaissance for the realistic beginning of the story and Romanticism for its fantastic continuation, on a rich tapestry of solemn figures, interiors and outdoor scenes; and how he makes her stand out from this background by the glow of her appearance, at once intensely alive and meditative, and presents her, to future young women, as the image of maturing womanhood.

THE OPUS OF THE AUTHOR-ILLUSTRATOR

Every now and then there appears in children's literature an author-illustrator who creates a sphere, a domain, a small world of his own: over a number of years and books, distinctive themes, motifs, and stylistic features mature and spread out; but at the basis of this development lies an identity arising from the integration of unmistakable elements. We have chosen the work of Ezra Jack Keats as our example of this.

Keats has illustrated many books written by others; he has also written and illustrated quite a few books of his own. From among these we shall concentrate on the series of books about that small crowd of children whose first hero is Peter, who is joined successively by his dog Willie, Amy, and Archie, and replaced later on by Roberto and Louie.

These books share common characteristics. They are written in a simple and concise language: Keats once referred to his admiration for the sparing style of Japanese haiku poetry. The plots relate realistic everyday events,[9] often spanning a very short time (except for *The Snowy Day* and *A Letter to Amy*); the plots change in nature and circumstance as the children grow, but they are always about small scale experiences, enlivened by sudden, unexpected happenings.[10] However, just as in haiku poetry, the simplicity of content and form is deceptive. If this were our subject, it could be shown that Keats's sparing language has a rhythm all of its own. It can also be demonstrated that his plots tend to have a rhythmic structure. *Whistle for Willie* is a good example. Its story starts in a minor key: Peter wishes that he could whistle for his dog. When he sees another boy whistling, his spirit drops. He encourages himself by turning round and round, until he is dizzy (fig. 71). When Willie, his dog, approaches, he tries to whistle. Unsuccessful again, his frustration deepens. Now he finds solace in drawing a long line

---

9. Ezra Jack Keats, *Jennie's Hat* (New York: Harper & Row, 1966), is one of his few fantasy stories.
10. The text is childlike (*The Snowy Day*), and slight (*Whistle for Willie*) as Georgiou says: Georgiou, *Children*, pp. 104–5.

When he stopped
everything turned
down . . .
and up . . .

and up . . .
and down . . .
and around
and around.

Fig. 71. Ezra Jack Keats, "Everything turned down . . . and up . . ."
From *Whistle for Willie* by Ezra Jack Keats. Copyright © 1964 by Ezra Jack Keats. Reprinted by permission of Viking Penguin, Inc.

with colored chalks all the way home. Right at his own door he is ready for another try. But no, nothing happens. At home he attempts to cover up his humiliation by pretending, to his mother, that he is father. Yet even putting on father's hat does not do the trick—still no whistle. So Peter, vexed with himself, descends to the sidewalks, walks along a crack, tries to run away from his own shadow. When, once more, Willie appears around the corner, suddenly a real whistle forms on his lips. Peter and Willie and the parents are proud.

There is a recurrent rhythm in this. Every time he fails in reality Peter withdraws into himself, into even deeper compensatory fantasy play: getting dizzy means losing one's balance, and then regaining it. Drawing a line on the sidewalk means attempting not to go astray. Putting on father's hat is an act of identification and of asking for help. Walking along a crack is a well-known defense mechanism, binding hostility that is, in Peter's case, directed against himself and which is also expressed in an attempt to get away from his shadow. In the end he is successful: from each withdrawal into fantasy he draws new strength; from the last, deepest frustration springs triumph. The story presents a learning experience and it includes a promise: if you don't give up and if you know how to temporarily retreat from reality and to gather renewed energy in your own imagination, within yourself, you will gain mastery.

The other stories in this series would, on analysis, reveal similar structures, though not all are based on such rhythmic balancing as is *Whistle for Willie*. All will, on nearer acquaintance, turn out to be much more than just small talk. Keats's prose hides depths. Just as in this story trying to run away from his shadow represents his being disgusted with himself so, in *A Letter to Amy*, Peter's confusion finds expression in his mixed-up reflection, which he sees in the wet street. The compensatory games he invents to master frustration in *Whistle for Willie* also appear in other stories, as early as *The Snowy Day*. There, after he tells himself that he is too young to join the older boys in the snowball fight, he overcomes his disappointment by no less than three solitary games, making a snowman, making "angels," (fig.72) and pretending to be a mountain climber. When, in *Peter's Chair*, he gives in to his mother and returns home, he covers up his embarrassment by playing an amusing trick on her.

The stories bring up the child's basic conditions. Even if you have understanding parents and wonderful friends, growing up is a busy affair and full of suspense, and not too easy at times. There are disappointments, like what happens to Archie in *Pet Show!* and *Hi, Cat!*; anxieties, like the new sister in *Peter's Chair*, the pangs of first liking a girl in *A Letter to Amy*, the ugly big boys in *Goggles*, and Louie's fright before and when he meets his dressed-up friends in *The Trip*; there are the wonderful surprises, the endings of *Whistle for Willie* and *A Letter to Amy*, and the near-miracles when, in the end, Louie gets Genie the doll in *Louie*. Each book presents one or more facets of the process of maturing by experience, of mastering life, in the guise of stories: now we are coming back to the surface whose immediacy and upper-level light-mindedness is exemplary.

Keats's heroes are genuine boys, to be sure. They play and talk and fight like boys. But they are also sensitive, taciturn daydreamers who easily retire into themselves and who know so well to transform their bewilderments into (as the grown-ups would have it) symbolic play. This is how they learn, from *The Snowy Day* through *The Trip*.

However, Keats the illustrator has none of the reticence of Keats the writer and his boy protagonists. The former's style contrasts the latter's. Together they create polyphony.

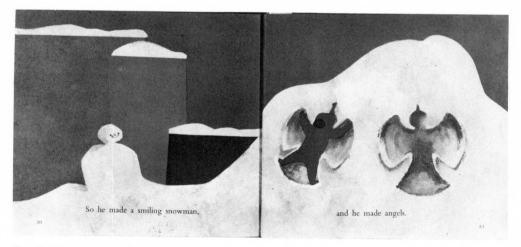

So he made a smiling snowman,   and he made angels.

Fig. 72. Ezra Jack Keats, "Angels"
From *The Snowy Day* by Ezra Jack Keats. Copyright © 1962 by Ezra Jack Keats. Reprinted by permission of Viking Penguin, Inc.

The illustrator's technique varies and frequently combines colors and cut out papers, painting and collage and photography and montage. His style is certainly influenced by Matisse and cubism and pop art. But at the base of its maturation lies a romantic expressionism. Expressionism in the sense that shapes and colors bespeak emotions; romantic in the sense of the assurance offered by the pictures that life, for children, is richer and more dramatic than we would ordinarily think.

While the verbal stories tell about everyday life's tricks and treats, the illustrations light up and illuminate the kids themselves and their environment, about which the text is silent. The derelict, neglected, dirty, poor urban neighborhood is both depicted and redeemed. For the children growing up there cityscape is home; it shines, gleams, and burns with warm colors because it is the sphere of their fantasies, where grafitti are part of their play, where backgrounds, walls, and objects are visual metaphors of their emotions. The houses in the street where Peter tries to whistle change in color and shape with his moods; when he gets dizzy from turning round and round, the traffic lights fly off their fittings (fig. 71). When happiness reigns things are more quietly realistic. Tension turns the background into more abstract and formally expressive structures, as in *The Trip* and *Whistle for Willie*. The rainstorm in *A Letter to Amy* is both an agent of the plot—so that Peter loses the letter to the wind—and a reflection of his emotional upheaval in that he thinks that it would possibly be wiser not to send the letter to Amy (fig. 73).

Color compositions are either a joyous riot, as in *Peter's Chair*, or a radiant symphony of limpid windows and swirling skies, from evening to morning, as in *Dreams*: colors are almost always strong, clear, dominating. When Keats uses muddy colors, as in *Goggles*, it is not because that is what the yard

Fig. 73. Ezra Jack Keats, ". . . his reflection . . . looked all mixed up . . ."

looks like, but because of the big boys' repulsiveness. The constant motif of the wall reflecting what goes on in the heroes' mind comes out here with particular intensity. When, during the fight, Peter's and Archie's anguish is greatest, the muddiness gives way to a passionate crimson, to return when the danger has passed. Even in *Peter's Chair* the envied sister's room has a wallpaper that sets it apart from the rest of the pictures.

Apprehension and sudden fright are frequently indicated by large shadows and silhouettes cast on the luminous walls: the big boys in *Goggles*; lonely wandering Louie; the rapidly and ominously growing shadow of the falling paper mouse in *Dreams*, frightening first Roberto and then the dog; the last pictures of *Hi, Cat!*, where Peter and Archie are silhouetted against the backgrounds—they have not yet gotten over the shock caused them by the crazy cat that ruined their games. Only at the very end does Archie calm down and realize, in talking to his mother, that the cat followed because she liked him. That is the way you learn.

Keats is also a master of the abruptly altered angle of vision, of close-ups, of the convincing expression centering on his heroes' noses and chins. One could continue and find more interesting aspects in this series of stories. It is just a sidelight on Keats's versatility that one could easily demonstrate, in his accruing opus, most of the formal relationships between text and illustration and the latter's functions and interpretative roles. At the same time the aesthetic and the socio-psychological confines of this series are clearly demarcated. The neighborhood, Peter's and his crowds' temperaments and the nature of their experiences, the persistent illustrative motifs, the dialogue between the husky text and the luxurious dramatic pictures spelling out what the text hints at—together they circumscribe a small artistic universum, such as genuine artists create in any art form.

The unity of this "world" and its symbols of representation and communication, over a number of works, can give children a taste of something that exists and develops in time, a taste replenished by repeated recognition. Small experiences strung together by the artist can represent a life style.

Nothing could substantiate this view of Keats better than *Apt. 3*. It does not belong to the Peter-and-his-friends' series. Sam, the boy whom the story is about, is a few years older. The plot will not capture the interest of those children who love Peter's crowd. Sam and his little brother descend the flights of their apartment house searching for the source of some sounds of music. They find it; it is the blind man's harmonica and they become friendly with him.

Yet *Apt. 3* belongs to Peter's and Archie's world aesthetically and psychologically. The halls and staircases of the deteriorating apartment building are what they may have to live with one day, if they are not lucky. The very title of the book projects alienation. But from behind the apartment doors, isolated from each other, leak signs of manifold lives. Sam is that kind of boy once more, sensitive to people and to sounds, the falling rain, music. It is a lyrical story, written in gentle language, in rhythms more expressive than we are used to with Keats (it even contains a verbal metaphor, appearing when the effect of the blind man's music is described). It tells of a meeting between two people of a kind, two who find solace in the spiritual appeal of music. Out of this meeting communication grows, friendship may grow. The blind man's despair and the squalor Sam perceives around him have heightened, not deadened, Sam's alertness for beauty. This is a bitterly optimistic story on catharsis, redemption by the miracle of art, differing in seriousness but resembling by its nature the experiences of smaller children—the snow crystals encompassing Peter in *The Snowy Day*, Louie falling in love with the rainbow-colored doll in *Louie*, and Louie again flying over the moon while looking at the colorful sights pasted in the old shoe box in *The Trip*.

The illustrations dramatize the lyrical mood, probably also making it more easily accessible for the young reader. The gestures and postures of the people in the story are down to earth, outspoken. The important visual motifs are the ones we know well. The apartment building is muddy and ugly. The large shapes of the boys, painted from a close angle, evoke intimacy. From the beginning there is visual metaphor. The parallel diagonals of the falling rain and the fire escapes make a melancholic pattern, over which some lucent specks of color float, representing the sounds that fill Sam with sad and lonely feelings. They reappear, spreading over the window panes when the harmonica makes sights and sounds from outside float into the blind man's room, and Sam floats with them. Sam himself is portrayed conspicuously. The shining colors of his red cap and blue vest make him stand out and beckon to us to follow him. There is a distinction about the boy, some intent hope and pride, when he sits on the stairs expecting the girl to come out of Apt. 2, or when his mind opens as he listens to the man's music.

Sam is older; and so his experience is riper, too. This is not a book for small children, and possibly not even many older ones will become attached to it. For those who will, it holds a thoughtful minor-key message about the communicative and liberating power of art.

Apt. 3 is a characteristic example of that Keatsian aesthetic "world" whose identity is based on the integration of unmistakable elements and intentions, that small universum recognizable by the aesthetic and psychological stimuli it offers.

EXPLICIT ARTISTRY IN CHILDREN'S BOOKS

One other manner of opening children's eyes to art is represented by illustrators who create pictures that are consciously presented as art, and still within the children's grasp. Such illustrators tend to work less out of a personal identification with childhood and more on the basis of a clear perception of what a good illustrated book for children should be like. Our example of this is *The Voyage of the Jolly Boat*, written and illustrated by Margret Rettich.

It is the story of Little Johan (Jan in the English version), whose father, a fisherman on a small island in the North Sea, died when Jan was eleven years old. He began to help his mother by working for fishermen in the village. One day, wanting to prove that he was strong enough to catch fish, he takes a tiny jolly boat and goes out to sea, together with his friend and his sister. They are caught in a storm and only three days later a ship saves them and takes them to Amsterdam, where they are shown around the city. Jan is adamant about bringing the jolly boat back home, as a proof of his manliness. So the three children set out on a tedious and dangerous voyage, over land, through canals and moors and the river until they, long believed lost, return home. The church bells ring for joy all day. Jan will be a good fisherman.

Rettich created the story from a short newspaper report of 1686 on an event that happened in October of that year. She narrates it in even-keeled prose as an unsentimental yarn. There are no overstatements, no emotions of the narrator are expressed, there is scarcely any figurative language. Like the ancient account it is based on, it is a factual description; it elaborates on what is supposed to have happened. It has none of the generality of the folktale. The children are characterized by their behavior. In changing circumstances they act as fits their individual personalities. Details fill in the successive stages of their journey; short dialogues, exclamations, briefly related reactions of adults to the children's predicaments highlight the moods.

Yet this evenness conceals intention. Most of the concise passages making up the story have a distinct common, though internally varying, structure: a statement of what is about to happen is followed by a circumstantial account of how it happened; then comes a closing phrase. Sentence structures support the conciseness: few long sentences, interrupting sequences of short and very short ones. Thus a recurrent rhythm is created which urges us forward like waves in the sea, and the epic purpose of the tale is revealed; its restrained diction admits an unreserved admiration for the obstinancy, courage, and resourcefulness of the children. Put between the identical sentences opening and terminating the story—"This happened long ago. Very, very long ago"—a chain of events occurs whose timelessness is in no need of comment. Heroism speaks for itself. It is a tale of *homo faber*, of acting, inventing, producing man and woman and, more specifically, boys and girls who become heroes in a small way because they persevere and, with a bit of luck, learn to overcome adversity and master their destiny. For Jan, their leading spirit, mastering destiny has a double meaning: returning home safely in spite of the manifold dangers, and proving that he is worthy of being accepted as a fisherman able to earn his family's livelihood.

The story reflects a fervent belief in the dignity of children who live in a world where most adults relate to them benevolently, but nobody wraps them in excessive care and consideration; they let them fight for themselves. Of course, underneath the briskly told events reverberates the archetypal motif of the young hero who sets out to prove himself and returns to replace his father.

The illustrations keep close to the text, illuminating the significant expressions and situations, and accenting the motif of the children's sensible, continual action under changing circumstances (fig. 74). Very distinctly and precisely the illustrations influence and change to an extent the even course and rhythms of the verbal story, highlighting certain passages, profiling the flow of events, orchestrating, so to speak, the textual melody. This is achieved mainly by modulations of spatial relationships. When the action is quick—Jan and his friend prepare the jolly boat for fishing; Jan steals bread and sausage from a farmer's house—small horizontal panels on successive pages indicate speed. Slower or longer events are depicted in somewhat bigger pictures of varying formats. Large and quiet stretches of time, such as the beautiful days spent in Amsterdam, the river carrying the jolly boat

Fig. 74. Margret Rettich, *The Voyage of the Jolly Boat*
From *Die Reise mit der Jolle* by Margret Rettich, published by Otto Maier Verlag Ravensburg © 1980.

along, or tense periods, the storm or the long moment when the boys almost sink into the moor and are rescued by Jan's sister, or the disappointment, when, near the end, neither high nor low tide get them home, are pictures spreading out over the pages.

The changing sizes of the illustrations constitute the most dramatic element in the book. The representation of people and the course of the plot are more in keeping with the epic character of the text. But in contrast the moods of the sea, the coastline, the river, the island, and the big city are painted with a subdued glow and with a spirited sense of natural pageantry. All the emotion is there. The land- and seascapes open wider vistas without overwhelming the viewer. They are slightly stylized (the Hokusai waves of the storm, for instance) and thus add depth, lend a touch of universality to the dignified representation in text and illustrations of the children's foreground existence.

Yet in spite of the influence the pictures exert on the dynamics of the story they do not blend with the text—the illusion is not perfect. One soon finds out that this is intended by the author-illustrator. She takes care to clearly separate the pictures from the text so that they will not overlap or even touch. She uses, moreover, some small devices to strengthen the impression that we have art before our eyes. The paintings are surrounded by thin but clearly recognizable contours, and in most pictures the brush oversteps the outlines and leaves some traces beyond them: the artist deliberately creates an effect of aesthetic distance. The pictures are here to be viewed as the small works of art which they are.[11] The quality of these stately panels, rich, realistic compositions, inspired by the images of the period they tell of, and by the hues of the sea, is such as to arouse, like pictures in an exhibition, our attention, to arrest our progress, not to speed it up. They suggest contemplation; that is, they offer an art experience.

ADULT EXPERIENCE IN CHILDREN'S BOOKS

Finally, let us explore one more facet of that developing art form, the illustrated children's book: the authors and illustrators who expand the limits of children's literature by introducing themes held to belong to adult experience and art expression. We are not speaking here of books which are, as we said earlier, above the heads of children. On the contrary, the two books by Wagner and Brooks which we take as our examples, *The Bunyip of Berkeley's Creek* and *John Brown, Rose and the Midnight Cat*, are authentic picture books, whose language is simple and convincing and whose illustrations have a touching and humorous subtlety. Also, text and pictures fuse successfully.

The Bunyip of Berkeley's Creek is a fantasy creature born of the mud with a

11. Rettich has earlier written and illustrated, in a similar vein: "The Story of the Waterfall," *Die Geschichte vom Wasserfall* (Ravensburg: Otto Maier, 1974). The two books reflect a common approach. The later one is still more mature in narrative and illustrative style.

strong urge to know who he is and what he looks like. He is uniformly
rejected by all the animals whom he meets and asks about himself, because
he is so horribly and disgustingly ugly. But he is persistent and goes on
asking, until he meets a man who bluntly expresses his opinion that bunyips
do not exist at all. Now the bunyip gives up. He retires to a deserted place
where nobody can see him, and is content with looking at himself in the
mirror. That very night the mud stirs once again and another bunyip is born,
turning up to ask who she is and what she looks like. But now there is
someone to reply. Joyfully, they are not alone, though they only have each
other.

The illustrations intensify the melancholic mood. The Australian landscape is boundless and desolate. The bunyip is pictured as being ugly
beyond relief. He is a fantasy creature; he wears trousers, owns a comb and a
mirror, looks at a newspaper, lights a fire at night. There is something so
modest and sad about him that one starts to like him quite early, in spite of
his revolting looks. There is something softly funny about him and about
Brooks's style, except for the horror when the bunyip meets *man*: the first
sign of him is a technotronical, caged-in contraption with boilers, pipes,
chimney, aerials; next comes the moment of pseudo-truth when a cold,
indifferent researcher, backed up by closed circuit screens and panels com-
putes the bunyip out of existence, without looking at him—for there is no
one to look at (fig. 75).

In style and intention, content and execution, and in quality this is, in
spite of any doubts one might have, a picture book for children. But it is an
odd one. Many ugly creatures rove about in children's literature; but either
they are the protagonist's foes, to be vanquished by him or her, or they turn

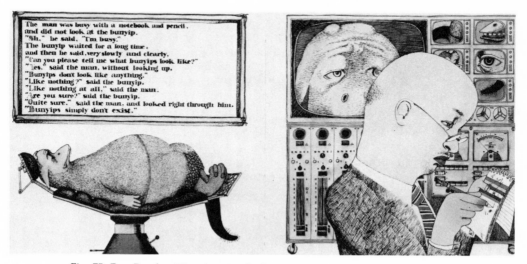

Fig. 75. Ron Brooks, "Bunyips simply don't exist"

From *The Bunyip of Berkeley's Creek* by Jenny Wagner, illustrated by Ron Brooks, Longman Young Books/Childerset, 1973.
Copyright © 1973 by Ron Brooks and Childerset Pty Ltd. Reproduced by permission of Penguin Books Ltd. and Bradbury
Press, Inc. Scarsdale, NY 10583.

(as do Grimm's and Beaumont's beasts) into beautiful human beings. Here the ugly beast is delivered from neither ugliness nor lowliness; only his loneliness is alleviated by the female bunyip who joins him (surely they will multiply). So they find identity, contrary to what the most repugnant creature along the creek, man, thinks. This is not an easy message for children to perceive and assimilate. However, let us reiterate, this is, probably because of the inner logic of the straightforward story and the superior quality of the illustrations, an authentic children's book. It is a thoroughly contemporary one, influenced by motifs of the grotesque and of alienation in modern art. Its hero is an essentially ambiguous figure: are children to identify with the bunyip's indomitable belief in his existence and refusal to accept that he is ugly, or to be uplifted by the understanding that if even such a ludicrous lowly creature can find joy in life, so can they? A double-pronged, existentially true approach to what anxiety means characterizes the book.[12]

Wagner and Brooks's other picture book, *John Brown, Rose and the Midnight Cat*, also has an undercurrent, and more, of anxiety. Rose is a plain, nice, elderly woman who has lost her husband and lives alone in her farmhouse. But John Brown, her dog, looks after her just as she takes care of him. The idyll is disturbed by a black cat who appears at midnight and wants to be let in. John Brown, out of jealousy or because he knows better, does everything to fight her off. When he perceives that Rose pines for the cat, he gives in. Now the three of them live together in the small house.

The illustrations gently build up and emphasize the moods, the widow's simplicity, John Brown's sedate wisdom, the quiet intimacy (fig. 76) that characterizes their staid, protected, eventless life together (with the late husband's picture standing in the background); until things change when the serious, intent, dark cat forces herself into the circle.

There are symbolic overtones to the pictures. The colors fluctuate between pink peacefulness and other, threatening shades. In one illustration the dog may be seen to draw a kind of magic circle to keep out the intruder and its dangers. The book ends on the cat.

Again, just as with the previous book, the unaffected story and the clear, warm pictures, and the way they are combined make this a superior children's book. But what does all this mean to children? Even the surface plot differs from what may usually rouse their interest. How does it apply to their life experience? Does it show them that one should accept strangers? But that is certainly not the point. That even in a quiet, solitary elderly woman's life the unexpected may intrude?

Of course, as we said, the truth is that even the surface story contains the motif of anxiety. First both Rose and John Brown are disquieted; then, when

---

12. Despite the many questions arising from this book, we still believe that an impossibly ugly *living* creature is a more desirable proposition for empathy and/or identification than a capital *A* (see James Krüss, *Die Geschichte vom grossen A.* [Stuttgart: Thienemann, 1972]), or a colorful piece of stone (Leo Lionni, *Pezzettino* [New York: Pantheon, Random, 1975]).

Fig. 76. Ron Brooks, "John Brown and Rose"
John Brown, Rose and the Midnight Cat, written by Jenny Wagner, illustrated by Ron Brooks, originated by Penguin Books Australia and published in the United States by Bradbury Press.

they settle down with the cat, the dog remains apprehensive. As in the story of the bunyip, Brooks's illustrations are infinitely responsive to the anxious mood. Without his innumerable small fine pen lines for the backgrounds the mood would not shine through.

On the symbolic level the theme (of which Wagner is aware) is the end of life. Rose is willing to let in death, over the objection of her protector. Or can the cat be interpreted otherwise, as the symbol of female instincts called in by Rose to strengthen her, as she feels her own life forces drained off by the protected eventlessness guided by the dog's sad eyes?

These are strange subjects for picture books. The first story, about the bunyip, treats the discovery of individual and collective identify as renouncement. Rose confronts children with the conclusive inconclusiveness of old age. Either book is a blend, text and illustration, of single-minded charm and deeply serious issues. Both are strong and probably healthy antidotes against the more powerful stereotypes in children's literature.[13]

Barbara Bader once said that if myth is a metaphorical statement of the truth, *Where the Wild Things Are* is a myth.[14] One is tempted to apply her

13. This discussion of Wagner and Brooks gained much from a talk with Professor Maurice Saxby.
14. Bader, *American Picturebooks*, p. 514.

vitalizing statement to these last two books. Have we already understood the skeptical message about humanity contained in them?

Some conclusions arise from the issues that were brought up in this chapter.

The illustrated book for children, including the picture book, has, in these days, become an open art form, branching out in various directions and competent to respond to any theme for any age, to assimilate any style, and to combine the configurations of its two media, its composite text, in inexhaustible variations and quite demanding modes.

It is an art form in the sense that it communicates its message in a way which is untranslatable into any other form of aesthetic expression. This is, after all, the sign by which an art is recognized and defined. Its superior examples, such as we have discussed here, present to children the nature and strategies of art, the interweaving of contents and meanings.

Recalling the various aspects of the illustration which we have looked at, we can say that it is through a wide range of individual styles and approaches, but relatively few basic conditions and means, that the illustrator creates the opportunity for a child's and youth's aesthetic experience to arise and his and her aesthetic sense to be fashioned.

The examples we have chosen for this last chapter are not inexchangeable. Many more like them exist; we have met some of them in previous chapters. But the ones we did choose have in common a respect for the child's right to be offered books that he will enjoy, and a similar respect for the deeper levels of the child's mind. However these artists may be motivated by their individual alloys of personality, talent, and involvement with childhood, they share a dignified approach to the child's world, to his and her experience and potentialities. They wish to stimulate children by applying to them the humanizing power of visual art.

Such is the nature of the superior aesthetic message that it influences the whole child. By heightening his sensibilities it develops his self-perception and his comprehension of the world he lives in, his ability to understand his own intimate experiences and to relate more meaningfully to others.

CHILDREN'S WORKS CITED

ANDERSEN, HANS CHRISTIAN. *Hazamir*. Trans. by Nathan Alterman. Illus. by Amos Hetz. Tel Aviv: Dvir, n.d.

BOLLINGER, MAX. *Knirps*. Illus. By Klaus Brunner. Winterthur: Comenius, 1961.

BRIGGS, RAYMOND. *The Snowman*. New York: Random, 1978.

BURTON, VIRGINIA L. *Choo Choo: The Story of a Little Engine Who Ran Away*. Boston: Houghton Mifflin, 1937.

CARROLL, LEWIS. *Priklyutcheniya Alicy v Strane Chudes*. Trans. by Borisov Zakhoderov. Illus. by H. Kalinovsky. Moskva: Detskaya Literatura, 1977.

CHARLIP, REMY, and JOINER, JERRY. *Thirteen*. New York: Parents Magazine Pr., 1975.

EFTIMIU, VICTOR. *Înşir-te Mărgărite*. Illus. by Jul. Perahim. Bucureşti: Editura Tineretůlui, 1968.

GARFIELD, LEON, and BLISHEN, EDWARD. *The God Beneath the Sea*. Illus. by Charles Keeping. London: Longman, 1970.

HALBEY, HANS A. *Es wollt' ein Tänzer auf dem Seil den Seiltanz tanzen eine Weil.* Illus. by Leo Leonhard. Aarau, Frankfurt a/M: Sauerländer, 1977.

ISADORA, RACHEL. *Ben's Trumpet*. New York: Greenwillow Books, 1979.

IWASAKI, CHIHIRO. *Staying Home Alone on a Rainy Day*. New York: McGraw-Hill, 1969.

KEATS, EZRA JACK. *Apt. 3*. New York: Macmillan, 1971.

———. *Dreams*. New York: Macmillan, 1974.

———. *Goggles*. New York: Macmillan, 1969.

———. *Hi, Cat!* New York: Macmillan, 1970.

———. *Jennie's Hat*. New York: Harper & Row, 1966.

———. *A Letter to Amy*. New York: Harper & Row, 1968.

———. *Louie*. New York: Greenwillow Books, 1975.

———. *Pet Show!* New York: Macmillan, 1972.

———. *Peter's Chair*. New York: Harper & Row, 1967.

———. *The Snowy Day*. New York: Viking Press, 1962.

———. *The Trip*. New York: Greenwillow Books, 1978.

———. *Whistle for Willie*. New York: Viking Press, 1964.

MAYER, MARIANNA. *Beauty and the Beast*. Illus. by Mercer Mayer. New York: Four Winds Press, 1978.

MAYER, MERCER. *There's a Nightmare in My Closet*. New York: Dial, 1968.

McKEE, DAVID. *The Magician and the Sorcerer*. New York: Parents Magazine Pr., 1974.

PROKOFIEV, SERGEJ S. *Peter und der Wolf*. Illus. by Frans Haacken. München: Parabel, 1958.

RETTICH, MARGRET. *Die Reise mit der Jolle*. Ravensburg: Otto Maier, 1980.

RETTICH, ROLF, and RETTICH, MARGRET. *Neues von Hase und Igel*. Ravensburg: Otto Maier, 1979.

RELLSTAB, URSULA. *Der Professor und der grosse rote Fisch*. Illus. by Beni La Roche. Basel-Wadenswil: Lüber-Stutz, 1968.

SENDAK, MAURICE. *Where the Wild Things Are*. New York: Harper & Row, 1963.

VAN ALLSBURG, CHRIS. *The Garden of Abdul Gasazi*. Boston: Houghton Mifflin, 1979.

VAN TUINEN, MARIANNE. *Circus Spaghetti*. Leeuwarden, Holland: Pers, 1979.

WAGNER, JENNY. *The Bunyip of Berkeley's Creek*. Illus. by Ron Brooks. Melbourne: Childerset, 1973.

———. *John Brown, Rose and the Midnight Cat*. Illus. by Ron Brooks. Harmondsworth, Eng.: Penguin, Kestrel Books, 1977.

ZAVŘEL, ŠTĔPÁN (ill.). *Un Sogno a Venezia*. Text: Micheline Bertrand. Trans. by Cesare della Pietá. Conegliano Treviso: Quadrogono libri, 1977.

Bibliography

ALDERSON, BRIAN. "A View from the Island: European Picture Books 1967–1976." In *Illustrators of Children's Books, 1967–1976*, edited by Lee Kingman et al., pp. 20–43. Boston: Horn Book, 1978.

ANDERSON, WILLIAM D., and GROFF, PATRICK. *A New Look at Children's Literature*. Belmont, Calif.: Wadsworth, 1972.

APOLLINAIRE, GUILLIAUME. *Calligrammes: Poèmes de la Paix et de la Guerre (1913–1916)*. Paris: Gallimard, N.R.F., 1925, 1966.

ARBUTHNOT, MAY H. *Children and Books*. 1st ed. Chicago: Scott, Foresman, 1947. (3rd ed., 1964.)

ARNHEIM, RUDOLF. *Art and Visual Perception: A Psychology of the Creative Eye*. Berkeley and Los Angeles: Univ. of California Pr., 1974.

————. *Visual Thinking*. Berkeley: Univ. of California Pr., 1971.

BADER, BARBARA. *American Picturebooks fron Noah's Ark to the Beast Within*. New York: Macmillan, 1976.

BAUMGÄRTNER, ALFRED CLEMENS. "Erzählung und Abbild." In *Aspekte der gemalten Welt*, edited by A. C. Baumgärtner, pp. 11–73. Weinheim: Beltz, 1968.

BENSE, MAX. In *Concrete Poetry: A World View*, edited by M. E. Solt. Bloomington, Ind.: Indiana Univ. Pr., 1970.

BETTELHEIM, BRUNO. *The Informed Heart: Autonomy in a Mass Age*. Glencoe, Ill.: Free Press, 1960.

————. *The Uses of Enchantment: The Meaning and Importance of Fairy Tales*. New York: Vintage-Random, 1977.

BINDER, LUCIA. "Die Illustration im Bilderbuch." In *Buch-Partner des Kindes*, edited by Waltraut Hartmann et al., pp. 131–34. Ravensburg: Otto Maier, 1979.

BINKLEY, TIMOTHY. "On the Truth and Probity of Metaphor." *Journal of Aesthetics and Art Criticism* (Winter 1974), p. 175.

CAMPBELL, JOSEPH. *The Hero with a Thousand Faces*. New York: Meridian, 1956.

CIANCIOLO, PATRICIA. *Illustrations in Children's Books*. Dubuque, Ia.: Brown, 1976.

CIRLOT, JUAN EDUARDO. *A Dictionary of Symbols*. Trans. by Jack Sage. 2nd ed. London: Routledge & Kegan Paul, 1973.

CLARK, KENNETH. *Landscape into Art*. Harmondsworth, Eng.: Penguin, 1949, 1961.

COHEN, ADIR. "King Matya I." In *Janusz Korczak hamehanekh*, pp. 160–65. Tel Aviv: Czerikover, 1973.

DAGUT, MORTON B. "Can 'Metaphor' Be Translated?" *Babel: International Journal of Translation* 22 (1976): 533–37.

DE TOLNAY, CHARLES. *Michelangelo: Vol. II: The Sistine Ceiling*. Princeton: Princeton Univ. Pr., 1969.

DIAMONDSTEIN, BARBARALEE. "Inside New York's Art World: An Interview with Robert Motherwell." *Partisan Review* 3 (1979): 385–86.

DODERER, KLAUS. "Illustration im Kinderbuch als Kunstprodukt." In *Bienále Ilustracií Bratislava '67–'69*, edited by Eva Šefčáková, pp. 141–43. Bratislava: Obzor, 1972.

————, and MÜLLER, HELMUT, eds. *Das Bilderbuch*. Basel, Weinheim: Beltz, 1975.

ERIKSON, ERIK H. "Ego Development and Historical Change." In *Identity and the Life Cycle: Psychological Issues*, vol. 1. New York: International Univ. Pr., 1959.

ESCARPIT, DENISE. "L'image et l'enfant." In *Image et Communication*, edited by Anne-Marie Thibault-Lalan, pp. 75–105. Paris: Éditions universitaires, 1972.

FELDMAN, EDMUND B. "Perceiving the Elements: Aesthetics." In *Art as Image and Idea*. Englewood Cliffs, N.J.: Prentice-Hall, 1967.

FOTHERINGHAM, HAMISH. *List of English Books on Anthropomorphic Machines*. Munich: International Youth Library, 1966.

FRANZ, MARIE LOUISE VON. *The Feminine in Fairy Tales*. New York: Spring, 1972.

FROMM, ERICH. *The Forgotten Language: An Introduction to the Understanding of Dreams, Fairytales and Myths*. New York: Rinehart, 1951.

————. *Man For Himself: An Inquiry into the Psychology of Ethics*. New York: Rinehart, 1947.

GARDNER, HOWARD. *The Arts and Human Development: A Psychological Study of the Artistic Process*. New York: Wiley, 1973.

GARLAND, MADGE. *The Changing Face of Childhood*. London: Hutchinson, 1963.

GEORGIOU, CONSTANTINE. *Children and Their Literature*. Englewood Cliffs, N.J.: Prentice-Hall, 1969.

GOMBRICH, ERNEST H. *Art and Illusion*. New York: Pantheon, 1960.

————. "The Visual Image." *Scientific American*, Sept. 1972, pp. 82–96.

GREGORY, R. L. "The Confounded Eye." In *Illusion in Nature and Art* by Richard L. Gregory and Ernest H. Gombrich. London: Duckworth, 1973, pp. 49–96.

GROTJAHN, MARTIN. *The Voice of the Symbol*. New York: Dell, 1973.

HALBEY, HANS A. "Die offene und geschlossene Form im Bilderbuch." In *Festschrift für Horst Kunze: Buch-Bibliothek-Leser*, pp. 533–38. Berlin: Akademie Verlag, 1969.

HEARNE, BETSY. "Mayer, Marianna: Beauty and the Beast" and "Goode, Diana: Beauty and the Beast." *Booklist* (Sept. 15, 1978), pp. 217, 223.

HENTIG, HARDTMUT VON. Back cover of J. Korczak, *König Hänschen I*. Trans. by Katja Weintraub. München: Deutscher Taschenbuchverlag, 1974.

HERMERÉN, GÖRAN. "Two Concepts of Illustration." *Representation and Meaning in the Visual Arts*. Lund Studies in Philosophy. Copenhagen, Oslo, Lund: Scandinavian Univ. Books, 1969.

HINDMARCH, IAN. "Eyes, Eyespots and Pupil Dilation in Non-Verbal Communication." In *Social Communication and Movement*, edited by Mario von Cranach and Ian Vine, pp. 299–321. London: Academic Pr., 1974.

HOLEŠOVSKÝ, FRANTIŠEK. *Ilustrace pro děti—tradice, vztahy, objevy*. Praha: Albatros, 1977.

HOLLANDER, JOHN. "The Poem in the Eye." In *Vision and Resonance: Two Senses of Poetic Form*, chap. 12. New York: Oxford Univ. Pr., 1975.

HÜRLIMANN, BETTINA. *Europäische Kinderbücher in drei Jahrhunderten*. Zurich: Atlantis, 1963.

————. *Die Welt im Bilderbuch: Moderne Kinderbilderbücher aus 24 Ländern*. Zurich: Atlantis, 1965.

JUNG, CARL GUSTAV. *Symbols of Transformation*. Trans. by R. F. C. Hull. New York: Pantheon, 1956.

KANDINSKY, WASSILY. *Concerning the Spiritual in Art and Painting in Particular 1912*. New York: Wittenborn, 1970.

KINGMAN, LEE, ed. *The Illustrator's Notebook*. Boston: Horn Book, 1978.

————; HOGARTH, GRACE ALLEN; and QUIMLY, HARRIET, eds. *Illustrators of Children's Books 1967–1976*. Boston: Horn Book, 1978.

KLEIST, HEINRICH VON. "Ueber das Marionettentheater." In *Saemtliche Werke*, vol. 3, pp. 213–19. Leipzig: Max Hesses Verlag, n.d.

KORN, A. L. "Puttenham and the Oriental Pattern-Poem." *Comparative Literature* 6 (1954): 289–303.

KÜNNEMANN, HORST. *Bibliographie Muse und Maschine*. Munich: International Youth Library, 1965.

————. *Profile zeitgenössischer Bilderbuchmacher*. Weinheim: Beltz, 1972.

KUNZE, HORST, and WEGEHAUPT, HEINZ. *Für Kinder gemalt: Buchillustratoren der DDR*. Berlin: Der Kinderbuchverlag, 1970.

LANGER, SUSANNE K. *Feeling and Form: A Theory of Art*. New York: Scribner, 1953.

LÜTHI, MAX. "Allverbundenheit." In *Enzyklopädie des Märchens*, edited by K. Ranke. Berlin: De Gruyter, 1975.

MASSIN, ROBERT. *La Lettre et l'image. Du signe à la lettre et de la lettre au signe*. Paris: Gallimard, 1970.

MCCANN, DONNARAE, and RICHARD, OLGA. "Stereotypes in Illustration." In *The Child's First Books—A Critical Study of Pictures and Texts*. New York: Wilson, 1973.

MCLUHAN, HERBERT. *The Mechanical Bride: Folklore of Industrial Man*. New York: Vanguard, 1951.

MELVILLE, HERMAN. *Moby Dick*. New York: New American Library, 1961.

MERKELBACH, VALENTIN. "Tendenzen im Bilderbuch der Zwanziger Jahre." In *Das Bilderbuch*, edited by K. Doderer and H. Müller, pp. 279–80. Basel, Weinheim: Beltz, Gelberg, 1975.

MOLES, ABRAHAM A. *Information Theory and Aesthetic Perception*. Trans. by J. E. Cohen. Urbana: Univ. of Illinois Pr., 1968.

NEUMANN, ERICH. *The Origin and History of Consciousness*, vol. 1. Trans. by F. C. Hull. New York: Harper/Bollingen, 1954.

————. *Die grosse Mutter: Der Archetyp des grossen Weiblichen*. Zurich: Rhein Verlag, 1956.

OVENDEN, GRAHAM. *The Illustrators of Alice in Wonderland.* London: Academy Editions; New York: St. Martin's, 1972.

PHILLIPS, ROBERT, ed. *Aspects of Alice: Lewis Carroll's Dreamchild as Seen through the Critics' Looking Glass 1865–1971.* Harmondsworth, Eng.: Penguin, 1974.

POLANYI, MICHAEL. "What is a Painting?" *American Scholar* 39 (1970): 655–69.

PROPP, VLADIMIR J. *Morphology of the Folklore.* Trans. by Lawrence Scott. Austin: Univ. of Texas Pr., 1970.

RANK, OTTO. *The Myth of the Birth of the Hero.* Trans. by F. Robbins and S. E. Geliffe. New York: Journal of Mental and Nervous Disease, 1914.

REIK, THEODOR. *Listening with the Third Ear.* New York: Farrar, 1949.

RIESMAN, DAVID; GLAZER, NATHAN; and DENNEY, REUEL. *The Lonely Crowd.* New York: Doubleday, n.d. Abridged by the authors.

ROSENBERG, HAROLD. *Saul Steinberg.* New York: Knopf, Whitney Museum of American Art, 1978.

SCHWARCZ, JOSEPH H. "Machine Animism in Modern Children's Literature." In *A Critical Approach to Children's Literature,* edited by Sara I. Fenwick, pp. 78–95. Chicago: Univ. of Chicago Pr., 1967.

————. "Meheymanutoh shel ha'iyyur besifrey yeladim." *Hahinukh* (Tel Aviv) 5 (1969): 427–42.

————. "Al hakitsch ba'iyyur." Problems in Children's Literature: A Symposium. *Eyyunim behinukh* (Univ. of Haifa) 3 (1974): 79–98.

SHAPIRO, MEYER. *Words and Pictures: On the Literal and the Symbolic in the Illustration of a Text.* The Hague, Paris: Mouton, 1973.

SMITH, JAMES S. *A Critical Approach to Children's Literature.* New York: McGraw Hill, 1967.

SMITH, KARL U., and SMITH, MARGARET F. *Psychology: An Introduction to Behavior Science.* New York: Little, Brown, 1973.

STEINBERG, SAUL. "Country Noises" (cartoon). *New Yorker,* Feb. 12, 1979, p. 29.

SUTHERLAND, ZENA, et al., eds. *Children and Books.* 6th ed. Glenview, Ill.: Scott, Foresman, 1981.

SWARZENSKI, HANNS. *Monuments of Romanesque Art: The Art of Church Treasures in North-Western Europe.* Chicago: Univ. of Chicago Pr., 1967.

TILLICH, PAUL. "Modern Man and Freedom." *Listener,* Dec. 14, 1961, pp. 1025–26.

WEGEHAUPT, HEINZ, ed. *Das schöne Kinderbuch.* Berlin: Kinderbuchverlag, 1977.

WEISMANN, DONALD L. *The Visual Arts as Human Experience.* Englewood Cliffs, N.J.: Prentice-Hall, n.d.

WIENER, NORBERT. "Some Moral and Technical Consequences of Automation." *Science,* May 6, 1960, pp. 1355–58.

Index of Illustrators

Italic page references indicate illustrations.